LONDON'S LADY DETECTIVE
MAUD WEST

Every kind of Detective
work undertaken with
Secrecy and Dispatch
DIVORCE SHADOWINGS
SECRET ENQUIRIES ETC.

MALE & FEMALE STAFF

ALBION HOUSE, 59-61, NEW OXFORD ST. W.

TELEPHONE:
MUSEUM 5120.

MANAGER - - H. ELLIOTT.

The Adventures of
Maud West, Lady Detective

'If you are inclined to regard the "Golden Age" detective stories as obviously a fantasy form – and never more fantastic than when the sleuth is a woman – Susannah Stapleton's book will astound you. "Maud West" was a real woman detective, but her story blurs the margin between possible truth and impossible invention till your head spins. If you are susceptible to Miss Marple and Harriet Vane you must read *The Adventures of Maud West*. You will never know the difference between fact and fiction again.'
Jill Paton Walsh, author of the Peter Wimsey/
Harriet Vane mysteries

'I rocketed through this terrific book. A brilliant literary sleuth tracks down a real one, uncovering a flabbergasting hidden life along the way. And if you thought that detective novels exaggerate the amount of inter-war crime, you are wrong.'
Lissa Evans, author of *Crooked Heart* and *Old Baggage*

'A deliciously entertaining, meticulous and affectionate investigation into one of the great unsung heroines of British detection, our very own real-life, female Sherlock Holmes. Criminally good. It's impossible not to love this book.'
Mel McGrath, author of *Give Me the Child* and *The Guilty Party*

'A powerhouse of a book, both a biography of one of the first women detectives, and a portrait of the Jazz Age, that society perched uncomfortably between Victoria and modernism. But Susannah Stapleton's more profound achievement is in encouraging her readers to follow along as she goes about the business of the historian and biographer, permitting us to watch history being uncovered in real time. *The Adventures of Maud West, Lady Detective* is, as one suspects Maud herself was, sweet, and wonderful company, and absolutely determined to discover the truth.'
Judith Flanders, author of *The Invention of Murder* and the Sam Clair mysteries

'Maud West is a gloriously English eccentric – think Miranda Hart meets Margaret Rutherford – brought to vigorous life by present-day sleuth Susannah Stapleton. Stapleton brings a keen eye for bizarre and quirky detail to this compelling tale of London's leading female private detective in the days before the Second World War. But it's also a charming and deeply felt love letter to a completely forgotten trailblazer who forged a complex life and successful career when many women were banished to the typing pool, the nursery or the kitchen.'

Sean O'Connor, author of *Handsome Brute*

'Susannah Stapleton's dogged sleuthing of Maud's own complicated, messy, spunky life reveals the wider story of a little-explored sliver of life between the wars: female detection with all its risks, boredoms, tawdry deceptions, disguises and necessary seductions. I loved it.'

Kate Colquhoun, author of
Mr Briggs' Hat and *Did She Kill Him?*

THE ADVENTURES OF

Maud West, Lady Detective

Secrets and Lies in the Golden Age of Crime

SUSANNAH STAPLETON

PICADOR

First published 2019 by Picador
an imprint of Pan Macmillan
20 New Wharf Road, London N1 9RR
Associated companies throughout the world
www.panmacmillan.com

ISBN 978-1-5098-6729-5 HB
ISBN 978-1-5098-6730-1 TPB

1 3 5 7 9 8 6 4 2

A CIP catalogue record for this book is available from the British Library.

The picture acknowledgements on p. 369 constitute an
extension of this copyright page.

Typeset by Jouve (UK), Milton Keynes
Printed and bound by CPI Group (UK) Ltd, Croydon, CR0 4YY

Visit **www.picador.com** to read more about all our books
and to buy them. You will also find features, author interviews and
news of any author events, and you can sign up for e-newsletters
so that you're always first to hear about our new releases.

For Sarah

Contents

Prologue

The Lady Vanishes

One evening in 1939, Maud West, London's leading lady detective, locked the door to her Bloomsbury office and promptly disappeared, never to be seen again. Her exploits over the past thirty-four years had taken her around the world, snooping in drug dens, grand country houses, mental asylums and more. She had unmasked blackmailers, caught adulterers, foiled jewel thieves and shut down cults, all on behalf of a client list that could have been lifted from the pages of Debrett's. The press loved her – a real lady sleuth in the golden age of crime – and newspapers across the globe reported tales of her derring-do.

And now she was gone.

As one would expect, Maud West had amassed a fair few nemeses over the years. But she wasn't abducted that night in 1939, nor was she killed or harmed in any way. She didn't hide out in a Harrogate hotel or wake up swathed in bandages, hurtling across Germany on a Hitchcockian train. She simply ceased to exist – if it could be said that Maud West had ever truly existed at all.

That said, she used to be easy enough to find. If there was no London telephone directory to hand, a quick glance at the personals column of any major newspaper would do the job.

LONDON'S LADY DETECTIVE **MAUD WEST**

Every kind of Detective Work undertaken with Secrecy and Despatch. Divorce Shadowings, Secret Enquiries, etc. MALE AND FEMALE STAFF.

Albion House, 59, New Oxford Street, W.

TELEPHONE: MUSEUM 5120.

See? There she is.

Chapter One

The Documents in the Case

. . . in all good faith to other women
who would become detectives, I would
utter one word of advice – Don't.

Maud West, 1914[1]

Maybe I should have walked away at the first sign of deceit; after the
incident with the bear-skin rug, perhaps, or during that ridiculous
car chase across Hampstead Heath. In Paris? Or Rio? There were
so many times I could have turned back and just left her to it. But
then I would never have met the Countess or the Prince of Lovers,
or learned how to rig an office safe with chloroform or whip up a
disguise using only a piece of orange peel and a wisp of goat hair.
I'd never have laughed with her or wept for her; I'd never have seen
what lay beneath. Besides, I'm not sure I even had a choice. There
was almost a sense of inevitability about the whole thing.

Looking back, you could say that our paths began to converge
on Boxing Day 1984, when the magnificent Joan Hickson, in her
first tweedy outing as Miss Marple, pottered into my family's sitting room to investigate *The Body in the Library*. Just shy of my
twelfth birthday, I was immediately and irreparably entranced –
by the whodunnit, yes, and the frocks, the hats, the gigolos and
jazz fiends, but, most of all, by the idea of all those delicious secrets
lying so perilously close to the surface. Before long, I'd sought
out the books for my own private feasts of sparkling cyanide and

arsenic-laced prawns, and taken up snooping on the side. By the time I was thirteen, I was eyeing up louche lipstick in the village chemist, sneaking the occasional cigarillo and dabbling in a bit of light blackmail. It was only the threat – and subsequent reality – of boarding school that put paid to an otherwise promising future as a Jazz Age reprobate.

Somewhere along the way, my talent for muckraking was guided into a career in history, where it was thought I could do less harm. But I never gave up the detective stories. If I learned anything from my two-year incarceration in a ladies' college, it was that there's nothing like a good murder to lift the spirits. As the years went on, I put this to good use in what became something of an annual ritual: in the darkest days of winter, I'd take a couple of weeks off work, build a nest by the fire and escape into a world of daggers, poisons, wrath and revenge. It never failed to beat away the winter blues. Until, that is, a few years ago.

All the usual elements were in place that winter: miserable weather, a build-up of petty resentments, a stack of green Penguins foraged from second-hand bookshops. Yet, however much I craved that state of rightness-with-the-world, where the bodies are all lined up, someone is on their way to the gallows and a cup of cocoa awaits before bed, I couldn't find a way in. As the first week wore on, a trail of half-read books lay scattered throughout the house, old friends abandoned mid-sentence: Harriet Vane motionless under the bed; Nero Wolfe sliding down the back of the sofa. I couldn't settle to anything.

Instead, my mind kept going back to a historical missing-persons case I'd recently completed. It had arisen out of some exhibition work I had done for a museum, and my quarry had been a minor nineteenth-century inventor whose fate had stumped a small band of collectors and enthusiasts for decades. The case had taken me on an exciting jaunt, on paper at least, from Liverpool to

Havana, with a small attempted coup in Spain along the way. There
had been exploding steamships, secret marriages, royal pardons,
family feuds and a sad, gin-pickled end. When I thought about it,
I'd been feeling a bit flat ever since. I missed the thrill of the chase.

I didn't want to read about detectives; I wanted to *be* one. But
when I tried to think of what to tackle next, the only mysteries that
came to mind were the Princes in the Tower, Jack the Ripper and
the Holy Grail, and my chances of solving any of those were slim
at best. Besides, I wanted fresh ground, a mystery of my very own.
And there was the problem. It had to be something that no one
knew about, including me.

The solution, of course, was right under my nose – or rather
under my bed and down the back of my sofa – but it took a while to
filter through into conscious thought. It surfaced late one evening.
I'd been yawning my way through the opening chapters of Gladys
Mitchell's *Death at the Opera*, waiting for someone to die so the
eccentric Mrs Bradley could start sleuthing, and was about to call it
a night when there it was, the question from which there would be
no turning back. Were there really lady detectives – proper flesh-
and-blood ones – in the golden age of crime?

I reached for my laptop. Google didn't know. I tried various
online encyclopedias and library records. Nothing. It was only
when I turned to the National Archives' Discovery catalogue that
I had my answer. There was at least one:

Reference:	1129/6
Title:	London's Lady Detective. Miss Maud West, who is London's only Lady detective examining handwriting through a magnifying glass to detect forgery in a case upon which she is at present engaged. From her offices in New Oxford Street, she travels all over the country on investigations. Dailypress Photographic Agency, 31, St. Annes Chambers, Broadway, E.C.4. Copyright "Dailypress".
Description:	Negative Sheet Number Y9/24

It was a description of a press photograph, the title presumably taken from a label on the reverse. There was no date, but the language sounded about right for the inter-war years. London's only lady detective? That had potential. The original was held at Manchester Archives, so I typed a short email requesting a copy and went to bed, planning to delve a bit deeper in the morning.

Half an hour later, I was up again. How had I never heard of Maud West? A quick search on her name suggested I was not alone. London's only lady detective had slipped into obscurity. She'd received a brief mention in one recent book (Virginia Nicholson's *Singled Out: How Two Million Women Survived Without Men after the First World War*) and a couple of related blog posts, but it appeared that even they knew nothing beyond the fact of her existence. What's more, they all cited the same source: *British Women in the Twentieth Century*, Elsie M. Lang's survey of pioneer businesswomen, published in 1929, a copy of which was somewhere in my possession.

I'd always had a soft spot for Elsie Lang. Her bread-and-butter work was writing about crumbling buildings (*Some Old English Abbeys*, *The Oxford Colleges*, etc.), the kind of gentle, pleasant labour I knew well. But, every so often, she would come out with something that revealed a fierce hinterland – a translation of Venetian poetry about the Medici women, for example, or this 1929 celebration of female liberation. Over the years, it had become something of a set text for those interested in twentieth-century women's history. As well as setting out in clear terms the struggles women had faced in getting a higher education, the right to vote, access to birth control, freedom from rib-crunching corsetry and countless other challenges, it was also a book of firsts – the first female MP, the first woman barrister, the first female racing driver, and so on. There were explorers, accountants, aviators and surgeons, but I didn't remember any detectives.

After numerous rounds of the house, rummaging through overcrowded bookshelves, I finally found my copy. And there she was, in the index: *West, Maud, 273*. What had Elsie said about her? And how had I missed it? Perhaps I'd never read to the end, because she appeared on the very last page, almost as an afterthought, squeezed in between a pageant producer and a company director in a list of career options for women. There were just six words:

Miss Maud West is a detective.

The game was afoot.

The next morning, I flicked through the pages of *British Women in the Twentieth Century* whilst waiting for the kettle to boil. Maud West may have warranted only six words, but the fact that she had made it into the book at all placed her in formidable company. Elsie Lang's women were the epitome of female achievement in a man's world. Some had degrees, others had worked their way up from the bottom of their respective fields, but they were all mavericks in one way or another. These were women who made the headlines, whether they were the lone female voice in Parliament or striding solo across the Serengeti. They were impossible to ignore.

I sat down at my desk and brought up *The Times'* online archive. Had Maud West been impossible to ignore? Had she made the headlines? After a bit of rootling around, it didn't look as though she had. There was nothing in the main news section at all, not even any mention of her giving evidence in court. There were, however, two advertisements. The first appeared a few times during the course of 1909:

> MAUD WEST, "LADY DETECTIVE." Tel. 8561 Gerrard.
> Are you worried? If so, consult me! Private enquiries
> and delicate matters undertaken anywhere with secrecy
> and ability. DIVORCE, SHADOWINGS, &c. Intelligent
> Male and Female Staff. REFERENCES TO LEADING
> SOLICITORS. High-class firm. Consultations free with
> Principal or Manager.—MAUD WEST, Albion House,
> 59, New Oxford-st., London, W.C.   ¦25

A high-class firm specializing in private enquiries and delicate matters? Add in the description of her peering through a magnifying glass in the Manchester Archives photo, and Maud West was shaping up to be a proper consulting detective of the sort I'd been reading about for years. Even that 'Are you worried? If so, consult me!' reminded me of the adverts at the start of Agatha Christie's Parker Pyne stories ('Are you happy? If not, consult Mr. Parker Pyne . . .'). The main difference, it seemed, was that Maud West had staff. London's lady detective was no part-time dabbler, working from home and occasionally calling on the assistance of a trusty sidekick or a raggle-taggle bunch of street urchins. She was running a serious operation with an office full of employees in the heart of the city.

The second advertisement read:

> DON'T miss MAUD WEST'S REMINISCENCES
> (London's Lady Detective), 6 p.m., to-morrow.—
> Exhibition of Women's Progress, Sunderland House,
> Curzon Street, W.1.

This was from March 1936, so she'd clearly had a long career – nearly thirty years, at least – and one interesting enough for reminiscences. Was there a record of the talk somewhere? What had she said? Thirty years was long enough to develop a good stock of anecdotes; she was bound to have had a few adventures and mishaps along the way. Had she worked with the police? Did she have inside knowledge of any of the big cases of her day? Or did she speak in more general terms about her work? And, if so, what did that involve?

I found an answer, in part, in the social column of the *Sunday*

Times. It only told me what she had been doing on one specific evening in November 1930 and it didn't really help in terms of understanding her work, as she was off duty that night, but it still took my breath away:

> Next Thursday the business women of London who belong to the Efficiency Club are to discuss "Efficiency in Murder." In the chair will be Miss Maud West, who is well known as one of London's lady detectives, and whose activities extend to the Continent. A lecture is to be given by Miss Dorothy Sayers, who will explain to the members of the Club and their friends how murder may most efficiently be committed with the least possible likelihood of discovery. Miss Sayers, in her books "The Documents in the Case" and "Strong Poison," has already given some idea of her views on the art of polite murder.

Maud West had met the mighty Dorothy L. Sayers: novelist, translator, theologian and founding member of the Detection Club, at which the top golden-age crime writers met to dine, collaborate and indulge in strange rituals involving a skull named Eric. At the very least, Maud had shaken her hand and introduced her to the Efficiency Club (whatever that might be). But was that their only encounter? Did they go for dinner afterwards and swap crime stories? Were they friends? Was it worth going to America, where Sayers' diaries and letters were kept, to find out? I felt the familiar tingle of worlds intersecting and ideas sparking.

But I was getting ahead of myself. I didn't even have a sense of who Maud West was, let alone what sort of friends she had. She was just a shadow, a faceless blur, her edges defined only by her fictional counterparts. I traced my finger over her advertisement and found myself wishing, not for the first time, that I could pick up the phone and dial a long-defunct number. I could almost hear the crackling of the line and a faint voice echoing across the years: *'Hullo? Gerrard 8561? Miss West speaking.'*

I mentally dropped the receiver back into its cradle. What would I say? I'd always had specific questions in mind during previous reveries, very precise whens and whys and what-on-earths. This was different. 'Who *are* you?' seemed a bit blunt, but that was what I wanted to know. Who was Maud West? Where did she come from? How did she end up in such an unusual job?

Put like that, these questions seemed such basic interview fare that I was certain that someone had asked them before. Some curious journalist must have spotted her adverts or gone along to her 'reminiscences' and wanted to follow up the story – and if it hadn't been the gentlemen of *The Times*, then what about their tabloid cousins? They were always on the lookout for oddities and odd-balls. How could they have resisted a lady detective?

From my home in Shropshire, I didn't have access to the digital archives of the more gossipy rags like the *Daily Mirror* or the *Daily Mail*. These were restricted to members of academic institutions and I'd need to go to the British Library to view them. Looking out of the window at the cold, relentless drizzle, the prospect didn't appeal. Fortunately, there were alternatives: the numerous open-access newspaper websites run by various bodies around the world.

I decided to start with Trove, the online archive maintained by the National Library of Australia. From experience, I knew that many overseas newspapers carried both fragments and whole reprints of articles that had originally featured in British national newspapers and magazines. I suspected that if Maud West had appeared in the British tabloids, however briefly, she would be found here.

My hunch paid off. But it wasn't just one or two articles I found; it was dozens. Over the next few days, my printer churned out piece after piece about Maud West. Encouraged, I checked a few more online archives and found articles in the *New York Tribune*, the *Times of India*, the *Singapore Free Press* and a number of foreign-language newspapers. I'd barely scratched the surface, but it was clear that news of London's lady detective had spread throughout the world:

MAUD WEST
détective à transformations

The Lady 'Tec.

LONDON'S FAMOUS WOMAN DETECTIVE.

Die Detektivin im Salon.

The articles ranged in date from 1913 to 1938. Some were just snippets, pointing out the curiosity of a female sleuth. *Time* magazine, for example, included her advertisement in a round-up of strange items found in a single issue of London's *Morning Post* from 1934.[2] But there were also signs of the interviews I'd been hoping for. Most of the quotes were second-hand, maybe even third-hand, but it was obvious that over the years more than one person had sat down with Maud West and asked about her work.

I found an answer to one of my questions almost immediately, in the *Perth Daily News* from 1926:

It was chance, not impelling desire, which made her take up this unusual work for a woman. Having nothing to do a solicitor relation asked her to help him solve a hotel robbery by going there as a waitress. In a spirit of adventure Miss West went. Although she knew nothing of waiting . . . by the time she had picked up enough of the art to pass muster she had discovered the thief. Her success led to other commissions, and eventually

to the suggestion that she should take up the work professionally. She did.[3]

There were also a few hints about the type of cases she took on.
According to some eastern European news reports from 1913, she
was hired to blend in with the guests at society parties to protect
her hosts' property from damage by militant suffragettes, whilst
an advertisement for a security agency in New Zealand listed her
alongside the famous Pinkerton's Detective Agency in New York
as one of their overseas agents for chasing debts.[4] Other articles
talked about how she gathered evidence of adultery for divorce
cases, work which could take her all over Europe. 'In shadowing
one lady just before the war,' she said in 1915, 'I had to travel to
Berlin, Paris, Moscow, Ostend, and back to London in the same
week.'[5]

On the whole, however, by the time these interviews had filtered
through to the international press, they had been distilled into
headline-grabbing pieces about 'the Woman Sherlock Holmes',
devoid of any useful facts and full of hyperbole. There was much
lamenting her lack of deerstalker and violin, and one reporter even
moved the location of Maud's New Oxford Street base to the more
convenient Baker Street, 'a stone's throw from the rooms of the
immortal Holmes.'[6] They revelled in the heady mix of glamour and
adventure that the life of a woman detective implied, describing her
office with its luxurious 'inch-deep carpet, Prussian blue papered
walls and New Art statuettes' and revealing the contents of the
overnight bag she kept there for emergencies ('revolver, hypodermic syringe, vial of dope, a half dozen disguises').[7]

The idea of a lady detective in disguise particularly captured
the journalists' imagination. Almost all of them homed in on this,
revealing that she had been known to dress up as a charwoman, a
gypsy, a nurse, a fortune teller and, as the *Adelaide Saturday Journal* reported in 1926, as a man:

[Maud West] has successfully occupied rooms at a fashionable hotel as a titled Englishman, and has followed her suspects into their clubs, has played baccarat beside them at the Monte Carlo Casino, and no one has suspected that the young person in silk hat and evening clothes was a woman . . .[8]

Maud West made occasional attempts to counter all this by explaining the day-to-day reality of her job: 'There is nothing mysterious or miraculous about the way I find out things. The whole secret is in the application of practical common sense. And the only motto for the successful detective is – Keep on trying.'[9] She said that the simplest disguises were often the best ('a pair of heavy earrings make me look frightfully common'), and explained the skill and experience needed for accurate observation.[10] Above all, she emphasized the hard work involved: 'A strong constitution is absolutely essential. One frequently has to go without meals, and the strain is very severe, for one never knows when one will be able to rest.'[11]

But the newspapers wanted thrills and spills, as was most evident in a particularly colourful set of articles I found in the Australian press. I had gone looking for tabloid journalism and I'd found it, only this wasn't the *Daily Mail* or the *Daily Mirror*; this was worse. According to the small print, many of these articles had been syndicated from a British magazine called *Pearson's Weekly*. Just seeing the name made my heart sink.

Journalistic integrity didn't even make it onto the agenda at *Pearson's Weekly*. Ever since it first appeared in the late nineteenth century, it had one mission: to make money. It was brazen in its pursuit of the Sunday reader, that downtrodden soul desperate for a few hours' respite from the daily grind, and a good chunk of the paper's income came from its legendary competitions which, along with the numerous advertisements, were designed to appeal to fantasies of a better life. There were pages of them every week with prizes ranging from briar pipes to houses and husbands, open to all on payment of a small fee. Everything else was just filler.

I even had some copies on my shelves, bound into a hefty volume covering 1934, which I had purchased purely for entertainment. The paper's motto was 'To Interest, to Elevate, to Amuse.' You couldn't fault it on interest and amusement, but elevation? Leafing through its pages, it was hard to find any actual news, unless you counted such pressing matters as 'What Has Happened to the Loch Ness Monster?' and 'Is Wireless Giving You A Sixth Sense?' Fiction, sport, celebrities and humour featured heavily, and there was also a fair amount of true crime: a behind-the-scenes series about Scotland Yard, for example, and a feature on Cairo's Narcotics Intelligence Bureau. Cautionary tales scattered throughout each issue warned of killer swans, luggage thieves, motor bandits and cheese smugglers.

I could see that this last batch of articles I had found about Maud West would have been the perfect match for *Pearson's Weekly*. They had dramatic headlines:

The Phantom Thief

World-Wide Pursuit of Cocaine-Drugged Countess

Some were accompanied by lurid illustrations:

As for the articles themselves, they described Maud West undertaking a series of adventures wilder than any I had imagined. I'd thought she might have been caught snooping in the wrong place occasionally, maybe even had a run-in with a disgruntled criminal or two, but these tales were something else. They took her from the slums of Whitechapel to smart Paris hotels, to New York's Lower East Side and the backstreets of Buenos Aires, all on the trail of a cast of characters that included runaway heiresses, defrocked vicars, amateur surgeons and continental blackmailers. The baddies carried guns and knives, and said things like 'Good heavens, we are nobbled.'[12]

The Maud West depicted in these articles was a woman of many parts. In some stories she was the feisty heroine, skulking about in the underworld and relentlessly chasing her prey until victory was hers. In others, she appeared as a kindly yet strict mother figure, sorting out troubled love affairs with calm authority. In a few, she played an almost comic role, diving under rugs and squeezing into tight spaces to avoid detection. One caper even included a *follow-that-cab!* sequence.

They were completely over the top, but there were no protests from Maud about their accuracy, no attempts to counter the sensationalism or put the record straight. The reason for this was simple:

CROOKS I HAVE FOILED.

⸻◆⸻

FROM THE NOTEBOOK OF A LADY DETECTIVE.
(By Maud West.)

She had written them herself.

*

What to make of it all? On the one hand, Maud West was a genuine detective, and a successful one at that. She was a businesswoman, a member of the brisk-sounding Efficiency Club, and had enjoyed a career lasting over thirty years. On the other, she was a hack writer churning out 'true' adventure stories for the gutter press. It was possible that the two overlapped, but, if so, at what point did fact turn into fiction?

I cleared the kitchen table and laid out her articles, shifting them around as I thought things through. At one end of the table I placed those which were believable: a case in which she had to retrieve a letter sent in error, for example, and a story about an innocuous, if complicated, love triangle. At the other end were those which tested the limits of credulity, such as a chase across the Atlantic that ended with Maud in a Brazilian drugs factory, jotting down the recipe for cocaine. Where did I draw the line? Did it go before or after any revolvers were drawn? Was dropping a sleeping draught into a suspect's coffee improbable or merely illegal? And how did I feel about Chinamen, that cliché of bad detective fiction?

I was torn between discounting the whole lot and arguing myself into a place where anything was possible. The more outrageous tales were unlikely to be representative of her daily life, but could they be highlights of a long and strange career? She had existed in a different time, after all, one that was less regulated and more conducive to adventure. Even my own grandmother had once been kidnapped by pirates in the North China Sea as a child, and she hadn't even been looking for trouble. Maud West was paid to seek it out and poke about in places that were best left unpoked. Viewed in that light, were her stories really so implausible?

Then it struck me. Caught up in all the drama, I'd missed the most obvious point of all. Of course the stories couldn't be true. Not word-for-word true, anyway. Libel laws aside, detective work involved sorting out personal problems and making embarrassing or awkward situations go away, those 'delicate matters' mentioned in her advert. The last thing Maud or her clients would have wanted was for the details to be splashed all over the papers. Her career would have been over before it had started.

So, why had she written them? Did she need the money? Was her work poorly paid? It seemed unlikely. Wealthy people in desperate situations would pay as much as was required to get things resolved, and there were clearly enough of them around for her to maintain a central London office and, if her adverts were to be believed, a body of staff. Was it a way of advertising? If so, it can't have been very effective. Her prospective clients wouldn't have been the sort to read *Pearson's Weekly*. I imagined they would stick to the broadsheets: *The Times*, the *Daily Telegraph* and the *Manchester Guardian*. Besides, even if they had come across one of her stories, it would hardly have inspired confidence in her discreet professionalism.

Maybe that hypodermic needle and vial of dope in her overnight bag provided a clue. I'd assumed they were tools of her trade, there for protection alongside the revolver, but what if she was blowing all her money on drugs? Had she got a taste for gambling in the casinos of Monte Carlo? Was she being blackmailed? Or did she just crave the attention, a trait that must have put her at a disadvantage in a profession where discretion was key?

I had no idea. But something didn't add up.

I decided to put Maud's stories aside for the time being and look again at the more straightforward evidence I had found in the overseas newspapers. A few hints enabled me to work out that she had set up her detective agency in 1905. Assuming that she had been a young woman when she had gone on her first, tentative sleuthing mission, and that it had taken her a few years to gain enough experience and confidence to go into business on her own, I figured that she must have been born sometime around 1880.

According to the 1911 census on ancestry.co.uk, there were nearly 300 people called Maud West in England at that time, not one of whom claimed to be a private detective. If I narrowed it down to those born in 1880, give or take five years, there were still over seventy, although only twenty of those lived in London. It didn't sound like many, but, without more information to go on, I'd need to start drafting family trees for each one, looking for the 'solicitor relation' mentioned in the *Perth Daily News* – a brother? a cousin? a grandfather? – and hope for the best. And that was assuming that Maud was there at all; she might have been working abroad on the night of the census. It seemed wise to wait for more clues before I started delving into her background.

On a more positive note, I had found a description of Maud. It had appeared in the *Adelaide Express and Telegraph* in 1914 and, to my relief, didn't describe a glamorous femme fatale decked out in scarlet lipstick and a low-brimmed hat, as in the illustrations that accompanied some of her articles. She sounded refreshingly normal:

> . . . Miss West is in appearance just a typical sturdy, athletic Englishwoman. Light brown hair, frank brown eyes, and a healthy complexion, all spoke of one who lived, or ought to live, an out-of-door, fresh air life. And this is probably one of the secrets of her success as a detective. She is just like so many other ordinary, middle-class English girls . . .[13]

By my calculations, she would have been in her early thirties at the time, so hardly a girl, but the fact that she was solidly middle class made sense if there was a solicitor in the family and Maud had been at leisure to practise her sleuthing skills before taking up the work professionally. I also wondered if her background was another clue as to why she went into business at all: however much her family loved her, a presumably unmarried daughter could be a financial burden. Maybe they had been keen to marry her off, and maybe, for whatever reason, Maud didn't want that.

By this point, I was itching to see a photograph of her. I wanted to look into those frank brown eyes and get the measure of her, but it was proving difficult. I'd received an email from Manchester Archives saying that the first photo I had requested would be delayed as they were reorganizing their storerooms, and I'd searched other archives catalogues and photographic agencies without success. As a last resort, I'd set up an eBay alert, which so far had only produced hundreds of twee dog postcards by the Edwardian artist Maud West Watson.

Then, one day, amidst all the terriers and poodles, there was a young man:

It was another press photograph, and it had a date: 22 February 1922. Heaven knows where it had been for the past ninety or so years – when it arrived through my letterbox, it was stained and battered and gave off a weird, formaldehyde-like tang – but at some point a sub-editor had daubed on a bit of white gouache and touched up the eyes, nostrils and cigarette with ink.

The scribbles and stamps on the back attributed it to the New York offices of a London photographic agency. There was also a faded label:

LONDON'S PREMIER LADY DETECTIVE
Miss Maud West, London's only woman detective,
has made quite a name for herself as a Sherlock Holmes . . .

So, this was Maud. Would I have bought a newspaper from her or walked past without a glance as she skulked in a doorway? Maybe. Was this her normal get-up? I couldn't discount the possibility that she preferred men's clothing, but the caption also stated that she was in 'mannish make-up', so I went with the idea that she was demonstrating her disguise skills. It was certainly attention-grabbing. In 1922, with the Jazz Age under way, cross-dressing wasn't unheard of, but it still had the capacity to shock the good people of Middle England.

Looking beyond the clothes, she was plumper than expected, but her overall appearance matched the description from the *Adelaide Express and Telegraph*. How old was she here? Forty? She hid it well. She hid a lot of things well. Her eyes, for example, were giving nothing away: they stared into the middle distance, refusing to meet my gaze. Despite that, Maud West suddenly felt very real. I couldn't imagine what strapping and corsetry was going on beneath her waistcoat, but underneath that there was a beating heart. Maud West wasn't just a lady detective; she was a living, breathing human being, full of complexities and anxieties and private passions. Who did she love? What did she fear? After the photograph was taken did she burst out laughing and whip off that ridiculous hat, or did she stand up, straighten her tie and ask for a light? Who *was* she?

The questions were piling up and I was no closer to finding any answers. It was time to head out and do some proper research. I needed to find the original articles that Maud had written, but there might also be case files or appointment books hidden away somewhere. I knew she had staff. Who were they? Perhaps one of them had left a diary or some letters behind. I could check the Home Office records at the National Archives to see if she had ever worked with the police, and look through ships' passenger lists for details of any trips abroad. Her revolver would have required a firearms certificate and, if the relevant register had survived, that might offer up a home address.

There were plenty of ways I could start building a picture of Maud's life and work, but first I wanted to settle a question that had been niggling at the back of my mind. Although many of the sources I had found stated that she was London's *only* woman detective, others had used the words *leading* and *foremost*. That suggested there were others. If so, who were they? And was Maud West really in a class of her own, or was it all just hype?

The Creeping Tiger

BY MAUD WEST

The facts were these. A certain well-known hostess asked me soon after the war to try to recover a packet of letters which had been taken from her private bureau. She did not suspect anyone, nor had she been blackmailed, but she confessed that if the letters fell into unscrupulous hands 'there would be the dickens to pay.'

'I have not had a moment's peace of mind since the letters went,' she continued. 'I do not suspect my husband, because he is totally ignorant of my foolishness. It all happened while he was on active service. Prompted, I suppose, by sympathy, I had become friendly with a man who was badly wounded. Our friendship ripened quickly and we wrote to each other. He died before the war ended. I kept his letters. Now they have gone.'

The problem she had set me did not seem easy to solve, but by persistent questioning I learned, after my third visit to her, that among her callers about the time the letters vanished was a man whom, before her marriage, she had jilted. He had been deeply in love with her at the time, and they had remained good friends.

Certain other circumstances which confirmed my suspicions caused me to try to make the man's acquaintance. I learned that though he had a fine flat he lived mostly at a West End hotel. The next morning saw me booked at the hotel, where I arranged with the head waiter to sit at a table facing my quarry. On the fifth day he smiled and with a courtly bow greeted me with a quiet 'Good morning.' I acknowledged his greeting smilingly and, after some customary remark about the weather, we discussed the news of the day.

This went on for several days, and then, with unexpected suddenness, he invited me to lunch. After a moment's hesitation I accepted. Later, to my dismay, he asked me to dine at his flat. I was getting heartily tired of the slowness of my inquiries, and in desperation I agreed. Before going there I arranged for two male assistants to be within earshot.

The dinner was splendidly prepared and set by his manservant, yet I did not feel as light-hearted as I appeared. With liqueurs and coffee we settled in front of a cosy fire in comfortable armchairs and talked about many foreign countries I had visited. At his request I accepted a second liqueur. This was my great moment, the one I had been playing for. As he went over to a cabinet to pour out the drinks, I skilfully dropped a sleeping draught into his coffee.

My nerves were strained to breaking point. Would he suspect the coffee? Would I have to rush to the window and call for help? Would my plans all fall to pieces? The seconds seemed like hours, and then with some casual remark he drank the lot! Very soon he relaxed and fell into a drugged sleep.

My actions now had to be very swift and silent, because I had to reckon on the possible return of the valet. In a corner of the room was a desk which had interested me all the evening. Fortunately it was unlocked. Quickly pulling the lid down, I made a thorough search and, to my delight, found the missing packet of letters.

In my haste and excitement I let the lid of the desk fall with what seemed a terrific crash. My heart stood still as I saw the sleeping man move. What was I to do if he awoke? Suddenly I dropped on my hands and knees and crawled under a huge tiger skin rug on the floor. I can only explain my action as being impelled by the elemental idea of hiding in the face of danger. Anyhow, having got under the rug, I crawled underneath it to the door, grabbed my hat and coat, and dashed into the street.

Next day, after returning the letters to my client, I paid another visit to my sleepy host. He was somewhat shame-faced and apologised for his unseemly conduct in falling to sleep. Edging towards the door I told him why I had accepted his invitation to dinner, how I had taken a packet of letters from his desk, and how I had crawled to the door under the rug. He did not seem to mind losing the letters at all. He said he had taken them in a stupid moment and had not intended to make use of them. But he thanked his stars that he did not wake up while that tiger was moving.[14]

Chapter Two

The Body in the Library

Brilliant deduction may be all very well, but
each detail must be logically checked and
verified before the fact is accepted . . .

Maud West, 1930[1]

It was good to be back in the British Library. As I settled into
my usual corner of the Humanities Reading Room, with its rows
of pale wooden desks and green leather chairs, I glanced around
at my fellow readers. There was something immensely comfort-
ing about the sight of all those figures bent in concentration over
their own private obsessions; it felt like coming home. The place
hummed with possibility. Stored within the mysterious depths of
the building were over 150 million items, from Leonardo da Vinci's
notebook to yesterday's *Sun*. If any lady detectives were lurking
in the shadows of history, there was a good chance I would find
them here.

But first, whilst I waited for my books to arrive at the issue desk,
I opened my laptop and brought up Wikipedia. On the train to
London, I had remembered coming across an American female
detective in a biography of Abraham Lincoln. She had little to do
with my current quest, but I was curious to see what impact she'd
had on the profession in America.

Her name was Kate Warne, and the article described how she
had marched into the Pinkerton National Detective Agency in

Chicago in 1856 and talked her way into a job as the nation's first female private investigator. Just twenty-three and recently widowed, she had cut her teeth on an embezzlement case before coming into her own during the Civil War by infiltrating secessionist tea parties and famously foiling an assassination plot on President Lincoln. There was also a photograph some believed to show her relaxing in a Union camp around 1862:

Trousers again. A theme was beginning to emerge. It wasn't one I had anticipated, but it made sense. In a world of rigidly defined gender roles, most of the power and excitement lay on the male side. History was scattered with stories of women who had passed themselves off as men to achieve their ambitions, whether it was to become a surgeon or run away to sea, so why not detectives?

At the end of the war, however, Kate Warne had dusted down her frocks and carried on her work as a woman, running Pinkerton's first all-woman detective bureau until her sudden death in January 1868. She was only thirty-five when she died, but her brief career had paved the way for women in all areas of investigation. Soon, even the police were exploring the idea of female crime fighters.

But that was America. In Britain, things were much more

conservative. I knew that when Maud West started out in 1905, the ranks of the British police were still firmly closed to women and would remain so until after the First World War, but were women already taking on private work?

The books I had ordered weren't much help. Despite promising titles – *The Lady Investigates* and *The Edwardian Detective* and so on – they all dealt with fictional sleuths. I also found two volumes of memoirs by a detective called Annette Kerner, who claimed to have been recruited into secret government operations in 1919 after running away from home to work as a singer in Switzerland. She eventually opened her own detective agency after the Second World War (at 231 Baker Street), but the stories she told of the intervening years were as crazy as Maud's. On further investigation, it transpired that she had taken up her pen after being declared bankrupt following a fraud trial in 1952.[2] I decided to give Ms Kerner a wide berth and retreated to the newsroom in search of solid fact.

There, it only took a brief search of the tabloid databases to establish that London was positively teeming with female detectives around the time Maud West was in business. They appeared again and again, giving evidence in court and surprising the readers of the *Daily Mail* by being clever and smart:

WOMEN DETECTIVES.

TWO CLEVER SISTERS.

KNIGHT'S WIFE FINED.

WHAT A LADY DETECTIVE SAW.

WOMAN DETECTIVE.

SMART WORK AT WEST END SALES.

They were store detectives. Catching shoplifters wasn't quite what I'd had in mind, but it was a start.

Department stores had first appeared in Britain in the mid-nineteenth century. They were the first public spaces created with women in mind, designed to offer a refined and leisurely shopping experience away from the grime of the streets. Their vast, glittering halls, crammed with tempting goods, were an immediate hit with the affluent middle classes, but they also attracted less welcome visitors, as the managing director of Harrods told the *Daily Express* in 1913:

> There are few problems which confront the large storekeeper more difficult than the problem of the shop-thief, for it is necessary for retail firms not only to have a watch kept on their own property, but also to see that their customers are protected from pickpockets. Every large store has its detective department, thoroughly organised, working to such a way that mistakes are never made.[3]

In order to blend in with the customers, the majority of store detectives were women, often former shop assistants who had stepped out from behind the drapery counter to do their bit in the fight against crime. And what a time it was for crime – the fashions of the day were practically designed for it. With a discreet slit in the seam of a dress, all manner of things could be squirrelled away. The newspapers were full of women who had been caught with astonishing amounts of loot beneath their skirts. One example was twenty-three-year-old Matilda Greenberg, whose suspiciously bulky appearance after a trip to Whiteley's in 1904 was found to be caused by sixty-five yards of purloined satin, still on the roll.[4]

But the store detectives didn't just have to deal with individual thieves. Members of shoplifting gangs, such as the notorious Forty Elephants, would swoop in and cause a rumpus whilst their colleagues stuffed furs and trinkets into their special 'grafter's bloomers', which were fitted with pockets and hooks. It was a high-stakes game. A habitual thief might expect to receive up to two years hard labour if convicted, so many came prepared for battle. As the head of Selfridges' 'secret service', Matilda Mitchell (described by her interviewer as having 'an altogether dominant face for a woman') said in 1913:

> The professional shop-lifter of the lower class is not an easy person to arrest. I have even known them carry scissors to stab the arm with or pepper to throw in the eyes.[5]

Things were looking up. If this was the level of excitement one could expect on a trip to the shops, maybe Maud's tales of guns and car chases weren't as improbable as they first seemed. I was curious to know how the detectives defended themselves. New York's early policewomen were taught ju-jitsu. Was it the same for London's store detectives? I had visions of shoplifters being hurled to the ground outside Selfridges, with hatpins flying and yards of silk floating down in cinematic slow motion. The closest I could find, however, was a photograph from 1927 showing a group of women in droopy knitwear learning how to make an arrest:

The man in the picture, Charles Kersey, was a former police officer who ran a training academy for store detectives 'up some rather dingy stairs' in Baker Street (again). According to an article from 1933, he taught his students self-defence ('And, with a blood curdling gesture, he indicates the best way of breaking the little finger . . .'), tutored them in how to give evidence and arranged visits to the police courts.[6]

Appearing in court was a major part of the job. I found one of Kersey's detectives testifying at Marylebone on behalf of three different stores on one single day in July 1919. Blanche Bolton had only been working as a detective for three weeks, but she'd been busy. For Marshall & Snelgrove in Oxford Street she described her 'somewhat violent struggle' with a woman who had lifted a customer's handbag, and reported how she had watched a well-known Russian pianist steal a cloak. She then gave evidence against a young lady 'of very good family' from Maida Vale who had been charged with theft from both Debenham's and Peter Robinson's.[7]

As many of the culprits were indistinguishable from the stores' genuine customers, the job required tact and skill. Blanche Bolton had followed the pianist Madame Levinskaya around Marshall & Snelgrove for an hour and a half before making her move. Rugby tackling an innocent duchess could have serious consequences, as one anonymous store detective – possibly Blanche herself – told the *Daily Mail* one week later:

> The general public does not, I think, realise the difficulties. One single mistake could lose me my job and ruin my career. In other callings one may make blunders that are not irretrievable. A detective cannot.
>
> If I were to arrest a person for stealing and the case could not be proved I should probably let my employers in for heavy damages, and they would have no further use for my services.[8]

Had the worst come to the worst, I thought it likely that she would have been able to find other work. Blanche Bolton's sister, for example, was said to have exposed some fraudulent palmists alongside her usual store work.[9] And, prior to joining Selfridges, Matilda Mitchell had worked undercover for the South-Western Railway Company and roamed the hills on horseback, tracking down unlicensed vets on behalf of the Royal College of Veterinary Surgeons.[10]

Women were clearly doing some fascinating work outside the confines of department-store life, but these glimpses were only ever little asides that were rarely followed up. Store detectives were presented as plucky and admirable, but as soon as they took on private work an awkward silence seemed to descend, especially in the more upmarket newspapers. But why?

All became clear over the next few days as I delved deeper into press reports and consulted academic journals. The general public may not have liked the idea of spies lurking amongst the corsetry in their favourite department stores, but they accepted that store detectives were there to fill a precise commercial need. The motives of the private detective, on the other hand, were much more questionable. As one leading barrister sniffed in *The Times* in 1905, it was 'a calling that stank in the nostrils of every honest man'.[11]

I recognized that tone of snooty contempt. It was the voice of the British establishment. Protecting the nation from rogue vets and nimble-fingered thieves was one thing, but grubbing around in a chap's private life? That was 'hideous' and 'so contemptible as to be almost outside the pale of humanity.'[12]

Yet it was the establishment itself that had made the profession an indispensable part of British life. Its folly lay in the creation of one piece of legislation: the Matrimonial Causes Act of 1857. In a word? Divorce.

Until 1857, the only way of obtaining a divorce was through a

Private Act of Parliament, a process so expensive that on average only two such Acts were passed each year. Everyone else had to make do with a lifetime of domestic misery or pursue other options such as abandonment, bigamy or arsenic. The Matrimonial Causes Act took divorce out of Parliament and into the civil courts so that, in theory, anyone could rid themselves of a tiresome spouse in a completely above-board and legal way.

It still wasn't easy. The fees kept it out of the reach of many, but even those with money had an additional hurdle to overcome. No divorce would be granted without evidence of adultery, and female petitioners had to prove an additional cause such as rape, cruelty or incest. This had some unintended consequences. As the hearings were held in open court, with the galleries inevitably packed with members of the press, the nation suddenly had some very fruity reading material to enjoy over breakfast.

Barely a year after the courts had started hearing cases under the new legislation, even the Lord Chancellor was having misgivings. He confided to his journal that 'like Frankenstein, I am afraid of the monster I have called into existence.' Queen Victoria agreed, describing the newspaper reports as on a par with 'the worst French novels'.[13]

Not only did the potential scandal of open court hearings give many would-be divorcees pause for thought (this deterrent being a deliberate aspect of the legislation), but it made it difficult to find people willing to testify. This was especially true of key witnesses whose livelihoods depended upon discretion, such as hotel managers and household staff. What was needed was an outside party willing to gather evidence and then take the stand in court. Enter the private detective.

All the main detective agencies employed women to assist with inquiries. They could visit places where a man's presence might be suspicious, to befriend landladies, eavesdrop on co-respondents or go undercover in factories and shops to investigate cases of pilfering and fraud. In 1894, the head of one of the largest detective agencies in London ran a special advertisement which appeared in the *Sporting Times*:[14]

SLATER'S WOMEN DETECTIVES.

Many men say women have been their downfall, but HENRY SLATER owes his success to his lady detectives for secret watchings, secret inquiries, &c.—a speciality in detective work, of which he is the pioneer.—No. 1, Basinghall Street, E.C.

As it happened, Henry Slater wasn't the pioneer he claimed to be, but then he wasn't really Henry Slater either (or Captain Scott or any of the other aliases he used), as was revealed when he appeared before a magistrate on a conspiracy charge in 1904.[15] He was a former legal clerk called George Tinsley, and the use of women detectives had been widespread for years. One case I found even predated the Matrimonial Causes Act. In 1854, Charles Frederick Field, a former inspector with the Metropolitan Police, was hired to gather evidence by a man suing his wife's lover for damages in a 'criminal conversation' case.* Unable to gain access himself to the terraced house in Cheltenham where the trysts were thought to be taking place, Field installed a female employee as a cook in the adjacent house and gave her a special gimlet with which to bore a peephole in the adjoining wall.[16]

All in all, it was a sordid business. But there was something about the freedom and excitement the work offered that seemed to attract a certain type of educated, middle-class woman. In 1892, the women's journal *Hearth and Home* reported with dismay that it had received a number of letters enquiring about detective careers: 'This reveals a very lamentable state of things. That there should be

---

* In such cases, a husband would seek financial compensation for the corruption of his wife, regardless of the affair's effect on the marriage ('conversation' being an obsolete term for sexual intercourse).

so many girls or women anxious to live upon the sins or misfortunes of their fellow-creatures is indeed a distressing situation.' In a bid to deter its readers from pursuing such 'objectionable' employment, it had contacted a number of detective agencies and found that 'the profession is overcrowded . . . one firm alone received eighteen hundred answers in response to a few advertisements for assistants.'[17]

Hearth and Home also grudgingly reported that the pay for female detectives was between five and ten shillings a day – a reasonable wage if the work was regular. A lady detective speaking to *Tit Bits* magazine, however, suggested it was not. She explained that she was paid on results and 'there are weeks which pass without our earning a sovereign.'[18]

But these women were still satellites to the male world of sleuthing, still largely rummaging around in laundry baskets and reporting back to the men in charge. I wanted to find the real troublemakers, the women who answered to no man. Surely, in a profession that by its very nature attracted those with more maverick tendencies, some of them must have broken away to work on their own terms? That is, unless Maud West really was a one-off.

Returning to *The Times* and other daily newspapers, I found that some women had indeed gone into business on their own. One of the most successful ventures was Moser's Ladies Detective Agency, which had been set up in 1889 by Henry Slater's greatest rival, the ex-Scotland Yard inspector Maurice Moser. This was an offshoot of Moser's main business and he had installed at its head his mistress, Charlotte Antonia Williamson. After two sensational court cases with their respective spouses, during one of which Moser's reputation was all but destroyed by Slater acting on behalf of Charlotte's husband, the couple had split.[19] But Charlotte continued as the head of the agency as 'Antonia Moser' before handing over the baton (and her name) to her daughter Margaret

Williamson in 1908. The business struggled, however, and was eventually dissolved in 1916.[20]

Other names, such as Margaret Cook and Grace Fielding, cropped up occasionally in news reports, but by the time the first full *International Police and Detective Directory* was published in 1922, only two out of the forty-five top detective agencies listed in Britain were run by women. One belonged to Maud West; the other to Kate Easton.

Kate Easton was a good fifteen years older than Maud. She lived at Gray's Inn, where there were solicitors and barristers galore to provide work, and had an office at the top of Shaftesbury Avenue. As far as I could tell, both women had set up their agencies in 1905, and each had a small army of male and female staff ready to do their bidding. For twenty years, their adverts battled it out in the newspapers, jostling for the attention of readers in a ping-pong of superlatives and definite articles:

Maud West – London's Lady Detective
Kate Easton – The Lady Detective
Maud West – London's Foremost Lady Detective
Kate Easton – London's Leading Woman in every Branch of Detective Work

And so on.

Maud won eventually, if only because Kate Easton retired in 1929. By then, of course, Maud had been sending photographs of herself to the press with the caption 'London's only lady detective' for quite some time.

Professional rivalry aside, both women had a lot to prove if they were to succeed. Detective work was a costly business and those who fell by the wayside appeared to do so mainly through bank-ruptcy. The work was well paid – for a week's observation, Kate charged six guineas, with one typical investigation bringing in a total of £94, an amount many office clerks would have struggled to earn in a year[21] – but a case could rack up substantial expenses with no guarantee of a successful outcome. Every detective had to deal with a quibbling client at some point. In 1912, for example, Kate Easton sued a woman who had hired her firm to watch an errant husband and then refused to pay on the grounds that someone had tipped him off that he was being followed.[22]

The trick seemed to be keeping these non-paying customers to a minimum by maintaining a good reputation and the trust of a large pool of wealthy clients. Unfortunately, most of these clients were to be found in 'good society' – the very place where the detective's work was publicly most reviled. All detectives, male or female, faced this dilemma, but Kate and Maud also had to face down the critics and naysayers who maintained that sleuthing was no job for a woman. Each had her own armour in this fierce battle for the hearts, minds and wallets of the British elite.

Kate Easton's armour was pure bluestocking defiance: 'I have always done a man's work, and I always will,' she declared in 1907. She explained that she had started out as a correspondence clerk for a large wholesaler, where she did a little ad hoc spying for her boss, before developing her sleuthing skills first for a solicitor and then for a male private detective, until she was finally able to open her own agency. She undertook the usual work of any private detect-ive: '. . . blackmail, divorce, evidence, robbery, I undertake it all; I have touched everything except murder.'[23]

Her client list also notably included suffragettes, such as Edith Wheelwright from Bath, who had been knocked out with chloroform by a female assailant and robbed of a pearl and emerald ring (an incident which the newspapers hinted was part of a wider internecine warfare between the suffragists of the West Country).[24]

Kate was herself a suffragist and joined the 'No Vote – No Census!' boycott of the 1911 national headcount.[25] On the night of Sunday 2 April, with Emily Davison famously hiding in a broom cupboard in the House of Commons and other suffragettes enjoying midnight picnics on Wimbledon Common and rambles around Trafalgar Square, Kate put her feet up at home and prepared to meet the enumerator with stony silence. He got nothing out of her, but she was well known enough at Gray's Inn for him to record her name, single status and profession. He also had a stab at her age, putting it at forty-five, but all other details on the form were left blank. A note at the bottom read, 'N.B. Information Refused by Miss Easton.'

The previous year, she had also been involved in the two hotly contested general elections of 1910, which saw the Liberals under Herbert Asquith cling on to power by just two seats in January and one seat in December. The secret ballot may have been in place for nearly forty years, but bribery and corruption were still rife, and undercover agents were commonly employed by parliamentary candidates to keep an eye on things. After the first election, Kate reported:

> . . . old clothes were necessary, as we had to encounter more than one shower of Election eggs, of course intended for the opposite side; but in the country we have had the most excitement. For instance, in the north they are rather brutal, and two men in my employ had narrow escapes during the last General Election. They had to watch a certain Yorkshire village to see whether there was any ground for a charge of bribery. It was a mining village, and somehow the miners found out who they

were. A crowd pursued them for two and a half miles along canal banks, and had they been caught, they would undoubtedly have been ducked, if not more relentlessly handled. Your Yorkshire miner is a bit of a tough, and his idea of fighting has no close similarity to the Queensberry rules.[26]

In her occasional forays into the press, Kate touched upon some of the unusual and dangerous situations in which she had found herself, such as renting a room in a brothel during a blackmail case, and getting herself admitted to an infectious diseases hospital.[27] But, for the most part, she just carried on without a fuss.

Maud, on the other hand, clearly loved fuss. She said she didn't ('My job's very dull, you know . . .') but the mounting evidence from the tabloids suggested otherwise. She sought publicity at every turn, arranging stunts to generate headlines:

REVOLVER SHOT AT A SEANCE.

LADY DETECTIVE TO SHOOT SPIRIT.

London, Saturday.

and circulating photographs of herself in disguise:[28]

MISS MAUD WEST.

It was all faintly ridiculous, but the more articles I found, the more I realized that Maud West was no dime-store detective. Looking beyond her tendency towards the absurd, there was a complexity to her that intrigued me. Her writing displayed a mix of world-weariness and empathy, of self-deprecation and border-line arrogance. And, whilst she showed a fabulous disregard for ethics when it suited her, I sensed a moral streak, too. There was also an air of genuine concern and passion for her work.

As a research subject, however, she was proving to be increasingly slippery. I'd even caught her in some outright lies. The first, of course, was that she was by no means London's only lady detective – and then there were the rugs. In her story from 1931 about drugging a jilted lover to retrieve some missing love letters, she had described diving under a tiger-skin rug to escape, yet I found another story from 1926 which described almost identical circumstances, only the man was suspected of will fraud and the rug was made of bear skin:

> The man must have been still too dopey to notice the strange antics of his rug, for I managed to get clear. The funny part, however, was that when I opened the door, with the rug still over me, I fell into the arms of my waiting assistant, who got the shock of his life. He thought his last hour had come![29]

I'd also come across more than one account of how she had begun her career as a detective. Initially, the latest articles I'd found seemed to corroborate the version in the *Perth Daily News*, which described how a solicitor relation had asked Maud to help solve a simple hotel robbery.[30] She expanded on this in the *Sunday Dispatch*:

> Nearly all the male members of my family have been connected with the law, either as solicitors or barristers. A study of criminology must have been in my blood, and it was after pestering

my people for some time that a solicitor uncle gave me my first enquiry job, which took me to Paris.[31]

It made sense. In divorce cases, at least, solicitors were often the ones to hire private detectives to gather evidence on behalf of their clients. On another occasion, she said, 'I was introduced to the law fairly young . . . because my father was a barrister. He wanted me to take up that side of it, but then he saw I seemed to have the aptitude for detecting, so he started me on this strange career.'[32]

A picture of Maud as a restless young woman, bored with her lot and desperate for adventure, was beginning to take shape in my mind – that is, until I found an entirely different story in *Pearson's Weekly*:

> Some few years after leaving school I undertook a case in an unprofessional capacity for a friend. It was quite an unimportant and very simple one, and I only mention it because it decided me, as I had then to do something to earn my own living, to start as a detective on my own account.[33]

What had happened to her solicitor uncle or her encouraging father? And, if she came from such an illustrious family, why did she need a job? Was she cast out, forced to make her own living? Had there been some sort of scandal or tragedy? Whatever it was, Maud evidently couldn't be trusted, even as a witness to her own life.

On the train back to Shropshire one evening, I mulled things over. If, as I believed, there was little truth to her stories individually, then what about her writing as a whole? After all, she had lived and worked in extraordinary times; she had witnessed women taking to the streets to demand the vote, the devastation of the First World War, the decline of the aristocracy, the tragedies and allure of the Jazz Age, and the gradual creep of Fascism. Throughout all this, Maud had spent her days dealing with people's secret fears and anxieties. If nothing else, through her articles and interviews, she had left behind a social history – admittedly, a slightly unorthodox one – of their struggles to come to terms with this ever-changing world. Maybe, underneath all the lies and fabrications, there was a truth to be found after all.

Looking at things from this angle, the way forward became clear. I would trace this chronicle of human follies and frailties from its beginning in 1905 to wherever it might lead, and, at the same time, I'd keep digging and digging until the real Maud West made herself known. It was going to be hard going, but Maud would have approved – if not of my aim, then surely of my method:

> Almost abnormal patience is required, for, on some occasions, months pass before the slightest progress is made. But the 'operative' as we call him (or her) must not lose keenness, and must bring the same energy to bear on the case all the time, however hopeless it may seem. Usually patience brings its own reward![34]

Maud was right. Although, as it turned out, I wouldn't have to wait long for my first reward.

The Lady with the Blue Spectacles

BY MAUD WEST

I remember one of my earliest clients was a lady who wanted me to find out all about another rather well-known lady in society. My client, who wore a pair of dark-blue spectacles, told me that she wanted me to find out as much as I could in twenty-four hours about the lady in question, and if the information was satisfactory (she did not define, by the way, what was meant by satisfactory) she would pay me £5, only I was to let her have the information by noon the following day.

She then gave me her, or rather a, name and an address in Kensington, and if she did not hear from me by the first post, arranged to call on me again the following day at noon. When she left I looked up the address she had given me in the directory, and ascertained that it was a stationer's shop. This led me to the conclusion I had already partly formed, that my client gave me a false name, and that the stationer's shop was probably a place where she received letters.

Now I did not much care about taking up a case for a client who gave me a false name and address, and had I been busier, I would, on making certain my client had done so, have dropped the case, but not being busy I thought it would be good practice to find out as much as I could about this blue-spectacled lady. Accordingly I took a hansom (this was before the days of taxis) to the address in Kensington, and ascertained that it was, as I suspected, a stationer's shop to which people could have letters addressed.

I was at the shop again the next morning at eight o'clock and waited about outside until about half-past nine when my client, who was wearing her blue spectacles, drove up to the door in a hansom. She had come to get the letter she hoped to receive from me (and which, of course, she didn't get) and in a couple of minutes she came out again and drove away, and the next minute I was following her in another hansom.

She drove to a house in Dover Street, and a few minutes later I made the interesting discovery that my client was a society fortune-teller, and it did not require any great powers of inference to guess that the lady about whom she was in so great a hurry to find out something was probably coming to her that day to have her fortune told.

Having ascertained the identity of my blue-spectacled client I hurried back to my office and there awaited her arrival at noon. She turned up punctually at twelve o'clock, and I shall never forget the way she started out of her chair when I told her that I did not care much about hunting up ladies' histories for fortune-tellers. She left my office, I think, with a much higher opinion of my ability as a detective than when she entered it.[35]

Chapter Three

Crooked House

I have, in the course of my work, become
acquainted with the history and methods of all
kinds of crooks and shady customers.

Maud West, 1919[1]

Starting at the beginning was easier said than done. According to Maud, she had set up her agency in 1905, but the earliest evidence I could find was an advert from July 1909 on the front page of the *Sunday Times*.[2] If this was indeed her first advertisement, she couldn't have chosen more colourful company with which to announce her arrival on the scene. The lottery of alphabetical placement had squeezed her in between two jailbirds-in-waiting:

GENTLEMAN (25), WELL-BORN, vague and of somewhat detached nature, studies during day but is unoccu-
pied during latter part of afternoons, welcomes suggestions
for employing this time.—Problem, c/o SUNDAY TIMES.

MAUD WEST, "LADY DETECTIVE." Tel. 8561 Gerrard.
Are you worried? If so, consult me! Private enquiries
and delicate matters undertaken anywhere with secrecy
and ability. DIVORCE, SHADOWINGS. &c. Intelligent
Male and Female Staff. REFERENCES TO LEADING
SOLICITORS. High-class firm. Consultations free with
Principal or Manager.—MAUD WEST, Albion House,
59. New Oxford-st., London, W.C. ¦26

RESIDENT PATIENT.—Married medical man, residing
favoured locality, London, wishes for invalid lady or
gentleman to accompany them six weeks' holiday and
afterwards permanently reside with them : every accommo-
dation. &c. Write Consultant, care of Willing's Advertisement Offices, 73. Knightsbridge, S.W.

The first shouldn't have been a crime, but it was. Even if the vague, detached gentleman failed to attract any 'suggestions' for his teatime doldrums, he could have been sailing very close to the wind as regards the Labouchere Amendment of 1885, under which even attempting to procure gay sex was punishable by up to two years' hard labour; the maximum penalty for the act itself was life imprisonment. Still, under those circumstances, what better thrill than to go cruising for company on the front page of the nation's most straight-laced paper?

The second may have been entirely innocent – a doctor who just couldn't get enough of wheeling people around in bath chairs – but it was hard not to imagine more nefarious motives.

As for Maud's own advert, I'd seen it before, but reading it again gave me an idea of a good place to start. If I wanted solid facts, what could be more solid than a building? Although Maud's interviewers couldn't decide whether her office had 'the aspect of a woman's boudoir rather than that of a detective bureau' or was just 'bright and ordinary', one thing was certain: it was located in Albion House at 59 New Oxford Street.[3]

My first stop, Google Street View, was of little help. At the time the images were taken, Albion House was shrouded in tarpaulins. As for other photographs, it appeared that many people over the years had stood with their backs to it to get a good shot of the ornate shop front of its neighbour, the famous umbrella merchant James Smith & Sons (est. 1865), but no one had ever turned their lens on Albion House itself. So, I headed back to London to have a look.

The building stood on its own miniature block, moated by New Oxford Street, Shaftesbury Avenue and two minor service roads. To the west was the umbrella shop, which backed on to a slim red-brick building overlooking a small square on Shaftesbury Avenue. To my surprise, I realized this was where Kate Easton had her office; I knew it was good to keep one's enemies close, but this was literally within shouting distance. To the rear of Albion House was the Neo-Romanesque Bloomsbury Baptist Chapel, built in 1886, and the building to the east, though grubby and unkempt, also retained many of its original nineteenth-century features.

Amidst all this stood Albion House itself, or rather a building that called itself Albion House. It displayed all the post-war charm of a lump of concrete. I had a pretty good idea what had happened, and it didn't take me long to confirm that, yes, at some point during the Blitz the Luftwaffe had dropped a high explosive bomb right on top of Maud's office, leaving everything else in the vicinity intact.[4]

Over the next few weeks, I haunted various London archives and libraries, trying to find information about the original building. But, despite looking at all manner of photographs, books, maps and plans, nothing was forthcoming. In a particularly low moment, I found myself studying drainage blueprints which had been submitted to the local authority following changes in public health legislation in the 1930s. These gave me details of where Maud West went to the loo, including a tiny illustration of one of the very toilets, but little else.

The breakthrough came when I started to look further into the past. Albion House, it turned out, was built on the site of an old Unitarian chapel which had been demolished in 1896. Whilst the new building was being erected in 1899, the *Building News* had published an architect's drawing of what it would eventually look like.[5] And what a building it was.

The Luftwaffe had robbed New Oxford Street of one of its most impressive landmarks. It was built of red brick and Portland stone; red granite pilasters separated the large shop windows at street level, and the whole thing was topped with domed turrets:

At least one of the windows on the upper floors had been Maud's office. But what about the others? According to advertisements I found from 1909, the ground floor held the London showroom of the Rover car company, which was offering its latest model, the 15 horsepower 'Landaulette', for £485.⁶ There was also a piano show-room and, as one travelled further up the building, a smattering of electrical and mechanical engineers, architects and surveyors. Being just around the corner from London's theatreland, Albion House was also home to the Music Hall Ladies Guild, a charity which ministered to female artistes – and their children – who had fallen on hard times through ill health or bad reviews.

But mostly, it seemed, Albion House was crawling with sharks and charlatans. One suite, for example, housed Professor Horspool's Vocal Academy, which was run by a retired vicar who, despite a noble motto – '*Magna est veritas et prævalebit*' (great is the truth and it will prevail) – and a reference from the Countess of Cardigan, appeared to spend a great deal of his time defending himself against accusations of being an 'impudent quack'.[7] In another, McKinley Alexander & Sons flogged penny shares in American railroad companies which, the *Financial Times* reported, offered no better chance of a return than a public lottery.[8]

The smaller rooms housed the snake-oil salesmen. From one, Harriet Meta hawked her miracle wrinkle cure as endorsed by the non-existent Countess Radsch of St James's, whilst in another Don José Acuna promised 'hair for the hairless' to those purchasing his secret Spanish remedy. Dr Franckel's Deafness Cure, which consisted of rubbing a black ointment called Ohrsorb Compound behind the ear, appeared to do nothing but raise eyebrows in the *British Medical Journal*.[9] Also on offer were Gould's Golden Pills ('for health and wealth') and the Isham Water Company's 'California Waters of Life.'[10] In Room 57, Mr Munyon, 'the Medical Millionaire', was making his millions one penny at a time by mailing out homoeopathic cure-alls.[11]

Maud evidently kept interesting company, but I had a curious sense of déjà vu. Munyon the Medical Millionaire? The Music Hall Ladies Guild? Dr Franckel? I was sure I had come across these people before – and, as it turned out, I had. They had all featured in one of the most fabled episodes of British criminal history.

It all began on 2 February 1910, when the treasurer of the Music Hall Ladies Guild failed to attend their weekly meeting. She was American and, although then retired from the stage, had once enjoyed minor success as a music-hall singer both in New York and London under the name of Belle Elmore. Some might have found her brash, with her bleached hair and almost obsessive love of new frocks and jewellery, but her vivacious personality had won her many friends who, in turn, kept rumours of her various affairs away from her husband.

The husband, whom Belle called 'Peter', also worked at Albion House. Short and balding, with a bushy moustache and slightly bulging eyes that peered out from behind wire-rimmed spectacles, he was also well liked, although his mild-mannered demeanour was very different to that of his wife. Until recently, he had been Mr Munyon's manager, but was now a partner in the Yale Tooth Specialists in Room 58. As a sideline, he also played the role of 'Dr Franckel', distributing Ohrsorb Compound to the deaf and gullible at three shillings a pop. He claimed to be a doctor, but the certificate on his wall was from a homoeopathic college in Michigan.

On the day of the meeting, his secretary Ethel delivered a letter to the Guild committee, explaining that Belle had been called away to America following a death in the family. It said she would be away for a few months and, as such, was resigning as treasurer.

At first, her colleagues thought nothing of it, appointed a new treasurer, and got on with their business. But, as time went by, they became increasingly suspicious of Belle's uncharacteristic silence – and of her husband's evasive excuses.

When, at the end of March, a notice appeared in the stage magazine the *Era*, announcing Belle's death from pneumonia, the Music Hall Ladies Guild swept into action. They wrote to Belle's stepson in California, in whose arms she had supposedly died, and learned that he had not even seen her, let alone been present at her death.[12] Meanwhile, their spies reported that Ethel had been spotted wearing items of Belle's clothing and jewellery.

The police were initially unwilling to help due to lack of evidence of any crime, but after three months of attention from the ladies of the Guild, Scotland Yard eventually dispatched Chief Inspector Walter Dew to Albion House. There, he interviewed Belle's husband, before visiting the couple's home at 39 Hilldrop Crescent in Holloway, where he found Ethel in residence. The relationship was unorthodox, coming so soon after Belle's death, but Dew was satisfied that everything was in order. And that would have been that, had the husband not panicked.

On 9 July, he sent a letter to his dental assistant asking him to wind up his affairs. The same day, he bought a wig, shaved off his moustache and hotfooted it out of the country with Ethel in tow, disguised as his son. The letter was signed 'H. H. Crippen.'

Inspector Dew immediately ordered further investigations, which ended with the gory discovery of a headless corpse buried in quicklime under the cellar floor at 39 Hilldrop Crescent.

What happened next became something of a legend: photographs of the fugitives had been circulated to the press, and the captain of the cargo ship SS *Montrose*, en route to Canada, recognized Crippen and Ethel as two of his passengers who had boarded at Antwerp. In a first for criminal history, he alerted Scotland Yard by ship-to-shore telegraph, which led to one of the slowest high-speed chases on record: by catching a faster boat, Inspector Dew was able to greet Dr Crippen and Ethel le Neve when the *Montrose* arrived in Quebec on 31 July.

The trial took place at the Old Bailey that October. After five days of testimony, the jury found Dr Crippen guilty of the murder of Belle Elmore, aka Cora Crippen, and he was subsequently hanged at Pentonville Prison. In a separate trial, Ethel le Neve was acquitted of being an accessory after the fact. Inspector Dew bathed in the glory of the title 'The Man Who Caught Crippen'.

But where was Maud West in all this? One of the most infamous crimes of the twentieth century had unfolded right under her nose and, as far as I could tell, she never mentioned it. Surely the Maud who dressed up as Charlie Chaplin and threatened to shoot ghosts wouldn't have missed this opportunity for publicity? According to the surviving police notebooks at Kew, she hadn't been interviewed as a potential witness, but even being a bystander would have been enough. 'The Cellar Murder' was plastered all over the papers for months, and the press were desperate for new angles. What was wrong with her? Was she piqued that no one had thought to consult her? Or – and I savoured the thought as it bubbled up – was she silent for another reason?

It was a long shot, but after hours of scrolling through articles about the case, I stumbled across an almost throwaway comment by Adeline Harrison, one of the members of the Ladies Guild:

> [The Guild] placed the matter in the hands, first, of a private detective, and then of Scotland Yard.[13]

As far as I knew, this had never been mentioned before or since. Admittedly, the Guild might have approached one of the more established London agencies, or Pinkerton's if they were trying to trace their friend in California, or even, heaven forbid, Kate Easton. But Maud was right on their doorstep. She must have known the parties involved, at least by sight, and she wouldn't have needed much of an excuse to go snooping around the building.

Had Maud West, 'the female Sherlock Holmes', failed to spot one of Britain's most infamous murder cases evolving right in front of her? In her defence, she was still relatively inexperienced at the time. Even Inspector Dew, with his twenty-eight years as a policeman (and twelve of those at the Yard), had almost let it go due to lack of evidence. It was only when they found the body that the case took off, and I couldn't imagine that Maud, even in her prime, would have gone on a midnight shovelling expedition in a private cellar on nothing more than a hunch. But, still, if she *had* been consulted, no wonder she kept quiet. 'The Woman Who Failed To Catch Crippen' probably wasn't the kind of headline she was after.

Whatever the extent of her involvement in the Crippen affair, Maud did admit to some mistakes during her early years as a detective. One of these occurred after a firm of solicitors asked her to follow a suspected blackmailer and report back on his activities. It would have been a straightforward task, had the man not twigged and, in turn, hired his own detective to tail Maud.

Late one afternoon, having spent the day trying to shake off her shadow, Maud stopped for a cup of tea, 'feeling very fatigued, depressed, and irritated.' Shortly afterwards, the other detective entered the cafe, but, instead of taking a table at a discreet distance, he sat down opposite her:

> At first he did not take the least notice of me, but after a few minutes, looking straight at me, he said: 'Miss West, I am getting tired of this. If you will come to my flat I will give you all the information you want. Mr A. (that was his client) is a real bad lot, and I don't mind if I give him away.'

She knew she ought to decline the invitation, but nonetheless decided to 'see what this particular move in the game meant.' It was, of course, a trap:

> We reached the flat in a few minutes . . . Directly I entered he turned and left the room; I heard the lock go 'click' and rushed to the door and rattled and shook the handle; I then turned back into the room and was crossing over to the window to see what my chances of escape that way were, when I saw an envelope directed to myself on the table.
>
> I opened it and found the following lines scribbled on a half-sheet of notepaper: 'Very sorry, but I had to get rid of you for a couple of hours; will be back at eight; there is no use in your trying to get away.'

When the detective returned, Maud knew immediately that something was wrong:

> He looked as white as a sheet and was very agitated. The first thing he did on entering the room was to take a drink of brandy,

then he turned to me, and said: 'You needn't trouble yourself
any more, Miss West, about the case: A. is dead.'[14]

What the detective had been up to remained a mystery. Maud
said he refused to give any further details, but she did later read in
an evening paper that Mr A had shot himself at his hotel. She also
discovered that he was wanted in New York for an unspecified
crime, and that he was due to be arrested that very afternoon on an
extradition warrant.

Clearly, she should never have gone to the flat. But, I wondered,
had she also made a slip – deliberate or otherwise – when recount-
ing these events? Although I had concluded that Maud's stories
couldn't be word-for-word true due to issues of client confiden-
tiality, I hadn't completely abandoned the hope that there might
be some hidden clue that would enable me to identify some of the
participants.

Maud once said, 'I have often done things that were most trouble-
some and sometimes tricky on the slenderest chance of picking
up a useful bit of information.'[15] The same could be said for my
own work, and there was a challenge in this particular tale that I
couldn't resist: she said that news of Mr A's suicide had appeared
in the evening paper. Perhaps this was true. After all, Maud could
never have imagined that one day someone might be able to trace
Mr A by searching the newspapers at the click of a mouse.

It soon became apparent, however, that shooting oneself in
a hotel of an afternoon was a surprisingly common pursuit in
Edwardian London. All manner of people were at it – Hungarian
counts, jilted lovers, bankrupt tycoons, provincial tourists – but
none matched the man in Maud's story. The closest I could find was
a strange case from March 1909, in which a distinguished-looking
man wearing a frock coat, silk hat and lavender gloves took a suite
at the Savoy under the alias of 'Dr George B. Pullman' of Chicago.

He subsequently arranged for a diamond merchant from the Burlington Arcade to bring a large quantity of jewellery to the hotel so that his 'wife' could choose a piece. When the jeweller's assistant caught him trying to make off with the diamonds down the hotel corridor, 'Dr Pullman' inexplicably drew a razor from his pocket and cut his own throat. His true identity was never revealed, but a letter from Switzerland, found amongst his belongings, suggested that 'Dr Pullman' had been implicating the writer in 'unpleasant things'.[16] Could this be Maud's blackmailer, trying to raise funds for a last-ditch escape from the New York police? Probably not, but it was tantalizingly close.

Somewhat heartened, I decided to take a closer look at another of Maud's stories from her early career, which also happened to involve a mysterious 'Mr A'. This one was a former curate at a West End church who 'had left it not in the best odour' and had recently returned to London after a spell abroad. Maud said she had encountered him after being approached by a wealthy picture dealer whose daughter 'had become very peculiar in her manner and general behaviour . . .' and seemed to be keeping some great secret.

After establishing that the young woman was a regular visitor to the former curate's flat near the Edgware Road, Maud started to keep watch. She noticed that, every afternoon, a small stream of well-dressed women would go inside and stay for nearly three hours. So, the next day she put on her best clothes and knocked on the door:

I sent in an assumed name, and was shown into a small, scantily furnished room. Presently a young gentleman with a marked American accent and wearing a well-cut black suit came to tell me that the Rev. Mr. A. was engaged at the present moment in 'worship' but that he would see me in about fifteen minutes if I cared to wait.

'But cannot I join in the worship!' I exclaimed. 'That is what I have come here for.'

The young man glanced at her expensive attire and jewels, popped out of the room, and returned with a request to follow him. Even Maud was unprepared for what happened next:

I shall never forget the sight that met my eyes. At one end of the room was a tall, very handsome man with a long beard, dressed in a scarlet robe and wearing a scarlet cap. He held a flaming torch in one hand. Round about him were about a dozen ladies, each of whom wore a sort of scarlet cape over their shoulders. The walls of the room were, I noticed, papered in blue-black ornamented with different figures in scarlet.

I was motioned by the young man to join the kneeling group of ladies, and did so. The Rev. Mr. A. took no notice of my entrance, but continued his prayer or address or whatever it was, for he spoke in some language that I did not understand. Suddenly the torch he was holding flamed up and then died down and went out. The Rev. Mr. A. said something, clapped his hands, and everyone got up and sat down on chairs; one of the congregation I saw was my client's daughter.

This charade, Maud discovered, was a lucrative one. In just a few weeks, the Rev. Mr A had managed to extract £150 from the young woman. He was subsequently visited by the picture dealer and persuaded 'to take himself and his orgies elsewhere.'[17]

The story had seemed so rich in detail that I'd had high hopes of finding a hidden clue. But, on further inspection, I saw that it was futile. Flaming torches? Scarlet robes? *Orgies?* Not the Roman kind, but still. There was little I could do with any of that. Furthermore, as the Rev. Mr A had been discreetly and conveniently shooed out of town, there would be nothing about the affair in the papers. I supposed there might be a dressmaker's diary lying forgotten in an attic somewhere with details of an order for a dozen scarlet capes and a little hat, but, until that turned up, there was no way of tracing him.

The characters in Maud's stories may have been stubbornly elusive, but in the process of trawling through the newspapers for matching cases, I had come across one of Maud's genuine, flesh-and-blood clients. He wasn't a particularly satisfied one, and she never wrote about him herself, but there was no doubt that he had existed. What's more, his story opened up another aspect of Maud's early career that she had omitted to mention.

Lieutenant-Colonel Monckton O'Dell Braddell was a senior medical officer in the Royal Army Medical Corps, stationed in the Punjab. I found the details of his dealings with Maud in various reports about the case of 'Maud West & Co. v Braddell', which came before the King's Bench Division of the High Court in November 1911. The suit concerned a bill of sixty-two pounds, which the colonel had refused to pay.

Braddell's first contact with Maud had been sent by cable from Rawalpindi on 21 November 1910. The message read:

Meet ship Scindia, 25th. Watch Mrs Braddell. Writing.

As promised, a letter followed, which explained, 'I am taking proceedings for divorce against her, and pending this I am advised to pay her expenses home and allow her so much. I only want to find out where she goes on landing, and if she goes to London the kind of life she leads.'[18]

One of Maud's staff, William Cheney, who had been working on a case in Lancashire at the time, was sent to Liverpool to meet the SS *Scindia*. When it docked, he found that Mrs Braddell had disembarked at Marseilles. She had, however, left some luggage on board to be forwarded to her father's address in Nottingham. Accordingly, another assistant – a Miss Magnen – was dispatched to track her down. The quibble over the bill seemed to arise from a dispute as to whether Miss Magnen had stayed in Nottingham for five days or twenty-two.

There was nothing surprising about the case, as such. It was a standard divorce investigation, and I already knew from researching Kate Easton that some clients refused to pay. What was odd, however, was that William Cheney was acting as a witness for the defence and siding with the colonel. In his testimony, he confirmed that he had indeed gone to Liverpool but that 'The alleged reports from him were false. Miss Magnen was not employed four weeks on this work – not [even] a week.'

Even stranger was the fact that, although Cheney worked for Maud West, he didn't work for 'Maud West & Co'. This appeared to be a completely different outfit. 'Maud West & Co.' was based in Regent Street and headed by a man called George Stafford Howell.

What was going on? Even the judge was confused. Stafford Howell, floundering under cross-examination, explained that 'There had been a dissolution of partnership of the plaintiff firm and a number of books and documents had been taken away, which he could not obtain.'

So Maud had once had a business partner, and the venture had evidently ended acrimoniously. The documents, I suspected, had not been 'taken away' but rather retained at Albion House when Maud booted him out, which must have occurred sometime between 21 November 1910, when Colonel Braddell's telegram arrived, and the court case exactly one year later.

As to why he was using the name 'Maud West & Co.', Stafford Howell simply said that 'some people liked to employ a female detective and the name was attractive.'[19] The judge was not impressed. He ruled that the account 'was a lie from beginning to end' and ordered Colonel Braddell to pay just twelve pounds for the actual work that had been done.

I couldn't find any mention of this partnership in any official records, but however it came about – and however it ended – Maud was plainly better off out of it. George Stafford Howell was a chancer. He admitted to the judge that he dropped the 'Howell' from his name when it suited him, and his business enterprises all seemed doomed to failure. 'Maud West & Co.' soon floundered, and he was forever in court, suing a respected East Riding farmer over a gambling debt, suing his home removals firm over a dented dish and some scratched wallpaper, and also being sued himself when he attempted to trade off the name of the famous Monte Carlo restaurant Ciro's when promoting his new tea shop in Piccadilly ('Ciro's now in London', read his advertisements).[20]

William Cheney, on the other hand, was clearly an asset to Maud. He had his weaknesses (in his youth, it appeared he had done time in prison for theft), but he also had a fine pedigree when it came to sleuthing.[21] His recently deceased father Thomas Cheney, a former officer in the Metropolitan Police, had been one of the most respected private detectives of his time. Looking through reports of his court appearances, it seemed that Thomas had been very much on the side of the establishment. In 1872, for example, he had helped a former police colleague identify a vicar from Clerkenwell who had been charged with 'frequenting places of public convenience for an unlawful purpose.'[22] Other reports in the press connected him to cases of fraud and jewel thefts, whilst his divorce work included a number of high-profile proceedings, such as that in 1907 between the British-born Baroness von Eckhardstein and her German diplomat husband.[23] In a strange coincidence, he had also once appeared as a witness alongside Dr Crippen, after one of Mr Munyon's employees was charged with theft in 1898.[24]

What a small world it was. I was finding links everywhere, which gave me hope that I would be able to find out more about Maud's own background. Her family was full of solicitors and barristers, she'd said that much, but where exactly had she come from, and how did she fit into this curiously interconnected world?

Of all the Maud Wests I had found in the census and other sources, none had leapt out as being definitively my Maud, although three had caught my eye for various reasons. The first was a suffragette from Maida Vale who had been bound over following a riot that had broken out after Emmeline Pankhurst's very public arrest at the London Pavilion in July 1913.[25] Although one of her fellow rioters 'emphatically denied that hat-pins had been used', it had been quite a violent scuffle and I could imagine Maud getting stuck in for the cause.

The second was the daughter of an Irish QC, called Dorothea Maud West, whose worthy spinsterhood seemed so pitifully dull that I could only hope that she *had* led a secret double life. She was also the only candidate I had found whose background tallied with Maud's statements that she came from a legal family.[26]

Finally, as a thrilling outsider, was a Maud West from St John's Wood, who had been sentenced to four years' hard labour in 1894 for a string of thefts, which included over £1,000 worth of diamonds. As one newspaper reported:

Absolute defiance was the attitude taken up by Maud West, a tall, well-dressed young woman, who was before Mr Cooke at Marylebone Police Court to answer three charges of robbery – one of an extensive character, and all alleged to have been committed with daring and ingenuity . . . During the hearing

Maud West kept up a running commentary on the evidence, and made a saucy reply when remonstrated with by the assistant gaoler.[27]

The age was off by a few years, but she undeniably showed the right amount of pluck. Besides, who better to catch villains than a former master criminal?

But, when it came down to it, I had to admit that my shortlist was little more than a wish list. So far, I'd found nothing to pin a detective career on any of them. I kept running into brick walls and was beginning to understand how Maud felt when she popped into that tea shop for a break: barely a month into my research, I, too, felt fatigued, depressed and irritated.

Why was I even bothering? Maud West was a proven liar – and she wasn't the only one. I'd never encountered so many slippery characters in the course of my work. At times, it seemed that hardly anyone in Maud's orbit was who or what they said they were. Even Albion House was masquerading as its former self.

Then, during a head-clearing walk, it came to me. It was so obvious, why hadn't I thought of it before? I brought up the *London Gazette* on my phone and typed 'Maud West' into the search box. The results were difficult to read on the small screen, but there it was in October 1933, buried in a batch of dry legal notices.[28]

It began, 'I, Maud West, of 59 New Oxford Street . . .' before descending into a turgid block of legalese. I skipped past all the 'heretofores', 'in lieu thereofs' and a number of 'and furthers', and scrolled down to what I knew was waiting at the end:

> such change of name is evidenced by a deed dated the 19th day of October, 1933, duly executed by me and attested and enrolled in the Enrolment Department of the Royal Courts of Justice on the 27th day of October, 1933.—Dated the 27th day of October, 1933.
> MAUD WEST, late Edith Maria Elliott.

Maud West wasn't a diamond thief, or a suffragette, or the daughter of an Irish judge. She wasn't even Maud West – at least, not officially until this notice appeared in the *London Gazette*. Her real name was Edith Elliott.

The Apaches of Saint-Cloud

BY MAUD WEST

The first time I was shot at coincided with my first business appearance in masculine disguise. It was a 'long firm' case, and I had been asked to discover where the man suspected to be responsible was in hiding, and also, if possible, find out where the goods had been stored.

What little was known about his movements pointed to him having escaped to Paris, where he was supposed to be living in the lowest dens and consorting with gangs of real Apaches – the toughest of the tough. It seemed quite obvious that if I were to do any good I would have to adopt a disguise. A woman might have excited suspicions and unwelcome attentions. From a cousin I borrowed a suit and cap, and off I went.

For days I lounged round some of the lowest cafés on the outskirts of Paris. Unfortunately, I only took with me one suit of clothes, and I couldn't very well go into a shop and order another. As it happened, this oversight very nearly wrecked all my plans. Unable to adopt any other disguise I must have aroused suspicion.

One dark night in a street near St. Cloud I was followed out of a café by a gang of men. Hurrying after me they surrounded me in the lonely street, and began using threatening language, while I could see one or two of them pointing revolvers at me through their coat pockets. They were many, I was alone; and in a flash I decided my only course was to pretend utter ignorance of the French language, so to everything they said I answered by shaking my head.

This drove them frantic, and soon they were all arguing among themselves, almost forgetting me in their furious endeavours to find a way of making me understand their oaths and threats. That was my chance. Taking to my heels I ran down the street. As I fled two shots rang out, and I heard the gang racing along after me.

I ran till I was almost exhausted, and then, turning a corner, I came upon the open door of a house. Hurling myself through it, I closed it quietly after me; stood listening as my pursuers dashed past, and turned to find myself in the presence of an astounded French family. I explained things to them, and we became such great friends that whenever I visit Paris now I always go to see them. For their open door I owe my life.[29]

Chapter Four

They Do It With Mirrors

I have played so many parts in my business life,
and represented so many characters, that my
friends declare that I've forgotten what my real
appearance and personality should be!

Maud West, 1926[1]

After all the hours I'd spent in Maud's company, it felt awkward
to start calling her Edith. Presumably there were those who did
(all those solicitors and barristers rattling around her family tree,
for a start) but I decided to stick with Maud until she did something Edith-ish – and as I turned my attention to the growing pile
of photographs I'd found of her in disguise, she was definitely in
Maud territory.

So far, in addition to the young man in the tweed cap and a somewhat bloated Charlie Chaplin, I'd tracked down pictures of her as
an old woman, a young fop, a bow-tied foreign businessman and,
my favourite, a country bumpkin with a gravity-defying beard:[2]

Two, however, stood apart from the rest. These were a pair from 1913 that showed Maud transforming herself into a man. They were by far the most straight-laced of the set and I was pretty sure that they had been the very first photographs taken of her in disguise.

Unlike her later studio portraits, they appeared to have been taken in a bedroom or dressing room of some sort. The first captured Maud standing in front of a long mirror, wearing a voluminous white shirt tucked into a pair of high-waisted trousers. Her long hair was pinned up into a bun and she was adjusting her tie. In the second, she was fully dressed and staring straight into the camera with one hand in her suit pocket and the other brandishing a cigarette; a hat now covered her hair, and a lens glinted over one eye. I couldn't find anything to fault in her outfit, from the hat down to her spats, but the end result lacked the ease and humour of her later efforts.

The photographs had appeared in the illustrated magazine section of the *Pittsburgh Press* on 27 July 1913, accompanying a piece simply entitled 'Maud West: Woman Detective'. This had reappeared the following week with an identical layout in the *San Francisco Call* and I had no doubt that further copies would turn up in other American papers, each with the same introduction:

> In fiction the woman detective is always young and fascinating; her skill in handling delicate situations and in solving the most puzzling mysteries arouses admiration. She is fearless and knows how to handle an automatic pistol. Prepare to be astonished: greet one in real life![3]

What followed wasn't so much an article as a jumble of anecdotes narrated by Maud herself. She took in many topics, from her enduring love of A. J. Raffles, the amateur cracksman and gentleman thief, to the importance of taking regular rest breaks. One minute she was admitting how she always looked under the bed at night and the next recalling how she'd faced down an irate blackmailer in her office ('I have my fingers on a pistol now that can spit ten bullets while you are firing one with that revolver of yours').

It was so different to the measured, albeit sensationalist, writing I'd found in her first set of articles, published just four months earlier in *Pearson's Weekly*. The first of those had appeared under the banner 'The Adventures of a Lady Detective' on 29 March 1913 on the women's page, alongside recipes and tips for getting rid of female moustaches, but the editor soon realized Maud West's broader appeal and moved the remaining articles to the main body of the paper. They had been well structured and well written, but this piece in the American press was a more rambling affair. What had got into her?

The answer to that question would arrive in due course but, in the meantime, there was another small mystery to keep me busy. In the midst of her torrent of thoughts was the following statement:

I once stayed at the Grand Hotel in Paris for a fortnight as a man. I did not wear a man's clothing all the time. Only when I was working. It is the easiest thing in the world to disguise oneself at a hotel and yet occupy the same room. I found no difficulty in avoiding the chambermaids as I went in and out.

She went on:

Often I make my changes of costume in my office here. Not long ago I came in at about 5 o'clock as a shabby old scrubwoman, removed all make-up and garments and was at the Ritz Hotel dressed for dinner by 7 o'clock. That is a pretty good contrast.

It was. But then so was this sudden depiction of herself as a master of disguise when compared to her *Pearson's Weekly* articles that spring. There, she had touched briefly upon the subject, saying:

I learnt a lot about the art of disguise in my early years . . . I learnt, not only how to successfully disguise myself by simple and rapid methods, but how to judge if a person I was following was disguised . . .[4]

Beyond that, however, she had given it no particular emphasis. Indeed, of the dozen or so cases she shared, only one had involved any disguise at all, and, even then, she didn't give any clues as to what that might have entailed, other than it needed to fit into a small handbag and be simple enough to adopt quickly in an abandoned cottage by the roadside.[5] A hat, maybe?

Yet here she was, lounging around in a smart black suit, languidly drawing on a cigarette, and explaining to the world how vital male costume was to her work. There were times, she said, when disguising herself as a man was the only option, such as when she needed to keep watch on a house or just loiter in the street: 'The woman, you see, cannot stand about like a man may.'

She had a point. For better or for worse, the details of a woman's clothing were always noticed. Whether fashionably dressed or deliberately plain, women were subject to split-second judgements about their appearance. The tiniest details lodged themselves in people's minds. A man's suit, on the other hand, rarely attracted attention and had the added advantage of allowing ease of movement. As Maud would later recall, 'the long, flowing skirts of pre-war days were a nuisance . . .'[6]

It all made perfect sense, although I couldn't help wondering why she hadn't mentioned it before. Maybe she really had graduated from hat-in-a-handbag levels of subterfuge to being able to pass herself off as a man within a matter of months. Or had something happened that summer that inspired her to add 'Master of Disguise' to her résumé?

A clue lay in her next appearance in the press. At the beginning of September, she featured briefly in a *Daily Mirror* article which opened with a series of questions:

Have you bought a bunch of flowers from a flower-girl in the West End of London or 'helped' a tramp 'along the road' recently? If you have, are you quite certain that you were dealing with genuine members of their respective classes? Have you any proof that the flower-girl was not a duchess in disguise, the tramp a marquis 'made up'?[7]

The country, the paper claimed, was in the grip of a 'disguise craze'. The manager of Clarkson's, the foremost theatrical outfitters in London, confirmed that they were making up twenty to thirty people a week. Their latest client had been 'the wife of a well-known member of the Government' who had made a bet that she could go unnoticed as a parlourmaid at a house where her friends were staying.

'I have had twenty-five years' experience of the business,' the manager said, 'and I have never known a busier time for disguising than the present.' Maud's contribution was a story of a provincial engineer who had disguised himself as a tramp to eavesdrop on a conversation between his wife and her lover in a London park.

Initially, I assumed that the whole thing had been cooked up by the *Daily Mirror* to fill a few column inches. But, after a few hours of searching through online regional newspapers in the British Newspaper Archive, I found that the people of Britain had indeed been raiding their dressing-up boxes in unusual numbers during the summer of 1913. There was the army officer from Aldershot, for example, who spent a day duping his friends in the guise of a distressed lady motorist, flirting with one over tea whilst the chauffeur was sent to attend to his car.[8]

Even men of God were joining in the fun. In the *Methodist Recorder*, one Wesleyan minister described how he had enjoyed a seventeen-day tour of the West Country disguised as a pauper. The sense of freedom had been intoxicating: 'As we steamed out of Waterloo, I put my head out of the window and reverted to a trick of jubilant boyhood; I couldn't help it, the occasion seemed to demand some worthy farewell.'[9]

The burglars masquerading as house painters and thieves as tramway inspectors were nothing new, although the escaped female convict posing as a Spanish countess seemed to be bringing an unusual level of drama to the standard prison break.[10] What was more surprising was that the police were joining in. In August, one constable had dressed as an artisan's wife and wheeled an empty pram around Lavender Hill in an attempt to catch a bookmaker in the act of street betting. Other similar cases included a police-man going undercover as a lady of leisure to trap a bag snatcher on Hampstead Heath.[11] The *Sporting Times* printed a poem on the subject which bore the refrain 'That's a rozzer with his old gal's clothes on!'[12]

The biggest headlines, however, were reserved for suffragettes, and I suspected that this was where the whole craze had begun. That April, the government had introduced what would become known as the Cat and Mouse Act to deal with the problem of hunger-striking prisoners. As the only alternative was to let the hunger strikers starve to death, the Act enabled the authorities to release such women on licence – and under constant surveillance – before returning them to custody once their health improved.

In the games of cat and mouse that followed, many suffragettes resorted to disguise to avoid recapture, much to the delight of the press. For instance, after being temporarily released from Armley Gaol on 17 June, Lilian Lenton managed to evade the police by dressing as a grocer's boy and making off in a delivery van. A few days later, she boarded a train for Dundee disguised as a children's nurse. On arrival in Scotland, she set fire to a castle and a railway station (her personal target being two empty buildings a week) before moving on to Wales. There, she hobbled into Cardiff station dressed as an old woman and caught a train down to the south coast, where she finally escaped to France on board a private yacht.[13]

It was all, by turns, both thrilling and amusing, but what on earth was going on? The suffragettes I could understand, but what about everyone else? Was the craze symptomatic of some deeper undercurrent in British society? The waters were choppy enough on the surface: on top of the disruptions to daily life by the activities of militant suffragettes, the country was entering its third year of industrial unrest. Strikes and rallies had become common as workers downed tools in one industry after another to demand better wages.

Such turmoil was one of the defining characteristics of the

Edwardian age, as the battle raged between old patrician values and new liberal possibilities, but this tension also manifested itself in more subtle ways. By 1913, for example, one could no longer be confident of a stranger's status simply by how they dressed or behaved. The brash Northern chap might be an influential industrialist, or the woman posting a letter bomb the daughter of a peer; even the prime minister, Herbert Asquith, had arrived at Number 10 from nonconformist Yorkshire roots. In short, no one could be trusted to stay where they belonged.

Those who found comfort in the old order were understandably alarmed by all this, but for many others it must have held a delicious sense of possibility. The boundaries that had once confined people to their 'proper' station in life had become less solid and, with the help of a cunning disguise, anyone could push against those walls and explore life on the other side. With the threat of exposure ever thrillingly present, a gentleman might become a chimney sweep, a docker a duchess, a countess a washerwoman – and, it seemed, a woman detective a monocled dandy.

Looking at Maud's later work, it was clear that she had learned a valuable lesson in how to promote herself during that summer of 1913. Her comments about disguise, along with the accompanying photographs, had elevated what could have been an interesting profile in a small magazine to an eye-grabbing piece worthy of syndication in some of America's biggest papers. Over time, she would take each element of that *Pittsburgh Press* article and improve upon it in her own inimitable style, adding a hefty dose of humour to the photographs she circulated and revamping the original illustration for use in her own advertising (see overleaf).

Above all, from that point forward, almost every interview she gave would start with her interviewer listing the various characters she had recently adopted.

But was any of it true? I wanted it to be. I wanted to believe

that Maud had gone undercover as a sailor, or had spent months
frequenting a village disguised as an old woman, 'ferreting out the
facts of a will tangle.'[14] I wanted to believe that her very first outing
in a borrowed suit and cap had brought her face to face with a gang
of Apaches, the infamous dandy hoodlums who had terrorized the
people of Paris for decades with their unique mix of savagery and
vanity. And I wanted there to be a small room at Albion House
crammed not just with wigs and dinner jackets and beggars' rags,
but comedy items, too, such as the 'somewhat loud plus-four suit'
that Maud said she used when she wanted to draw attention to her
presence on a case.[15]

It just all seemed so unlikely. But then, so had the disguise craze,
and that had turned out to be true. Maybe disguising oneself wasn't
that difficult after all. I'd never really considered the mechanics of
it. In fiction, heroes and villains tended to slope off one page only
to reappear transformed on the next, but what about real life? How
was it done?

*

The best place to start, it seemed, was with Willy Clarkson, the 'amusing, odd and fascinating little man' who owned the theatrical outfitters that had featured alongside Maud in the *Daily Mirror* article.[16] He was, without doubt, the best in the business and, due to a hunger for publicity that almost rivalled Maud's, had left behind quite a body of material about the tricks of his trade.

His list of theatrical clients read like a roll call of the best performers of the day: Sarah Bernhardt, Dame Nellie Melba, Enrico Caruso, Ellen Terry, Lily Langtry, Rudolph Valentino and so on. Other clients included Sir Arthur Conan Doyle, the royal family, two prime ministers and numerous members of the aristocracy. Detectives from Scotland Yard had used his services for decades, but he had also been the unwitting purveyor of wigs to Jack the Ripper and Maud's erstwhile neighbour Dr Crippen.

Willy had learned his trade in his father's shop in Drury Lane, where Charles Dickens was a regular visitor. The author had immortalized Clarkson senior as the barber Poll Sweedlepipe in *Martin Chuzzlewit*. Even the family's pet bullfinch had appeared in the novel and now lived on, albeit in stuffed form, on the top floor of Willy's own Wardour Street shop.

By all accounts, Willy was something of a hoarder. Sir John Gielgud recalled visiting Wardour Street as a young actor:

> Clarkson's shop was rather spooky; poorly lit, with stained-glass windows on the steep stairs to the first floor, dusty and cluttered with suits of armour, weapons, play bills, masks – a positive Aladdin's Cave of theatrical paraphernalia . . . Clarkson lurked in the recesses of the shop, but nearly always darted out when he heard the bell which rang as the front door was opened.[17]

Somewhere amidst all the clutter, there must have been a dressing room where Willy and his staff worked their magic on the various customers who came to him for help with disguise. As Clarkson's manager had explained to the *Daily Mirror*, this consisted mostly of 'wigs, beards, moustaches and glasses, [although] not the "smoked" kind, which always makes you look at the wearer.' The clergyman was the most popular disguise for men, he said, followed by the tramp, and then 'someone who might be mistaken for a doctor or a barrister'. Despite the company's record in aiding and abetting some of Britain's finest murderers, he seemed unconcerned about the uses to which such disguises might be put: 'the majority of our customers explain that they want to be disguised for the purposes of private theatricals.'[18]

This was similar to the excuse that Maud said she used when buying a new wig: 'In my wardrobe,' she wrote in 1926, 'I keep a flourishing stock of moustaches, beards and wigs; and I am positive that the wig-maker who creates a new "postiche" for me thinks I am one of the cleverest amateur actresses in London! In fact, he said to me one day: "My dear lady, you do get cast for a fine variety of parts, don't you? What is it today? An elderly countrywoman with sparse grey hair? Yes – certainly; I can soon arrange that for you."'[19]

Was this wig-maker Willy Clarkson himself? Maybe. His shop was just a ten-minute stroll from Albion House, and he'd helped out lady detectives in the past. As one anonymous female sleuth had said in 1909, 'Give me half an hour at Clarksons and you'll not know me.'[20] He was also famously bad with names, calling everyone a vague 'darling', and was used to dealing with strange requests with the utmost discretion.

That said, little was considered strange at Clarkson's. It was a place where inhibitions could be cast aside. One of the most common requests from female clients undertaking 'private theatricals' was to be transformed into a man. The staff had become quite expert at it, although, as the manager said, it was a difficult task: 'You have to "pad" a lot to hide a woman's figure.'

Did this explain why Maud had seemed strangely plump to me when I had first seen a photograph of her in disguise? It wasn't just strapping that was concealing her bust under that wool jacket; she'd essentially been upholstered. I couldn't help thinking, however, that if she found long skirts a nuisance, running around in a padded suit didn't sound particularly comfortable, either.

Nor did all the bits and pieces that needed to be glued to a person to affect a disguise. The *Daily Mirror* journalist had tried out three of Clarkson's most popular looks. The clergyman was simple and only took five minutes: 'Clerical attire, a little tuft of greyish whisker on each cheek bone, blackened eyebrows, and a couple of lines on each side of the mouth . . .' The tramp took fifteen, as it included the addition of nose paste, a kind of putty which had to be welded onto the face and then blended with greasepaint. Finally, he became a 'typical Belgian', which seemed to involve little more than a crepe beard and moustache and an alteration to the parting of his hair. I could almost hear Poirot's little sniff of disgust.

To test each disguise, the journalist popped out for a quick walk, and the *Daily Mirror* duly reported that 'In none of his roles did he attract the slightest attention or curiosity on the part of people in the vicinity of Piccadilly.' Going by the accompanying photographs, however, I could only assume that it had been a particularly foggy day.

Yet there was some evidence that suggested a Clarkson's disguise could stand up to pretty close scrutiny. In February 1910, the young Virginia Woolf (then Virginia Stephen), her brother Adrian and the artist Duncan Grant had joined two other friends in an audacious hoax masterminded by the lifelong prankster Horace de Vere Cole. Their target was the Royal Navy's new state-of-the-art battleship, HMS *Dreadnought*. Willy Clarkson had provided the disguises, transforming Virginia and her friends into Abyssinian princes with the help of dark greasepaint, elaborate robes, false beards and moustaches. The group then set off on the midday train to Dorset, where the *Dreadnought* was at anchor. As they made their way to the coast, an accomplice sent a telegram to the Commander of the Home Fleet:

> Prince Makalen and suite arrive 4.20 pm today Weymouth . . . Kindly arrange meet them on arrival. Regret short notice forgot wire . . .[21]

The result of the ensuing scramble at Weymouth was a credit to the Royal Navy, who greeted the party with full pomp and ceremony. After the band had played the British and Abyssinian national anthems, the group were treated to a tour of the ship by officers in full dress uniform, with Adrian Stephen acting as 'interpreter', mixing passages from Ovid with a smattering of Swahili and Greek. When a rising breeze threatened to send their moustaches flying, the group beat a hasty retreat back to London, but no one suspected a hoax until Cole leaked the story to the newspapers a few days later.[22]

The *Dreadnought* hoax highlighted an aspect of human psychology I had overlooked, namely that people see what they expect to see. The Royal Navy had been told to welcome a group of foreign dignitaries, and that was who they piped on board. Had I fallen into a similar trap and been led astray by the absurdity of Maud's publicity photographs and more fantastical stories? Of course she hadn't spent weeks living in London's Chinatown disguised as one of its native inhabitants or hobnobbed in high society as 'a titled Englishman',[23] but, as I looked more closely at some of the articles she had written, without mischief in mind, I realized that there might be at least *some* truth to her claims.

In these more earnest moments, Maud could be surprisingly

pragmatic about the use of disguise in detective work. In 1924, for example, she acknowledged that she worked as part of a team and if a case required a man to undertake some street surveillance she preferred to send an actual man to do the job.[24] Being a woman, however, had its own advantages. 'Generally, I start off as myself,' she said in 1938, 'because few wrong-doers suspect a middle-aged woman to be on their tracks.'[25] Even in her younger days, she admitted that 'most of my success as a detective is due to the fact that I do not look like one.'[26]

That said, a simple costume could open many doors, whether they led to the scullery of a Mayfair mansion with the aid of a housemaid's apron or into East End hovels via the navy serge cape and bicycle of a district nurse.[27] As Maud discovered, the latter ran the risk of being hailed to help with childbirth and patching up broken bones,[28] but, she said, a woman detective must be able to turn her hand to 'anything and everything . . . She must be able to be Lady X for five minutes and Nurse So-and-so the next.'[29]

The list of female roles Maud said she had undertaken herself was certainly wide ranging:

> actress, factory hand, flower girl, fortune teller, gold digger, gypsy, housemaid, millionairess, mother's help, opium addict, parlourmaid, scrubwoman, secretary, shop girl, vamp, waitress

One of her favourites was that of a journalist in search of copy, which gave her 'a ready excuse for my presence in an unlikely spot at an unlikely hour.'[30]

Even when there was a chance she might be recognized, the false moustaches usually stayed in the cupboard in favour of simpler methods. In 1914, she said, 'Dressing one's hair differently makes a great difference; darkening the eyebrows and lashes; a little rouge on the cheeks and lips, and there you are!'[31] By 1938, she had simplified this even further: 'Sometimes I alter the shape of my face merely by pushing a piece of orange peel beneath my upper lip.'[32]

Maud wasn't the only detective to use fruit in this way, as I discovered when I stumbled across *Crook Pie,* a book of essays on criminology from 1927. It was written by John Goodwin, who had been an Assistant Provost Marshal for the Military Police during the First World War and had subsequently undertaken work for the intelligence services, Scotland Yard and private inquiry agencies. *Crook Pie* contained a chapter on private detectives, as did his earlier book *Sidelights on Criminal Matters.* As the latter had a foreword by Sir Basil Thompson, Director of Intelligence at the Home Office and formerly head of the CID at Scotland Yard, I decided Goodwin was a source to be trusted.

'During the whole time I was engaged in police and Secret Service work,' he wrote, 'I rarely saw a disguise used.'[33] But, he said, it was a different matter when it came to private detectives, for one simple reason:

> Their method of working practically compels it at times, because, whereas when the official police are 'shadowing' a person several detectives work together, the private detective has to work alone. He thus runs a greater risk of being recognised by his quarry; and once he has been recognised he might as well go home.[34]

He described various simple ways they disguised themselves, including Maud's fruit-based method:

> A fig inserted in each cheek will 'fatten' a thin face, while a third pressed against the palate will even disguise the voice. A little pad of cotton wool on each shoulder will raise them and this will, in itself, make a world of difference, while a little lead

shot placed in one boot or both will alter one's gait or produce a definite limp . . .[35]

None of the techniques Goodwin described required much preparation or elaborate costume, so where did this leave Maud's insistence that she could pass well as a man and that she did so regularly?

She certainly had good reason for doing so, not just for the anonymity it afforded or to gain access to male-dominated spaces, but for her personal safety. Being a woman rendered her 'liable to annoyances of all kinds, from the bounder, the drunken man, and so on.'[36] In male clothing, she explained, 'I was more likely to be free from molestation.'[37]

Did I believe her? She had the right build for it. As she said herself, her broad shoulders and large features lent themselves easily to male disguise.[38] The key was being able to adopt the correct stance and an 'easy, confident manner.'[39]

These more sober statements on the matter suggested that – away from the camera, at least – Maud didn't rely on the kind of disguise one could buy from Willy Clarkson. There was no nose paste or greasepaint involved; her approach was far more subtle, and it resulted from years of practice.

'The ability to act and to impersonate other characters is absolutely necessary,' she said, explaining that she could alter her face 'quite easily by simply adopting another expression for the time being, and without using any sort of make-up whatsoever.'[40] She also knew how to disguise her voice: 'after considerable practice I think I am able to imitate the tones of the majority of women, and many men, sufficiently closely to pull off the business I want to.'[41]

I could imagine her practising. Any woman bloody-minded enough to fight her way to the top of a male profession surely also had the willpower to spend hours in front of the mirror perfecting a manly gait or an arthritic shuffle or doing vocal exercises to extend the range of her voice. By her own accounts, her perseverance paid off. She mentioned one prospective client who refused to believe that she could transform her appearance sufficiently for the job in hand, so Maud arranged to meet her that evening at a restaurant:

> When I approached and greeted her in the entrance hall I had so changed my appearance that she became indignant and insisted I had mistaken her for someone else. When I assured her that there was no mistake she was still sceptical; then finally I told her who I was and she could scarcely believe her eyes. All through dinner she kept saying to me: 'Well, I should never have believed it possible!'[42]

Maybe Maud's wig-maker wasn't so far off the mark in thinking she was one of the cleverest amateur actresses in London. The only difference was that her stage *was* London. She even had a stage name – *Maud West* – and, through the pages of the popular press, she was writing her own reviews.

A very clever actress, indeed.

Somewhere waiting in the wings, however, was the woman I really wanted to meet: Edith Elliott. I'd had a small breakthrough in that regard. Whilst exploring the possibility that private detectives were used to track down absconders under the Cat and Mouse Act (I found no evidence either way), I'd come across an article from 1909 about the suffragette Laura Ainsworth, one of the movement's earliest hunger-strikers. She was suing the Home Secretary for assault after being force-fed in prison and, although the details of her ordeal were gruesomely familiar, what really caught my eye was the name of her barrister: Mr George Elliott KC.[43] Could this be one of Edith's relatives? Her father, even?

Further investigation showed that Mr Elliott was one of the most renowned and popular defence barristers of his time. Widespread obituaries after his death in 1916 listed various celebrated cases he had defended. His clients were 'the cream of criminal classes' and had included a number of very imaginative murderers. The *Daily Mirror* also published a photograph which showed him to have a round face and wide nose – just like Edith – and noted that he had once joked that 'most of his clients had died violent deaths.'[44] Could laughing in the face of moral complexity be a family trait?

The Times said he was fifty-six when he died, so he was about the right age. Furthermore, he had left behind two sons and three daughters. Unfortunately, when I dug deeper, I found that he'd got married relatively late in life and his three daughters were all too young to be Maud. Still, there was always the possibility of unmentioned offspring from an earlier marriage, and he also had various brothers, uncles and cousins for me to check out. With a rare enthusiasm, I fired up my family-tree software and got to work.

The Diamond Necklace

BY MAUD WEST

A few years ago I went down to a great country-house where there was a big gathering of many well-known men and women in society. A diamond necklace had been stolen from a lady; the matter had been kept very quiet and no one except the lady in question and the host and hostess knew anything about the affair.

I was introduced as a guest, and, of course, no one in the house had the least idea that I was not one. My hostess was quite frank with me regarding the whole matter. She told me that she did not suspect any of the servants, and could only come to the conclusion that it was one of the guests, and she mentioned the name of one and the reason for her suspicion. I asked for a list of the names of the guests, and saw among them the name of a certain gentleman upon whom my suspicions at once fastened; for I knew, though, of course, his hostess did not, that a similar offence had been brought home to him some years back. He was not, I may say, the person whom the lady of the house suspected.

My suspicions were further confirmed when that night this gentleman told his hostess that he would have to depart the next day. I left directly after he did, for I determined to shadow him, and it was most important that I should not lose sight of him for a moment for the next couple of days.

I had, of course, to disguise myself. In order to do this I walked to the railway-station, which was about a mile from the house. I carried a small handbag and effected my disguise in a disused cottage by the roadside. I reached the station a few minutes in advance of the gentleman I suspected, and went up to London in the same train with him. Three hours after arriving in London I succeeded in obtaining conclusive proof that he had stolen the necklace. I followed him to a pawnshop and on his leaving it, ascertained that he had pawned the diamond necklace for £200.

He was not prosecuted, but I believe he had to leave the country.[45]

Chapter Five

The Shadow in the House

It is of the greatest importance that a client should
know, when engaging a private detective, that
confidence is being reposed in the right person.

Maud West, 1915[1]

Suffragettes were cropping up a lot in my research – first with Kate
Easton, then the disguise craze and now George Elliott KC – so
it was hardly surprising that Maud, too, had tales to tell. She first
mentioned the subject on the record on 23 May 1913, barely a
month after the Cat and Mouse Act received royal assent and just
weeks before Emily Davison was trampled beneath the hooves of
the King's horse at the Epsom Derby. 'I have had practically all my
staff employed at big social functions during the last six weeks,'
she told a journalist. 'Hostesses have shown me letters they have
received threatening damage to their property, and without a doubt
there is a very bad "scare" in Mayfair and Belgravia.'[2]

The nation had been feeling the effects of campaigns against the
government by the WSPU and the Women's Freedom League for
some time, but with a new suffrage bill before the House of Commons the WSPU had recently entered a new phase of guerrilla
warfare aimed at the population at large. This campaign, Emmeline Pankhurst stated, 'would stop short only at attacks upon
human life.'[3] Her army of women set fire to postboxes, destroyed
golf courses, poured purple dye into a water reservoir, severed

telephone lines and smashed windows, all the while leaving a string of notes in their wake with the simple message:

VOTES FOR WOMEN

Maud had experience of these notes herself. At one evening reception at a peer's home, she said, a picture had been badly damaged: 'The canvas was cut with a blunt knife, and "Votes for Women" was written on a piece of paper found on the floor.' At another party, a rare piece of tapestry was slashed beyond repair. The WSPU would explain this tactic the following year after an attack on Velázquez's *Rokeby Venus* in the National Gallery, by suggesting that it gave the painting 'a human and historic interest' and 'new value as a national treasure.'[4]

As for Maud's own vandals, suspicion was everywhere. Some said they were militants who snuck into parties uninvited, although Maud thought it more likely that they were normal guests 'strongly in sympathy with the suffragettes.' Or was it the staff? 'At an entertainment a few days ago,' she said, 'I was instructed to keep a special watch on two of the maids, whose sympathy with the suffragettes had been more ardently than discreetly expressed.'[5]

That summer, Maud also mentioned that she had been asked to keep an eye on townhouses whilst their owners retreated to the countryside.[6] This was understandable. The WSPU had developed quite a taste for empty buildings. That July, for example, the Sunlight Soap baronet Sir William Lever would return from a visit to Knowsley Hall, where Lord Derby was entertaining the King and Queen, to find his home near Bolton razed to the ground. A small portmanteau containing a note and suffragette literature was found nearby.[7]

I suspected, however, that Maud offloaded the work of house-sitting onto her staff. When it came to looking after her upper-class clients, surely there was far more fun to be had by joining them at their weekend parties in the country? That was, after all, the stuff of classic detective fiction: a country house, a sleuth, a gathering of strangers. Who knew what could happen?

The answer, as it turned out, was very little that would make it into a crime novel. Maud claimed to have found all manner of things in country houses, from stashes of stolen jewels to a factory for printing banknotes,[8] but there were no bloody corpses and the only locked room I'd found so far was the one containing the great detective herself whilst her rival tracked down the suicidal 'Mr A'. The country-house setting did, however, offer her the opportunity to give her literary talents full rein:

> It was night. I waited in the shadow of some trees, through which the moon shone and made eerie outlines. I heard a twig crack. I held my breath. Next moment I got a terrible shock. Someone had come behind me, and before I realised what was happening a figure of a man dived upon me and pinned me down. I struggled free, drew my automatic, and fired, wounding the man in the leg.[9]

The man was a burglar who was subsequently carried into the house for more traditional justice to prevail. Or so she said. In one of her less melodramatic moods, she admitted that the work was usually more mundane:

> I may have to watch a lady who has been suspected of stealing some of her hostess's valuables, or I may be commissioned to find out if one of the party is cheating at cards, or I may have to obtain evidence to be used in a divorce case or action for slander.

That private detectives were regularly employed by large estates was confirmed by an anonymous retired valet writing in *Pearson's Weekly* in 1912. 'It may seem a rather shabby and mean sort of thing for a gentleman to employ detectives in the guise of servants to spy on his guests,' he wrote, 'but it is sometimes necessary.'[10]

One example the valet gave came from his time in service with a Member of Parliament, who enjoyed hosting long weekend parties for the political elite at his country residence, an enjoyment that was dimmed somewhat when things started to go missing: first a diamond ring and then a carved ivory statuette. Two detectives were drafted in to act as footmen at the next gathering. Nothing happened over the weekend, but as the guests were preparing to leave on the Monday morning the detectives saw one of the guests, a well-connected political agent, take a valuable snuff box from one of the drawing rooms. After being summoned to the library, the valet said, 'The guest tried to bluff the matter out, but after a bit of "plain" talk from the master, he admitted having taken it, and also confessed that his wife had stolen the ring and the ivory statuette.' The pair soon left the country.

Maud had her own snuffbox story, which I found making its way around the European press in the summer of 1913. She was often asked, she said, to keep an eye on guests who were known kleptomaniacs. One was a wealthy woman who only ever stole snuffboxes and when she was invited to the party of a friend who had a particularly fine collection of old French specimens, her hostess took the precaution of hiring Maud to keep an eye on her. There were no fancy uniforms or gatherings in the library for Maud, however. She simply positioned herself outside the room containing the boxes all evening and when the woman tried to enter she engaged her in a long and tedious chat. The woman was eager to escape. 'But I didn't relent,' Maud wrote, 'so she fled the room containing the temptations empty-handed.'[11]

Kleptomania had first been identified as a psychological disorder in the early nineteenth century, but over time – perhaps in response to department stores' experiences with shoplifting – it had transformed into a 'disease' that mainly affected upper-class women. Theories about its cause ranged from sexual repression to congenital criminality, although not everyone was convinced it existed at all. In 1907, one unnamed lady detective declared, 'Kleptomania is nonsense.' The true source of such thieving, she said, was to be found in high society's fondness for drink, drugs, and, above all, ostentatious materialism:

> Society women, frenzied with the desire to outdo one another, will resort to tricks of dishonesty to which a servant would never stoop. The very superiority of culture and intelligence will impel an educated woman to venture upon a daring scheme that a poor servant would not have the brains or courage to plot much less to execute.[12]

I suspected that Matilda Mitchell and her store detectives would have had something to say about the capabilities of the lower orders when it came to cunning schemes, but whether it was genuine kleptomania or plain old larceny, protecting property kept private detectives busy. Any big social gathering, Maud said, would attract thieves, but summer garden parties were the ideal target: 'When all the guests are outdoors, the thief enters the house on the pretext of wanting to take a look inside, and ideally pilfers small yet valuable items.'[13]

Each year, she said, she went to one particular garden party with a dozen assistants dressed as maids who helped with serving tea whilst keeping an eye on nimble-fingered guests. These thieves, she said, were either 'typically shady characters' that had somehow wormed their way into well-to-do circles or 'themselves aristocrats who are in dire financial straits and can think of no alternative to stealing.'[14]

The aristocracy was undoubtedly beginning to feel the pinch. Increased taxation, reforms to the House of Lords and falling land prices were just some of the things nibbling away at their lives of leisured luxury: during the twentieth century, around 1,500 stately homes would be demolished due to lack of funds for their upkeep. But Maud suggested that the financial difficulties which prompted aristocratic guests to sneak their hosts' knick-knacks off to the pawnshop didn't arise from leaking roofs or the need to shore up the north tower. 'In most cases,' she said, 'it is gambling debts that drive them to such a desperate position.'[15]

High-stakes gambling had long been a favoured pastime of the upper classes. By 1910, the games of choice were poker, baccarat and bridge, although, as Lady Wolseley said in 1911, 'there have been so many bridge scandals that one is not surprised to find the game going out of fashion.'[16]

I imagined such scandals taking place after dinner, all port and cigars and manly bravado, but the evidence suggested that many of the culprits were women. As one private detective explained in 1908, 'It is no uncommon thing for ladies to go to afternoon tea nowadays in order to play bridge, at which large sums of money are won and lost.'[17]

He described how the hostess of one such regular gathering had approached his firm, convinced something was amiss after she lost nearly £3,000. 'Here, then,' he said, 'was a case in which a woman detective, if any, alone could be used.' Accordingly, he sent one of his female employees, herself a keen bridge player, to join the party. Over the course of several afternoons, she identified the cheat. 'Needless to say,' he concluded, 'the money was returned and the guilty woman's company barred in a good many houses after that.'

Such work also kept Maud – and her dressmaker – busy. One of the perks of being a lady detective, it seemed, was having a large collection of evening wear on hand for when one had to pose as the friend of a client. 'My dress bills for this purpose amount to a good sum in a year,' she said, 'and I have to constantly renew my wardrobe, for I must take a care to appear but seldom in the same frock or gown.'[18]

She recalled one occasion on which she had to rummage through that wardrobe at short notice:

> I simply received a telephone message in the morning from Mrs— to say that she wanted me to come to her house that evening at seven o'clock and to stay to dinner. When I got to the house my client informed me that she wanted me to watch a certain Mr— when he was playing cards after dinner.
>
> . . . After dinner the party adjourned to the drawing-room and began to play poker. I did not join the game, and neither did my hostess. To make a long story short, I watched the game for nearly four hours before I discovered the gentleman in an actual act of cheating. What he did was to slip some cards from the bottom and middle of the pack to the top when taking up the cards to deal, and being a finished card-manipulator, he could do this so quickly that no one who was not watching him very closely could possibly detect him.[19]

When confronted by his hostess, the man confessed to having cheated on eight other occasions and promised to refund the £1,100 he had swindled from various members of the party during the previous month.

Not all card sharps went so willingly. Society was still bristling with the echoes of the famous Baccarat Case of 1891 in which Edward VII, then Prince of Wales, had been dragged into a slander action that arose out of an accusation of cheating. Of the cheat himself, the Scottish baronet Sir William Gordon-Cumming, *The Times* intoned, 'He has committed a mortal offence. Society can know him no more.'[20] Sir William was dismissed from the army, forced to resign from his London clubs, and spent the remaining thirty-nine years of his life as a social outcast.

Social ostracism was apparently the penalty for offending the moral codes of high society. Maud, the retired valet and the anonymous private detectives had all mentioned it. The upper classes may have been largely responsible for creating the laws and institutions that kept the wider populace in check, but when it came to their own affairs, it seemed that they preferred to deal with matters in-house. Whether it was pilfering snuffboxes, cheating at cards or something worse, the sentence was social death. Well-born wrongdoers were banished, if not to the colonies, then to the Continent, which in many eyes was just as bad. As Maud herself wrote:

> [Society scandals] never or rarely see the light of the Law Courts; they simply end in the disappearance of some of the chief figures in them from the social world. Occasionally you may catch a reflection of some of these society dramas in some such announcement in the press that Lord— or Mrs.— has sold or let his – or her – house in town and intends living abroad for the next few years.[21]

On checking the newspapers, there were indeed suspiciously few reports of toff-on-toff crimes. Some of the other scandals I came across, however, shed a little more light on the breadth of work undertaken by private detectives in high society.

In 1906, for example, Lady Gwendolen Cecil, daughter of the third Marquess of Salisbury, employed a private detective to gather evidence for a libel case against a woman who had been distributing pamphlets which claimed that Lady Gwendolen had secretly given birth to an illegitimate daughter some years previously. The woman, a former organist at the Cecil family estate, alleged that the father was the estate chaplain and that she had been coerced into raising the child as her own.[22] Her claims were demolished in court.

Another brief scandal erupted in 1912 when it was discovered that badges for admission to the Royal Enclosure at Ascot, highly sought after and non-transferable due to the vetting process, were being sold on. Viscount Churchill, who was in charge of the Royal Enclosure, hired a female detective to befriend the society lady thought to be responsible. After a few meetings, telegrams and a pleasant drive to Ascot, the detective successfully acquired a badge and spent the day in the Royal Enclosure – 'where, I hope,' Churchill's barrister said when the matter came to court, 'she enjoyed herself.' The lady running the racket was merely served with an injunction and her anonymity, in the press at least, was preserved.[23]

In general, however, the upper classes managed to keep a tight lid on their affairs. They were aided in this not just by private detectives but also by the press. Although anything that emerged in court was considered fair game, the newspapers usually steered clear of the private lives of the elite in exchange for glamorous yet benign snippets for the society pages. There were also England's strict libel laws to contend with, so when gossip did appear, for example in the higher-class weeklies such as the *Bystander*, it was phrased in such a way as to be impenetrable to those not already in the know.

Such gentlemen's agreements had served all parties well for years, but in January 1911 a letter in *The Times* suggested that this was about to change. It came from an anonymous 'householder' whose butler, on placing an advertisement for a new position, had received the following reply from an American journalist calling herself Harriet:

Noting your advertisement in the *Morning Post* I shall be pleased to hear from you if you have half an hour to spare once or twice a week and would care to turn it into cash by writing me a long, gossipy letter about the well-known people in English Society who stay in the houses where you are employed. I pay liberally and settle each month for the letters received the previous one.[24]

'Harriet' suggested that the butler could 'double or treble' his salary in this way, and included a list of society names of particular interest to her. A postscript enquired whether he had any friends amongst the staff of leading London clubs or hotels. A few days later, a West End physician claimed to have received a similar letter asking for 'racy stories' about his patients, 'advance rumours of any *cause célèbre*, divorce, &c.' and details of 'the financial shifts and difficulties of any well-known people.'[25] Another was sent to the eighteen-year-old daughter of a peer with a special request for information '*à propos* of the rumoured intention of King George and Queen Mary to discourage the reception of American *nouveaux riches* in English Society.'[26]

The impertinence of these requests hit a nerve. The letters page of *The Times* was aflame. Was 'Harriet' a hoax? Some thought so; others clearly believed every word. A butler from Park Lane weighed in to complain about the besmirching of his profession; another correspondent tried to steer the debate towards the upper classes' 'perfectly sickening' habit of posing for press photographs, whilst the secretary of the Secret Commissions and Bribery Prevention League sought information about similar journalists so that they might be prosecuted for the attempted corruption of the humble British servant.[27] The American newspaperman and literary agent Albert Curtis Brown made a valiant attempt to defend his stateside colleagues, only to be shot down by an English journalist who pointed out that Brown himself had traded in unsubstantiated gossip about the royal family on a number of occasions.

The most interesting response, however, came from an anonymous correspondent who wasn't convinced that 'Harriet' worked for the press at all. He quoted her desire for information about 'financial shifts and difficulties' and said:

> I cannot help thinking that the last few words contain the pith of the whole matter, and that the information obtained in this way is placed at the service of the well-organized systems of spying and sneaking called private inquiry agents whose subscribers are West-end money-lenders and others who find it profitable to make themselves acquainted with the private affairs of people of some social and professional standing ... This must be better business than selling information to American papers.[28]

Whether or not this explained the 'Harriet' letters, his premise rang true. A few years earlier, the *Belfast Evening Telegraph* had run an article which described how both professional and amateur lady detectives, often recruited from within society itself, were employed 'with the object of elucidating matters of the first importance to financiers, promoters of trusts, and concessionnaries [sic] of all kinds.'[29] This could involve anything from upcoming political moves that might affect the stock exchange to the stable secrets of leading racehorse owners.

Private detectives were sitting on a goldmine. All that gossip overheard whilst undercover at parties or playing cards, not to mention information gathered during other routine investigations, was valuable currency. Why keep it locked away if there were buyers ready and waiting?

Of course, none of that precluded them selling some of that information to journalists as well. Although I had no evidence that any money had changed hands, one of Maud's own appearances in the American press seemed to be just the kind of thing 'Harriet' was after. The story in question appeared in both the *Washington Post* and the *New York Tribune* on 16 June 1914, having arrived by special cable the previous day: [30]

ROYALTIES GIVE
MILITANTS $5,000

Maud West, Society's Detective, Mentions Duchess and Princess of Teck.

The Duchess and Princess of Teck were both sisters-in-law to the Queen, so not the sort one gossiped about, but Maud didn't stop there:

> I am reliably informed that several other royalties besides the Duchess and the Princess have contributed subscriptions, in many cases as high as $5,000. It is simply a form of blackmail. Royalty is paying merely to escape molestation. [31]

Maud's allegations piggybacked on the news that police had seized the list of contributors to militant funds during a raid on the WSPU headquarters on 23 May. There was jubilation in Parliament and the press at this coup, although as one organizer of the WSPU pointed out, the list appeared in their annual report 'and may be bought by anyone for 3d.' [32] Nevertheless, the government announced that it would seek to prosecute those who had contributed funds. [33]

When the story bounced back to the British press, Maud's name had been removed along with any mention of the royal family. She did, however, speak anonymously about 'two foreign royalties now in London' and 'several well-known hosts and hostesses':

Some of my clients who have told me that they have paid money to the militant funds I know are certainly not in sympathy with the militant movement, and now that the subscribers are threatened with prosecution they are rather wishing that they had not done so.[34]

As it happened, the government was forced to back-pedal quickly on its stated intent to prosecute after it took a closer look at the subscriber list and realized that it included a good number of Britain's elite.

I decided to take a look myself and spent a day in the Women's Library at the London School of Economics going through the WSPU annual reports and subscription lists in the *Suffragette* newspaper. There was no mention of the Duchess or Princess of Teck. It was possible that their contributions were buried amongst the hundreds of anonymous donations, but, if so, they hadn't paid very much. Certainly no one had given anywhere near $5,000.

The two 'foreign royalties' were easier to spot, although one of those, Princess Sophia Duleep Singh, was a known suffragette and the other, Her Highness the Ranee of Sarawak, was an old friend of Oscar Wilde, so hardly a shocking addition to the list. Not having an intimate knowledge of high society at the time, it was impossible to know how many 'society hostesses' were included. There were dozens of titled subscribers, but the majority had also collected funds from others on top of their personal donations, so presumably were supportive of the cause.

I was left with two theories. Either Maud had access to financial information not included in the official WSPU accounts and had decided to leak that to the press, or she was selling secrets that weren't true. I didn't know which was worse.

*

Could one ever trust a private detective? The correspondent in *The Times* didn't seem to think so, nor did Sir Richard Muir, the famous barrister who had said that the calling 'stank in the nostrils of every honest man'. Common adjectives used in court included 'sordid', 'dirty' and 'dishonest'.

Others, however, were more sanguine. The *Belfast Evening Telegraph* had concluded its article about lady detectives with the statement: 'So long as espionage is not employed for the purpose of harassing private people or of carrying out some improper scheme, it is not likely to give any offence or do any mischief.'[35]

The problem was that it was often employed for those very purposes. With no system of regulation in place, setting oneself up as a private detective was the perfect cover for all manner of swindles and frauds. Take the case of David Watson, an inquiry agent who specialized in the recovery of stolen property. In 1913, it emerged that he had been arranging many of the thefts himself. His downfall came after he 'recovered' a jade ornament stolen from Liberty a little too swiftly.[36]

There were worse crooks to be found – those detectives dabbling in blackmail and extortion, for example – but what caught my eye about Watson's case was a statement that he made in court. In a bid to put a final nail in the coffin of his respectability, the prosecution had raised the fact, or possibly fiction, that he had once lived in sin with a countess. In response, Watson said:

> Is there anything marvellous in that? I called myself an inquiry agent, and I don't set myself up as an emblem of moral rectitude. The necessary stock-in-trade of an inquiry agent is that he should be a man who has seen something in the world and has known something about it.[37]

This was, in a nutshell, the problem with private detectives. They had to be willing to act in an underhand manner and understand the baser elements of human nature; they had to know how to cheat at cards, dig up dirt and bury secrets – and the fact that they had that knowledge, with all the attendant questions of how they acquired it, made them inherently suspect.

It also made them eminently employable. When clients found themselves in a tight corner, it was useful to have someone on hand who would be willing to bring matters to a neat resolution – whatever it took.

In 1905, for example, the Hon. Mrs Chetwynd found herself alone and living in Paris following a divorce. In a series of legal rulings, she had lost custody of her two young daughters, first to her husband and then, due to his subsequent death and that of his mother, to the horticulturist Christopher Leyland (of *leylandii* fame), who lived at Haggerston Castle in Northumberland. Quite naturally, she wanted them back. She hired Thomas Duguid, a sixty-year-old inquiry agent, to make this happen. Duguid had got as far as buying off the housekeeper at the castle and making the acquaintance of the coastguard on Holy Island (his intention being to whisk the girls away by boat to Spain) when the police knocked on the door of his lodgings and caught him with a notebook outlining his plans.[38]

When it came to the trial, the press was conflicted. Here was a rogue private detective of the sort it instinctively despised, yet he had gone rogue for a cause that many considered justifiable. As the *Bystander* put it: 'That a mother should desire possession of her children and that, if usual means fail her, she should have resource to the unusual, is easily understood . . .'[39] The pressure of public opinion meant that when Duguid was sentenced, he received a lenient nine months.

Did Maud kidnap children or deal in stolen goods? Probably not, although she undoubtedly broke the law in other ways on behalf of clients. Alongside committing perjury by fabricating evidence in the divorce court, it seemed to be part of the job. She would never admit to such behaviour in print, of course. Who would? If anything, she seemed to be trying to distance herself from it. Her story of turning away the fortune teller who wanted her to dig up society secrets took on a new significance in light of my recent discoveries.

But who was she trying to impress? Her articles, in all their gossipy glory, still seemed a risk to her reputation, and a pointless one at that. Everything I had read suggested that the upper classes would have chosen a private detective through word of mouth. At a pinch, they might have selected one of the established agencies via the classified ads, but they certainly wouldn't have flicked through their cook's weekend paper to find out which lady detectives seemed *au fait* with the ways of their fellow aristocrats. The same went for business clients or financial speculators.

Rereading the stories I had collected so far, I noticed one thing they had in common. However outlandish they got, the majority started from one of three scenarios: an investigation into suspected infidelity, an attempt to track down a missing person, or an allegation of blackmail. These weren't exclusively upper-class problems; anyone with a bit of money might seek help in such distressing situations.

Maybe, through her writing, Maud West the 'society' detective was courting an altogether different client group: the middle classes. They were, after all, the people most likely to be impressed, rather than appalled, by her tales of working for Lady This or the Honourable That. Nor did they widely enjoy the type of social connections that allowed for discreet personal recommendations when it came to hiring help.

Somehow, Maud had to make her agency stand out amidst the multitude scattered throughout London and provincial towns. Yes, she was a woman, but was that an advantage or a disadvantage? At least through her stories she could control that particular narrative and argue that she was as good – better, even – than a man. By using glamour and humour, and playing with the tropes of detective fiction, she could lodge herself in the minds of prospective clients, all the while repeating the message that she was available for divorce, missing persons and blackmail investigations.

This theory also made sense of a sleight of hand I had noticed in one of her early advertisements, which had appeared for a few years below her usual offering on the back page of the *Daily Telegraph*:[40]

MAUD WEST.   "LADY DETECTIVE."
READ THIS!   "Vanity Fair" writes on July 7, 1909:
"Clients entrusting their business to Maud West can rely upon absolute secrecy and exceptional ability."
Maud West, Albion House, 59 and 61, New Oxford-street, London.

I'd eagerly looked in *Vanity Fair* to find the article which would surely cement Maud's position as the favoured lady detective amongst the upper classes. But there was only a small filler item at the bottom of a page about the centenary of Darwin's birth, which gave her office address and the statement 'Readers can rely upon absolute secrecy and exceptional ability.'[41] It was essentially another advertisement; presumably she had come to some arrangement, by whatever means, with the editor for its inclusion. When I had first come across it, it had seemed a half-hearted effort for a detective trying to boost her credentials amongst the well-to-do subscribers of *Vanity Fair*. But now, viewed as a ruse to secure a society 'endorsement' with which to impress the middle-class readers of the *Daily Telegraph*? Genius.

Could one ever trust a private detective? Probably not.

*

One morning, wondering whether my investigation was even 'worth the candle', as Maud would put it, my inbox pinged. The scan of the photograph from Manchester Archives, the description of which had started my whole quest, had arrived. I perked up.

Going by the clothes and slight sagging along her cheek and jawline, Maud must have been in her forties or early fifties when it was taken. As the caption indicated, she was sitting at her desk, examining a piece of handwriting through a magnifying glass. I enlarged the photo on my screen, taking it all in.

I couldn't tell what she was looking at – a forged document or just a laundry bill she had lying around? – but I was satisfied. The photograph seemed a genuine portrait of a woman at work, in a rather ordinary office. There was no evidence of the overflowing vases of flowers or New Art statuettes that some journalists had mentioned, just plain walls and a glass-panelled door.

As for the detective herself, she was well turned out – her nails were neatly manicured – but she didn't look as though she'd made any special effort for the occasion. She'd recently had a cigarette;

the ashtray peeked out between the papers on the desk, of which there were just enough to suggest a busy workload whilst hinting at a neat filing system elsewhere. She was clearly a woman in command.

I surveyed my own desk. Was I a woman in command, a worthy match for the slippery Maud West? My own filing system comprised various unstable ziggurats of loose papers, a sprawling database into which everything digital got dumped, countless sticky notes and a jumble of tea-stained notebooks. From where I sat, still in my pyjamas, it seemed doubtful.

Whilst making an effort to tidy up, I picked up the printout from the *London Gazette* that I'd made a few weeks earlier. I hadn't paid any attention to it since then and just added it to one of the piles as I chased other leads. But now, taking a closer look, I realized what a mistake that had been. Legalese may be dull, but it has its purpose. I turned back to the photograph and, yes, I'd missed it there, too: a small detail, but suddenly glaringly – *gleamingly* – obvious. *You see what you expect to see.*

Elliott nose or not, Maud was unlikely to be George Elliott KC's daughter – or any blood relative, for that matter – because Elliott wasn't the name that she'd been assigned at birth. There was no getting away from it:

> I, MAUD WEST, of 59, New Oxford Street, in the county of London, and 8, Great Russell Mansions, Great Russell Street, in the county of London, Married Woman, heretofore called and

Edith Elliott, aka Miss Maud West, was married.

The Prince of Lovers

BY MAUD WEST

Some time ago I received a visit from a M. Dupont, a well-to-do merchant in Marseilles. I had acted for him in one or two matters and was glad to renew our friendship.

'Well, Miss West,' he began, as he planted his portly form in the office arm-chair. 'I have come to see you on behalf of my good friend L. and his wife. They are compatriots of yours, and well blessed with the goods of this world. L. is a successful merchant with branches in Paris and Tours. He has a charming wife, but is afflicted with a little devil of a daughter.

'She is nineteen and has just left a finishing school. She is a head-strong, determined, and romantic little idiot, who possesses a certain amount of brains and a wonderful face and figure . . . She means to travel and see the world, and unless they agree she will get a job abroad.

'Unfortunately she has control over a certain annual allowance, and her parents fear that unless they accede to her request she will run off and land herself in trouble.'

'That is not an unusual thing for a young woman to threaten, Monsieur Dupont,' I said. 'All young women feel like that at some time or other. I did. I ran off when I was nineteen . . .'

'I know . . . I know . . .' interrupted my friend. 'And you

made a success of it, because you are cautious and not a fool. But Violet is not like that. She is madly romantic and would be easy prey for an adventurer.'

'What do you propose to do about it?' I asked.

He smiled. 'Rather it is what you propose to do, Miss West,' he said. '. . . I have suggested to L. that he consents to his daughter's request. She is keen to visit England . . .'

We eventually arranged a plan, and M. Dupont went back to France . . . I had my own ideas regarding this young woman. I had seen her photograph, and besides being extremely good-looking there was a determined cut to her pretty mouth . . . I arranged with my agent in Paris, Jules Darracquer, that when the girl left home she should be shadowed until she arrived in London.

Now our young lady, instead of travelling from her home near Tours to Le Havre, and taking the boat to Southampton, as arranged, broke her journey at Paris, where she engaged rooms at an hotel on the Boulevarde Montmartre. Three days later I received this alarming report from Darracquer:

> Re. V. L. Seems have no intention of continuing journey. Frequenting restaurants and dance clubs in Montmartre district. Has made acquaintance of Prince of Lovers. Hotel office reports several large cheques cashed. Advise action. Darracquer

Darracquer must have known I would be alarmed when I read the words 'Prince of Lovers,' for this nickname disguised the identity of an individual who has caused a great deal of trouble to lots of people – invariably women! He was the son of a Marseilles waterfront tough, a member of the gang of apaches. The man, whom we will call Moquelain, had discovered that there were safer ways of earning money than by gangster methods. He was good-looking, tall and lithe. A professional gigolo and blackmailer, he was just the sort of person to cast a spell over the romantic mind of Violet L.

There was no good to be done by getting in touch with the French police, because Moquelain was too clever to have laid himself open to a charge. To warn the girl against his overtures would have been simply foolish, for he had probably told her some romantic tale about himself. There seemed to be only one course, and as I had been instructed that money was no object, I took it. I wired Darracquer:

Buy off Prince of Lovers. West.

Unfortunately, Darracquer made a false move. Instead of paying Moquelain for some ostensible business which would take him to the other end of France, he was foolish enough to tell the gigolo that the money was being paid provided he did not see the girl again. This was playing straight into Moquelain's hands, although Darracquer believed that all was well . . .

In the meantime the girl had arrived in London and occupied a small flat her parents had secured for her in a block of mansions, in which one of her women relatives also lived. I promptly made arrangements with the hall-porter that I should be given particulars of all Miss L.'s callers. I took an empty flat in the building and installed therein a pretty and charming girl, a member of my staff . . .

Events moved swiftly. Within two days, my assistant had become friendly with Violet. Within a week of her arrival I was invited to tea with the two girls, as my assistant's 'aunt'. This state of peace did not last long, however, as next day the hall-porter telephoned me that a 'Monsieur Moquelain' had arrived to see Miss L.

That evening Moquelain called again and took Violet L. to a theatre. When the couple returned my assistant met them 'accidentally' outside the flat. Violet introduced Moquelain to her and, when he had gone, after promising to call next day to take the girl to lunch, told my assistant that she was engaged to Moquelain and they intended to marry secretly.

Next day at twelve-thirty, Moquelain arrived. The porter was asked to call a taxi to take the pair to lunch, and as instructed, telephoned to my office the name of the restaurant to which they had gone.

I did a little telephoning myself, then went to the restaurant, securing a table in the corner from which I could see and not be seen. At a table for two sat Moquelain and Violet L., their heads together in deep conversation . . .

I watched discreetly, and had not long to wait! As the orchestra finished a soft melody, an over-dressed and over-painted woman who had been sitting at another table rose to her feet . . . She pushed her way between the tables towards the pair, attracting the eyes of everyone in the place, for she had obviously once been beautiful.

Then she stopped, and in a voice which everyone could hear, addressed the 'Prince of Lovers.' 'So I've found you at last, my beauty, have I?' she began. 'And now I have found you I intend to keep you. What are you doing here with this girl . . . ?'

Her voice rose higher and higher.

Moquelain got to his feet.

'I do not know you, madame,' he began, in French.

'What?' shrieked the other woman in the same language. 'You don't know me – your own wife? That's pretty good!' Then she proceeded to call the gigolo everything possible, and it was only after the maître d'hôtel had summoned two waiters and removed her that peace reigned again.

My plot had succeeded, and long before the woman had finished her harangue, Violet L. had picked up her fur and left the place disdainfully . . .

The 'Prince of Lovers' did not appear again, as I suppose he thought it hopeless after the episode; and that if he ever reads this he will at least appreciate the acting of his supposed 'wife', who was really an actress, and certainly earned the fee I paid her for the dramatic scene![42]

Chapter Six

To Love and Be Wise

It is wonderful how easy it is to vanish in London.
Often-times it is round a corner and out of sight.

Maud West, 1913[1]

So Maud was married. It was an unexpected development. Nothing I'd read had even hinted at there being a man on the scene. If anything, I'd expected her partner to be a woman, someone with a career of her own who would understand Maud's need for freedom and not be overly concerned when she headed off to the office and didn't return for three months (at one point Maud said she owned forty pairs of shoes and nineteen toothbrushes, all collected on such impromptu travels).[2] But no, the someone who put up with Maud forever haring off in unsuitable footwear was a man.

The home address in the *Gazette* notice was also a surprise, although for an entirely different reason. Great Russell Mansions was an ornate block of flats directly opposite the British Museum, one of my favourite teenage haunts. I knew the block well and had once planned to live there myself. It wasn't a particularly realistic plan as I was only sixteen at the time; nonetheless, I'd spent many hours idly sorting out the decor as I sat on the museum steps eating hot roast chestnuts, nursing a crush on Tiglath Pileser III and plotting all the adventures I'd have in the Mesopotamian desert to fund it all. If only I'd known, not only about the impending Gulf War, but about Maud. Back then, I'd have found some way to get into Flat 8 to have a nose around.

It was just the type of building I imagined Maud inhabiting: a magnificent six-storey confection of red brick iced with ivory stone architraves; the kind of place that had a rickety cage lift and a corpse in the stairwell. As for the flat itself, I'd envisioned a chaotic crash pad with discarded moustaches stuck to the bathroom mirror and a revolver stashed in the teapot. Evidently, I'd got that wrong. There had to be at least some level of domesticity to match her new status as a married woman. Did the Elliotts have a maid? It seemed likely, so I tasked her with tidying up the image in my mind. Before long, the disorderly gloom was transformed into a stylish, sunlit apartment in which the happy couple could share witty breakfast repartee over the morning papers.

It was a charming scene, but something was still wrong. What type of man would sit there merrily tucking into his devilled kidneys as he read about the various people his wife had seduced in the course of her work? Maud was quite open about this: 'I've made love to crooks before now,' she said cheerfully in 1926,[3] and so far I'd counted two waiters, an unspecified number of army officers and a woman in a nightclub. Mr Elliott, whoever he was, had to be self-assured and admire pluck and courage in a woman above any notions of convention and respectability. Not a buttoned-up Lord Peter Wimsey, then, but maybe a Raffles? Or was he more of a Tommy to her Tuppence?

Whoever he was, I couldn't wait to meet him. How that was to happen, however, remained unclear. It should have been simple. A wedding ring, a surname, an address, a year: such things send a researcher straight to the electoral roll. But the list of registered voters at Great Russell Mansions in 1933 was of no help:

1424	R	O	O'Sullivan, John Ignatius N.	7
1425	Rw	Dw	O'Sullivan, Hylda Mary	7
1426	Rw	Ow	Elliott, Edith—J	8
1427	R	O	Mill, Henry—SJ	9
1428	Rw	Dw	Mill, Annie	9

In one respect, it was a pleasing picture of how the long fight for women's suffrage would pay off – the 'Ow' next to Edith's name meant that the voting rights in Flat 8 were hers and hers alone, and the 'J' meant she was eligible for jury service – but where was her husband? Her change of name notice had appeared in the *Gazette* months after the roll for 1933 had been completed, so he can't have died or she would have described herself as a widow. She'd also moved in quite recently, as she wasn't there at all in 1932. Had Mr Elliott found out about the woman in the nightclub, cast his eyes over the piles of shoes and toothbrushes and packed his bags? Had there been a *final straw*? Or was this just Edith's personal crash pad after all? Did they have another home elsewhere?

Matters of the heart had also kept Maud and her fellow detectives busy. As one anonymous female detective wrote in May 1911, 'Love claims a lot of the lady detective's attention. Why not? There is no territory in which a woman's tact is more successful.'[4] The voice and tone were wrong for Maud, but they matched what I'd seen of another detective's writing. *Kate Easton?* I scrawled. If I was correct, for once the two women agreed on something, because two years later Maud wrote in the *Pittsburgh Press*:

It is surprising how many engaged or about to be engaged persons – both men and girls – commission me to make inquiries about their fiancés. It is quite a common thing. Occasionally I have to administer motherly advice, but I have managed to help in several emergencies of a delicate nature, and I have frustrated some nefarious designs. I am rather in favour of inquiries of this kind – it is better to be sure before marriage than sorry afterward.[5]

In April of the same year, she gave three examples of this type of work in *Pearson's Weekly*, although in each case her client was not the person about to be married but a concerned parent.[6] The practice of chaperoning had all but ended with the invention of bicycles that could outrun any maiden aunt, but few parents were willing to give their offspring complete freedom when it came to choosing a life partner. The first example involved a fiancée who, it was rumoured, had a conviction for shoplifting. Miss M— was the daughter of a naval officer and a few rungs below her husband-to-be on the social ladder. Her prospective father-in-law was unconcerned about this aspect of the relationship, but wanted Maud to lift the cloud of suspicion over Miss M—'s past before he would allow the marriage to go ahead.

After checking with other detective agencies and doing a bit of hunting of her own, Maud identified one case of a shoplifter who had given a false name and address after stealing a handbag from a department store a few years previously. The woman had subsequently served two months in prison, so Maud visited the gaol to look through the photographs of prisoners they held. One was an indisputable match with the picture she had of Miss M—.

'I had now found out all I had been commissioned to do by my client,' she wrote, 'but the case interested me strangely, and I determined to pursue my investigations a little further.' She shadowed Miss M— and eventually struck up a friendship with her at a library in Kensington where the woman was a regular visitor. Maud soon became convinced that the conviction had been a mistake:

> Her own story in the dock had been that she had taken the bag inadvertently without meaning to do so, but her story, a common one of the professional shoplifter, was not believed. I believed it however and anyone who knew the girl, I am sure, would have done the same thing.

Her client had only briefly met Miss M—, so Maud advised him to get to know her so he might form his own opinion about the incident. The wedding bells soon rang out.

There was no happily-ever-after for Maud's second pair of lovers. Her client on that occasion had been a country squire who was convinced that his son, a curate, was secretly involved with a woman in London. Maud soon uncovered the curate's regular visits to the house of a well-known society lady who had a very attractive daughter. Her client, however, was unimpressed:

'Oh, I know all about that affair! No; there is someone else I am certain.'

'Why are you certain?' I asked.

'Because,' was the reply, 'I believe my son would marry the young lady to whose house he goes so often only that there is someone else.'

Maud resumed her searches. The other woman, it turned out, was the curate's wife. The pair had married in Oxford when he was a student and she a barmaid, and he had kept this a close secret. Shortly after she reported her findings, Maud wrote without comment, the curate committed suicide.

The final case involved 'an officer from a Guards regiment' which, as I was learning, was Maud-speak for 'complete bastard'. Guardsmen were notorious. The breeding, uniform and military discipline of elite Guardsmen could mask all manner of deviant traits – and the only point in this particular suitor's favour was that he would have turned up to the wedding with his boots polished to perfection. Maud's inquiries revealed him to be 'one of the greatest blackguards I have ever encountered in the whole of my professional career, and I have known some bad ones indeed.' Not only had the officer left his regiment in disgrace and turned his hand to blackmail and swindling, but he'd been married before, to a governess he had picked up at a weekend house party: 'The girl had £300, which he took after they had married; and then he deserted her, and she had died in great poverty in Brussels.'

That alone would have been enough to put an end to the wedding preparations, but, Maud claimed, he added another black mark to his file when he made an unexpected appearance at Albion House one evening. She immediately knew he meant trouble, and discreetly reached for her revolver:

'How dare you,' I said, 'come into my private office like this?'

'I have just come to tell you,' he said, making a step towards me, 'that it is not safe for anyone – a girl especially – to go fooling around making inquiries about a man like me.'

'I have found out quite enough about you,' I said, 'to stop all chance of your being able to marry Miss—.'

His face went white; he raised his fist and made a quick step towards me, and then I brought the revolver to bear point-blank on his temple, and he stopped.

'You are an infernal coward!' I said. I was in such a rage with him that I could almost have shot him.

She refrained, and instead marched him to the stairs and waited until she heard the entrance door below click shut. Needless to say, the marriage did not go ahead.

Maud would come across all manner of relationships over the course of her career. As *Pearson's Weekly* wrote in 1921, 'Miss West has seen behind the scenes of hundreds of love affairs, strange and mysterious, tragic and comic.'[7] Her articles on the subject certainly suggested she had seen it all, from the agony of childhood crushes ('Oh mumsy, what is the matter with me, I feel so miserable?') to jealous septuagenarians. She'd intervened in torrid romances and read letters between indifferent couples:

MY DEAR C. – You must not run away with the idea that I am desperately in love with you. I am no more desperately in love with you than you are with me. But we are good friends, I believe, and it suits us both, I think, to marry. This is the plain fact . . . You are not a Venus any more than I am an Adonis – last night you seemed disappointed that I did not kiss you; how absurd it is; I don't like kissing; I never did. Another thing, don't call me 'darling' or 'dear,' I have a name, so have you and names were given to us to be addressed by.[8]

As it happened, Maud seemed rather in favour of such alliances. 'I am not sure indeed that matter of fact lovers don't make the happiest marriages,' she wrote. 'They are not blind to one another's faults and defects, and if they appreciate each other's good qualities the chances are they will be happy.'

What about her own marriage? Was it happy? Had it started from a similar practical basis, or was it a whirlwind romance? A possible clue lay in her story about the Prince of Lovers. Maud had defended Violet, the 'romantic little idiot' who wanted to travel the world in search of adventure, reminding her old friend Monsieur Dupont that she herself had run off when she was nineteen. Dupont had responded, 'I know . . . I know . . . And you made a success of it, because you are cautious and not a fool.'[9] On first reading, I had taken that to mean that she had simply left home in search of adventure when she was nineteen, but had she actually run off with a man? If so, and she had 'made a success of it', was that man Mr Elliott?

A small spanner was thrown into the works of this theory when I came across an almost identical story called 'Scoundrels in Love', which Maud had written in 1930. It was the tiger-skin vs bear-skin rug debacle all over again. This story also ended with a showdown in a restaurant, although it involved *two* French girls and the Prince of Lovers had been split into two conniving suitors posing as doctors.[10] There was no mention of M. Dupont or Maud running off at nineteen. Complete invention, or two sensationalized versions of a real-life case? It was impossible to tell.

It did, however, lead to another clue about Maud's marital affairs. I'd found 'Scoundrels in Love' by following a hint in an Australian newspaper, which in turn led to eight other articles that Maud had written for British regional newspapers in 1930. The first in the series was called 'How I Took Up the Work'. There, she had given yet another account of her very first case. In this version, it was her solicitor uncle who suggested that she pose as a maid at a French hotel to investigate a robbery, as she was 'the most innocent-looking person he knew.' In return, she had a surprise for him:

> I jumped at his offer for two reasons. First of all I am inclined to like any sort of adventure, and, secondly, and perhaps more importantly, I had a short time before got married secretly. My husband was not at all strong, and we needed all the money we could get.[11]

Was this when she was nineteen? And why was it a secret? Had she married the male equivalent of an Oxford barmaid, or was *she* the unsuitable one for some reason? And in what way was he 'not at all strong'?

As I pondered all this, somewhere in Australia an unseen hand was adding another clue to the Trove database, which I found a few days later. In December 1938, the journalist and soon-to-be war reporter Margaret Gilruth had written a profile of Maud in the *Hobart Mercury*, which included the statement, 'Actually, she has a husband of independent means who asks her at intervals to give up her work.'[12]

Was this the same man? As far as I could tell, Gilruth was a source to be trusted, so either Maud's sickly, unsuitable husband had developed into a man of substance, or she had married more than once. Perhaps that first husband had slid into an early grave or into the mire of the divorce courts. Either way, I could find no notice of any such wedding, divorce or funeral in the papers, and searching the civil marriage registers for the right Edith marrying the right Elliott sometime between 1900-ish and 1933 was a daunting, if not impossible, task.

As I let all this percolate, I decided to look at some of the methods Maud would have used in her own investigations. The most common appeared to be shadowing, surreptitiously following someone day in, day out, often in disguise, to see where they went and who they spoke to. The anonymous lady detective – the one I thought might be Kate Easton – said that it took up three-quarters of her time, whilst Maud described the focus required:

> Shadowing is one of the most difficult and arduous of our duties. One must keep one's eyes simply glued on the person one is following. If one allows one's attention to be distracted, even for an instant, one's quarry is liable to be lost.[13]

Sometimes, the detective would stay still: a stake-out, although the term wouldn't be used until the 1940s. Maud just called it observation and said it involved:

> Eyes glued to the doorway for hours on a stretch, never a blink through rain and cold lest in an instant of relaxation the quarry slip past.[14]

Neither sounded much fun, requiring a great deal of time, patience and, presumably, a strong bladder. Fortunately, if Maud's stories were anything to go by, there were shortcuts available. These included breaking and entering:

... we heard the occupant ... coming up the stairs. There was no time to be lost. My assistant scrambled into a cupboard, while I crept under the bed. As I am not the slimmest of mortals, it was rather a tight fit.[15]

Bribery:

... after a long conversation with each of them and a promise of financial assistance, I persuaded them to carry out my wishes.[16]

Bluffing:

My plan was what we call a 'try-on,' but it succeeded.[17]

And mysterious, unspecified moves:

How I succeeded in doing this is too valuable a professional secret to give away.[18]

There was a lot that Maud didn't want to give away. Not just professional secrets, or her true identity, or the fact that she was married, but, I suspected, the full range of the work she undertook. Her stories about love and love affairs, for example, failed to mention the more mercenary services inquiry agents offered in that area. According to the *Belfast Evening Telegraph*, detectives were sometimes hired by fortune hunters to provide information about the movements and habits of American heiresses and other wealthy women. It claimed that one man had recently charmed his way into a marriage worth £10,000 a year by using such information to book himself into the same hotels as the object of his wallet's desire as she toured the Italian lakes. He then obtained an introduction through 'a remote but mutual friend who was diligently hunted up for the purpose.'[19]

Nor did Maud mention her business clients much, unless they provided a useful background to some improbable adventure. But they must have provided a significant part of her income. As the anonymous lady detective had said:

> Business princes believe in shadowing. They say it helps them weed out the drones from the workers and fraud from honesty. So whenever an employer becomes suspicious we are called in.[20]

Female detectives, she said, were in particular demand when it came to following commercial travellers. They would shadow them from town to town, taking the same trains and checking with each shop they visited that they hadn't been quoting inflated prices and pocketing the difference.

Hadn't John Goodwin said something about this? I dug out my copy of *Crook Pie*. Yes, there it was, although he gave it a slightly different spin: 'Sometimes a business firm will employ a private detective to "shadow" its agents, or travellers, to find out whether they appear to be living within their means or whether some of the firm's money is "sticking to their fingers."'[21]

He also gave other examples of work private detectives undertook on behalf of commercial clients. Insurance companies, for example, would hire them to investigate 'bogus burglaries, "arranged" fires, fraudulent deaths, "stolen" cars and other insurance frauds ...', whilst employers with large unionized workforces had been known to employ detectives to gather intelligence on possible strike action or unrest.[22]

Maud herself said that her very first commission as a professional detective had come from a firm in the City. She had been hired to stay at an expensive West End hotel in order to check up on a man from New York with whom they were doing business. After a week of fruitless shadowing, she had struck up a conversation with him in the lounge after dinner one evening. Through polite chit-chat, she elicited his plans for the weekend, which involved a visit to Hampshire and what turned out to be the country retreat of the head of a rival firm. This revelation, she said, saved the firm thousands of pounds – some of which presumably ended up in her pocket.[23]

Goodwin also gave further details on the art of shadowing. In addition to core staff, he said, detective agencies also employed local 'wires' or 'narks' in major towns and cities to assist their work. These were not detectives as such, but were recruited from 'Hawkers, newsboys, taxi-drivers, hotel porters, waiters, cloak-room attendants, chambermaids' and so on. They would gather information, run errands and also put up visiting detectives when they were passing through town.

He described a case in which a detective had shadowed a man from London to Bath to Oxford to Birmingham and back. In Bath, the detective arranged for a local nark to pose as a blind man selling bootlaces and matches opposite the man's boarding house. As the city had two railway stations, the detective took a room at a hotel between the two. It was arranged that when the man emerged from his boarding house with luggage, the 'blind' nark would dispatch a child to the hotel with either six boxes of matches or six bootlaces to denote in which direction, and therefore to which station, the man was heading.

Such methods as with those Maud described all took time and were generally employed in commercial investigations, divorce shadowings and other substantial cases. But, as the journalist Basil Tozer reported on behalf of the *Daily Express* in 1914, detective agencies also offered speedier services to businesses and individuals needing a quick credit check or information about a person's character.

For his article 'London's Secret Service: Wily Ways of Private Inquiry Agents', Tozer had written to a private detective agency requesting information on two people. A comprehensive report on one came back within twelve hours, the other within twenty-four. They included information about income, outstanding debts, past history, current living arrangements, levels of sobriety and other habits. He found this 'quite disconcerting' and set out to find out how it was done.[24]

Much of his findings were as one would expect. Basic information was taken from 'books of reference', by which I assumed he meant street directories, membership lists and publications such as *Who's Who*. Being primarily a sports writer, Tozer focused on what these might say about a person's recreational interests – 'A is fond of golf. B is a billiard player. C is a hunting man. D delights in football, or possibly cricket. E is an ardent playgoer . . .' – but any information such as club memberships or a business address would be a useful starting point.

The next step was to visit the individual's home or office. This would be carefully timed to ensure that the person was out at the time, so that the detective, using some form of cover, could get into conversation with a domestic servant or office clerk:

> With extreme tact and cleverness he draws his victim on to talk; he puts questions to him – or her – which do not appear to be questions; he suggests, insinuates, interpolates an amusing comment or some quaint story here and there, just to keep the ball rolling, and finally departs with his memory well stocked with information, leaving his victim in blissful ignorance of the fact that his brains have been carefully, secretly, and thoroughly picked.

The same technique might be used in restaurants or tea shops to grill acquaintances or business partners. In an era accustomed to communal public eating this was relatively simple: 'It is so easy to get into conversation with such people during the course of a meal, if you happen to sit at the same table.'

The detectives, he said, were 'affable and most plausible gentlemen, with a considerable amount of tact', before adding, 'some of the representatives are quite attractive women.' The latter, he explained, had the advantage in that they were able to mine hairdressers, manicurists, chiropodists and other 'great gossips' for information:

> Lady A. spends an hour being manicured, and keeps up an animated conversation with the operator. She is followed by Mrs B., who also prattles irresponsibly. The next, a regular client, lets out all sorts of secrets about Lady A. and one or two other people . . .

If the female detective had also set herself up as a regular client – I thought of Maud's neatly trimmed nails – all this information was hers for the taking.

As Tozer concluded, 'It really is all very simple when you come to look into it – the way everything about everybody is known to the secret service.'

Could any of this help with my search for Mr Elliott? Not really. All those methods assumed one knew the name of the person one was investigating, or at least had a chance of following them in order to find out. What would Maud do in my situation, I wondered, other than to tell me to stop poking about in her private life?

She did have one other trick up her sleeve. It was something she mentioned often as a particular strength of female detectives: intuition. I couldn't see how it could help me, with so little information from which to intuit anything, but, as logic was getting me nowhere, I decided to give it a go.

What niggled? What made no sense? There were many things, but the one that stood out at that particular moment was the fact that she had legally changed her name in 1933. Why wait until so late in her career to make Maud West official? There must have been a reason. Had she got into trouble under her real name? Was she trying to distance herself professionally from something in her private life, something that involved her husband, perhaps?

A search of archive records and digitized newspapers for 'Elliott private detective' yielded no answers to those questions – so much for intuition – but it did bring up something else, or, rather, *someone* else: an inquiry agent named Henry, or Harry, Elliott.[25]

As with most private detectives' appearances in the press, Harry Elliott was generally to be found in court giving evidence in divorce cases. During one of those appearances it was stated that he worked for a woman detective.[26] Could this be the Mr Elliott I had been looking for? Had Maud married one of her employees? This didn't tally with Margaret Gilruth's statement that she had a husband of independent means, but Harry's earliest appearance in the press in 1912 certainly suggested that he was capable of generating the kind of headlines that Maud would enjoy:

DETECTIVE UP A TREE.

Divorce Court Sequel to Leicestershire Marriage.

Harry hadn't been the one up the tree (that was his colleague spying on a woman in her underwear), but he'd watched as a policeman yanked his partner out of the branches.[27] I figured that men capable of climbing trees in 1912 would have been able to fight for King and Country two years later, so I searched the National Archives catalogue to see if Harry's First World War record had survived. If it had, it was likely to include details of his next of kin.

Luckily, he was the only Henry or Harry Elliott listed in the Discovery catalogue who was also a private detective. I'd need to see his actual record to get all the details, but the catalogue description did include a home address to get me started: *Pearley, Finchley Avenue, Church End.*

The 1918 electoral roll for Church End, part of Finchley itself, showed that Harry was indeed married to a woman named Edith. Coincidence? Maybe. Edith was a common name, after all. As I cast about for anything that would give me a definitive answer, I realized that there had been a clue under my nose the whole time. Pinned above my desk was the advertisement that Maud had created in the 1920s using the gender-morphing illustration from the *Pittsburgh Press* and, next to the telephone number, was a name: *Manager: H. Elliott.*

It still wasn't enough, but it gave me an idea. If Harry Elliott was the manager *and* married to the boss, he was likely to have an official stake in the business. And if he did, along with all the other rate-paying business owners at Albion House, he would have had the right to vote in local elections in Holborn as well as his home borough. I returned to the electoral roll, this time for Albion House – and there they were in 1922, complete with a home address:

> Elliott, Henry
>   (abode, Pearley, Finchley Avenue, N.3)
> Elliott, Edith
>   (abode, Pearley, Finchley Avenue, N.3)

I'd found him.

Even better, the file listed in the Discovery catalogue wasn't just the standard war record outlining campaigns fought, medals won and pensions received. It was much rarer than that, one of a tiny sample of medical tribunal records that had survived routine destruction. Harry had appealed against his conscription and I could expect to find the reason why and other details of his personal life when the copy I'd requested arrived. Things were looking up.

The Chelsea Artist

BY MAUD WEST

To all appearances she was a young artist with a studio in Chelsea, though, unlike most artists, she seemed to have ample means. I had been asked to keep her under observation by the wife of an English naval officer, who had frequently been in the woman's company.

I discovered that the Chelsea artist made extensive tours of the country in a splendidly appointed car, which was chauffeur driven. After many hundreds of miles of shadowing, I learned that she showed a decided preference for seaports and the society of naval officers. At once I got permission from the authorities to strengthen my reserve watches.

One day, in male disguise, I was following the woman and a naval officer companion, when, to my dismay, my car developed engine trouble. Fortunately the mishap occurred in a main thoroughfare, and I was able to hail a passing taxi cab. I told the driver to keep the car in sight at all costs, but the chase ended at the woman's house. As her place was already under observation I told the driver to drop me at my address.

The sequel was, to say the least, unexpected. The taxi driver had obviously seen through my disguise and, being suspicious, he went back to the woman's address to tell the naval officer that he had been shadowed by a woman masquerading as a man. True to naval tradition, the officer acted promptly. Within half an hour I was under arrest as a suspected spy.

Hectic hours followed. Inwardly I abused myself for being so foolish as to leave my address an open secret. All my pleading for release failed because, in the nature of my work, I dare not carry documents showing my identity. However, on the arrival of a certain police inspector who knew me, my identity was secretly divulged to the necessary officials and I was released.

The naval officer who had informed against me in all sincerity was cashiered for his indiscreet association with the Chelsea artist. She herself was arrested and proved to be a highly-paid enemy spy.[28]

Chapter Seven

A Kiss Before Dying

In my profession you can never afford to let the
least chance of what I call 'scoring a point' slip.

Maud West, 1913[1]

By 1914, Maud's career was going from strength to strength.
She hadn't yet achieved the distinction, even in her own mind,
of being London's leading lady detective but she appeared to be
edging closer. In a story in a New Zealand paper that spring, it was
reported that a female investigator had been engaged to unravel a
particularly thorny case – 'one of the greatest crime mysteries of
modern times', no less. The journalist declined to say what the case
might be, nor did he name the detective, saying only that she was
'the only one in London who controls a firm of her own'. This was
plainly untrue, but it did narrow the field, and various other clues
in the interview suggested he was speaking about Maud rather than
one of her known rivals. What clinched it, however, was this:

> 'I get some pretty nasty experiences, but' – and a business-like
> pistol appeared apparently from nowhere, and a moment later
> disappeared by the same route – 'I'm not afraid.'[2]

It had to be her.

This was confirmed when I tracked down the original article in
the *Daily Express*.[3] It was by Basil Tozer again, presumably following up on the wily ways of private inquiry agents. The lady sleuth

was still anonymous, but not only was there the photograph of Maud dressed as a dandy from the *Pittsburgh Press* but also a photograph of her supposedly in her own clothes:

HERSELF.

She shared a few more details of her family, saying her father was a solicitor (did he become a barrister later? I wondered), as were her brothers – 'so I suppose I may have inherited their power, or whatever you like to call it, of putting two and two together and thinking things out logically, which, after all, is one of the principal essentials in this profession.'

The article also mentioned a couple of new disguises – a Salvation Army 'lassie' and a club commissionaire – but what interested me most was the mention of her colleagues. I'd been finding it difficult to track down the 'experienced male and female staff' mentioned in her adverts. Her ill-fated collaboration with the shifty George Stafford Howell had flushed out two of them – the old-school detective's son William Cheney and the mysterious Miss Magnen – and I was waiting on more information about her husband and office manager Harry Elliott. But who else was there? What help did she have?

Thanks to Tozer's barely concealed amazement that a woman with 'such wonderful hair' and 'strangely-intelligent' eyes could be in charge, the interview kept returning to that very subject. There were no names, but one of her staff made a dramatic entrance half-way through the interview when Tozer asked what she would do if he tried to strangle her there and then. In response, she made two quick taps on the wall with a pencil:

> ... and on the instant a man pounced into the room who looked as though he could have punched out Wells and Carpentier simultaneously. She smiled at him, and he retired.

Was this Harry? Her regular staff, she said, comprised seven men and five women, 'but I have "first call" upon other specialists in this kind of work when business is exceptionally brisk.'

As she spoke, the London Season was under way. This was always her busiest time, she said, and presumably she was making good use of the extra help to cover the endless round of balls and receptions that launched the most eligible – and gullible – young women into society.

That year, however, London didn't settle into its usual summer torpor once all the tiaras had been packed away and the last debutante safely returned to the shires. The nation had been watching events in Europe warily since the assassination of Archduke Ferdinand on 28 June. By early August, with the German army on the rampage in Belgium (whose neutrality Britain was sworn to protect), the country had little choice but to enter the fray.

As the war took hold, central London was transformed into something resembling a giant army camp. Temporary buildings sprang up in all the great parks, alongside training grounds, experimental bombing sites, internment camps and allotments. At night, the street lamps were dimmed to a faint glimmer, bathing the city in a dreary gloom punctuated only by searchlights scanning the skies for Zeppelins. When the air was still, the sound of distant explosions rumbled across from the front line in France.

The stern face of Lord Kitchener loomed out of posters saying,

'Your country needs YOU', whilst a banner outside Charing Cross Hospital barked 'QUIET for the WOUNDED'. Yet the streets were anything but quiet. They were full of soldiers, for a start, clomping through on their way to the front, or limping back on leave. Noticeable, too, were the number of refugees from war-torn Europe. And then there were the ordinary Londoners, jolted out of their normal daily routines to savour the novelty of this strange, new world. Of these, it was the young women who caused the biggest stir. Eventually, they would step into absent men's shoes as bus conductors and railway guards, and work long shifts in munitions factories, but in the meantime, many were taking advantage of wartime opportunities of a very different kind.

Nowhere was this more evident than in the area around Waterloo Station, or 'Whoreterloo' as it became known.[4] There, hordes of girls followed soldiers fresh off the trains from France, promising good times under the railway arches and in pay-by-the-hour boarding houses. The police were used to dealing with prostitution in the area, which had been a red-light district for decades, but this was different. Many of these newcomers were very young, and nor were they asking for payment.

Such 'khaki fever' wasn't just restricted to London. Similar reports came in from all over the country, wherever army camps and civilians collided. Despite much hand-wringing and moral panic, at first no one quite knew what to do about it. In the background, however, two competing factions of middle-class women were mustering, each sensing an opportunity to further their own aims. In one corner was Louise Creighton, widow of the former Bishop of London, and the National Union of Women Workers, seeking to uphold moral and social purity through their Voluntary Women Patrols (VWP). In the other was Margaret Damer Dawson and a group of ex-militant suffragettes, whose more feminist agenda was to ease women into permanent police work via their military-inspired

Women Police Volunteers (WPV). Damer Dawson would soon break away from the WPV to create a third group, the Women Police Service (WPS). Between them, they trained thousands of volunteers, who spread out in towns and cities and put an end to any amorous activity they encountered either through direct intervention or, more simply, by their libido-crushing presence.

The first official recognition that women could be effective law enforcers, however, came in August 1915 when Edith Smith, a thirty-five-year-old former midwife and WPS volunteer, was sworn in as Britain's first female police constable. Her remit was to address the problems of promiscuity surrounding the army camp at Belton Park in Lincolnshire on behalf of the Grantham police, a task she undertook with rigorous efficiency over the next three years. Despite the reservations of the Home Office, other police forces soon followed suit and hired WPS volunteers to do similar work, most notably in munitions factories.

Few, however, were given the powers of arrest that Constable Smith enjoyed and, as their numbers increased, a debate broke out regarding their suitability for the work. Were they capable of dealing with drunken servicemen? Was it decent for them to give evidence in court about homosexual acts they had witnessed in Hyde Park?[5]

In 1916, the *Daily Express* contacted Maud for her views on the qualities women could bring to Scotland Yard if they were ever let through the doors. She said that a 'clever woman' would have the essentials of 'keen intuition and tact', but added that few who applied to her proved fit for the work. It demanded such a range of personal attributes – 'very robust health, a quick intellect, sympathy, tact, and a large amount of self-reliance' – that they were rarely found in one person. The desirability of foreign-language skills and some knowledge of the law drained the pool of suitable candidates even further.[6]

In time, Maud would have more to say on the topic of women

in the police, but during the war her hands were full with her own wartime work, so the debate raged on without her. Establishing precisely what that work involved, however, proved trickier than expected.

In April 1918, the *London Evening News* ran a two-part exposé of gambling in the West End, which it described as 'the most fattening of war trades' and 'a cleverly organised robbery business'. Chemin de fer – a form of baccarat – was the game of choice, but that was all London's backstreet saloons had in common with the smart baize tables of Nice or Monte Carlo. Here, with the blinds drawn and harsh electric lights glaring overhead, distinctions between night and day became meaningless, encouraging the clientele to play on past the point of exhaustion. Drinks might be spiked with drugs to excite, calm or incapacitate depending on the fortunes of the house, whilst resident card sharps ensured that even the most clear-headed gambler had 'less chance than if he or she went on to the stage to upset the professional illusionist.'[7]

At particular risk were young officers, often fresh out of school and brimming with a fateful combination of bravado and naivety. To make matters worse, *The Times* reported, many of the touts who lured these young men off the streets were working hand in glove with unscrupulous moneylenders, whose printed circulars paid particular attention to 'young men with expectations'.[8]

Maud's own experience of the wartime gambling scene came about, she said, when friends of two such victims approached her to identify and expose the 'vultures' who were running a number of clubs in the backstreets of Piccadilly. To achieve this, she turned to her box of disguises to blend in with the gambling crowd. After sleeping during the day, she would emerge into the night as a man called 'Jimmy' or slink forth as a gold-digging temptress, moving from club to club, gathering evidence as she went:

Time and time again I tricked youngsters befuddled with drink at critical moments. Many of them must have wondered the following day when their minds had cleared of their orgy of drinking what had become of their companion and the 'fair charmer' of the previous evening.

She was keen to point out, however, that it was not an enjoyable task:

At this period I learned more of the vileness with which human nature can be associated than I had ever before experienced. Only constant alertness enabled me to get out of some of the most horrible and difficult situations unscathed ... the men one met in such places were unlikely to have much pity if they discovered my identity.

For protection, she wore some rather unusual accessories:

I never doubted the efficiency of a small but very useful revolver, or a certain dress ornament which contained a tiny but spiteful stiletto. Furthermore I always carried on a bangle two detachable beads composed of a soluble narcotic. With these I could promptly dope the drink of any too embarrassing suitor. On one occasion only did I find it necessary to lose one of my bangle beads. My armoury, I am glad to say, was never in action.[9]

She soon discovered that many of the touts employed to introduce young soldiers to these clubs were members of the armed forces themselves – some of high rank – who had desk jobs in London. 'Familiar with army routine and customs, and naturally quick in judgement,' she wrote, 'these uniformed pests were able, by the use of a few appropriate phrases, to secure their acceptance as "Hail fellows, well met.'"

Her method of identifying these men was simple. She took note of any military men in the clubs 'whose spending capacity was suspiciously unlimited' and then arranged for them to be trailed. Once she had gathered enough information, she sent the evidence to the military authorities and 'the whole crowd suddenly found themselves drafted for active services.' The civilians who ran the dens, she said, received long terms of imprisonment.

I didn't believe a word of it. Deadly jewellery? Vamping it up around teenage boys? A smooth-talking alter ego called Jimmy? Maud may have had some experience of wartime gambling dens, but surely not like this.

Her next wartime story got off to a better start, with a statement that was undoubtedly true:

> My staff at this time had been reduced, some being on active service and others carrying out duties of national importance.[10]

Many businesses struggled during the war as experienced and valued staff signed up to fight. Private inquiry agencies, however, suffered a double blow. As a major employer of retired police officers, they also had to contend with many of their remaining staff being recalled to former duties on the beat. So few detectives were left, in fact, that the newly formed British Detectives Association was forced to suspend its meetings.[11] As she had not been invited to join this male enclave, presumably Maud was unconcerned about this particular development, but she was finding the strain of increased work 'almost intolerable'.

'To avoid a breakdown,' she continued, 'I went to the east coast to recuperate.' It seemed a strange choice of destination, considering the German bombardments of Scarborough and Great Yarmouth, but a spa guide from the time assured me that it was just the place for a little rest and relaxation. Cromer, for example, had an excellent climate – 'bracing, dry, and invigorating' – and the serene landscape of 'cliff, moor and wooded dell' was a balm to frazzled minds.[12]

Unfortunately, her plans for a quiet seaside holiday never materialized. She'd barely had time to unpack her bathing suit before she was approached by 'a certain authority' to undertake a secret commission: 'My job was to track down, if possible, the cause for certain leakages of information connected with war operations.'

For the first few days and nights, she kept close watch on various buildings in the town before selecting one – 'a well-known mental home' – for closer examination. With the help of her new government friends, she was soon admitted as a patient suffering from the strain of war work. 'After being there a few days,' she wrote, 'I noticed that the doctor in charge was certainly not the type of man who should have nervous cases under his care.' He happened to be foreign, but it was his angry outbursts and fits of irritability which were of most concern to Maud. These, she observed, occurred only when patients were upstairs: 'I was forced to the conclusion that something up there was causing him anxiety.' The very top floor was out of bounds, so naturally she made a beeline for it at the first opportunity:

Creeping upstairs in the early hours of the morning and going to the door of the room facing the sea-front, I brought out a special key. With a feeling of satisfaction I felt the levers of the lock slip back. Cautiously opening the door, I found the room in comparative darkness, but the friendly light of the moon revealed all I wanted to see. There, on a long bench, was an ingeniously camouflaged and completely equipped wireless transmitter and receiving set.

She tiptoed out of the building to report her discovery and stayed to watch as the doctor and his chief assistant were bundled quietly into a car and whisked away into custody.

This wasn't the only tale Maud told of her encounters with enemy agents. There was the Chelsea artist, of course, but also a case in which she exposed a network of German spies posing as commercial travellers for a Dutch import firm. The firm had contacted Maud to undertake a week's surveillance on each of its twenty salesmen. It was a suspiciously large commission, so Maud had contacted a colleague in Holland to make inquiries. She received in return a report on the true nature of the export firm, and decided to play 'a little game' of her own:

> The gentleman who had interviewed me on behalf of the firm was no doubt laughing up his sleeve at the gullibility of an English woman detective who was obliging him by reporting on his spies . . . So I called in my secretary and dictated a series of reports on the different agents, which showed them to have been indulging in the most fatuous activities, after which I was able to leave the whole thing in the hands of the right people to deal with . . .[13]

It didn't take me long to establish that these tales were all complete fiction. Firstly, there was the small matter of the Official Secrets Act, which would have prohibited the publication of any genuine account of such work. More damning, however, was the evidence I found in various declassified MI5 files held at the National Archives.[14] The enemy agents described therein were an eclectic bunch, and although a number had indeed masqueraded as travelling salesmen hawking all manner of non-existent goods, from cigars to Peruvian sardines, not one ran a psychiatric hospital or went around seducing naval officers.

Furthermore, the files revealed that due to counter-espionage measures put in place before the war, there were very few spies to be found in Britain at all: only thirty-one were captured on British soil between 1914 and 1917. Maud claimed to have caught twenty-three. It seemed unlikely that she had personally outwitted three-quarters of Britain's known spy population without a mention in the history books, but I thought it wise to check the accompanying list of payments to secret service staff and informants, anyway. She wasn't there.

To give Maud her due, there may have been a shortage of real spies, but imaginary ones were to be found in abundance. As soon as war was declared, the ever-present distrust of 'the other' had gone into overdrive and curtains twitched across the land as patriotic souls scrutinized the behaviour of their neighbours. Fanning the flames of this 'spy mania' were the likes of William Le Queux, a writer with a long history of xenophobic scaremongering.

Sitting in his country pile in Devon, Le Queux was determined that the people should know exactly what they were up against. 'I am no alarmist,' he wrote in the introduction to *German Spies in England*. 'This is no work of fiction, but of solid and serious fact.'[15] He claimed to be an expert on German espionage due to years of research for the invasion fantasy novels that had made him famous and even had the 'displeasure' of including a number of enemy agents on his Christmas card list. He told of gun emplacements disguised as tennis courts, hidden wireless stations signalling to German submarines, and foreign-born governesses, porters, prostitutes and businessmen all conspiring to bring Britain down through their 'dastardly work'. It was such a hit that his publishers could barely keep up with demand.

Pitted against Le Queux and his fellow doom-mongers were more rational minds. The journalist Sidney Felstead, for example, was given access to secret-service files at the end of the war to produce a factual account of how Britain dealt with its unwelcome visitors.[16] It was hoped that *Spies At Bay* would put an end to the myths once and for all, but the sober reality of intelligence gathering and postal censorship could never compete in the popular mind with tales of widespread peril. The idea of the enemy within was so firmly embedded, in fact, that Maud could still provoke a quiet thrill over a decade later when she recounted her wartime adventures to the readers of the *Sunday Dispatch*.

So that was that – or so I thought. I had packed away all my papers relating to Maud's wartime adventures when my father called. He wasn't unfamiliar with the world of intelligence, having done time at GCHQ, and was now studying First World War history with the Open University during his retirement. Some time previously, he had leapt upon a curious article I had found during my first trawl of British newspapers and asked if he could investigate.

The article had appeared in Scotland's largest Sunday newspaper in August 1917 and concerned a pamphlet ostensibly written by the German steel magnate August von Thyssen (motto: 'If I rest, I rust'). The *Post Sunday Special* (soon to be rebranded as the *Sunday Post*) had printed the pamphlet in full, along with an explanation of its provenance:

> . . . the pamphlet was suppressed [in Germany], and Herr Thyssen was fined for writing it. A copy of the pamphlet came into the hands of a client of the well-known lady detective, Miss Maud West. Some little time ago the former was at Cassel, where the pamphlet was printed. He saw a copy of it at the house of a friend, who allowed him to make a translation . . .[17]

The pamphlet explained how German industrialists had not only been blackmailed by the Kaiser into contributing to war funds under threat of business ruin but had been promised mining rights in Australia and Canada once the war was won. It was a startling allegation, but didn't seem to have been picked up by any historians. My father hadn't known what to make of it, so had boldly consulted the Regius Professor of History at Cambridge, a leading expert on the politics of the First World War. On reading the text, Sir Christopher Clark's immediate response was that it was not from Germany at all. The contents were so inaccurate as to be laughable and the diction and tone were wrong. Instead, it appeared to be a 'not especially sophisticated' propaganda exercise. In other words, it was fake news, which had fallen somehow into Maud's hands and from there into a newspaper published in Dundee, one of the biggest hotspots for anti-war agitation. Five months later, it was read out in the US Senate.[18]

I couldn't imagine she'd written it herself. Despite being laughable, it was an elaborate argument designed to bolster anti-German sentiment by highlighting Germany's turpitude and the threat to Britain's current and former overseas territories, and that hardly came within her purview. Was her 'client' perhaps John Buchan, then head of the Department of Information, or his colleague Charles Masterman, who had set up its predecessor, the War Propaganda Bureau? Or did she have contacts elsewhere? It was a small world, after all, with a myriad of connections between the nascent intelligence services, Scotland Yard and private detective agencies.

Such covert favours, if they existed, wouldn't have taken up much of Maud's time, however, so the question remained as to the exact nature of her war work. If she hadn't been haunting illicit gambling dens or catching spies, what had she been up to?

Her peacetime work must have carried on to some extent, although much had changed. Many country houses had been put over to hospitals and convalescent homes, thereby shutting down the weekend playground of high-bred thieves and swindlers, and the WSPU had decided to step down their campaign of direct action after having one last go at the paintings in the National Gallery in August 1914. Even the Parisian Apaches had swapped their dainty shoes for hobnailed boots and headed off to the biggest scrap of all time, much to the relief of the French police.

But people were still falling in and out of love and I suspected that Maud was just plodding on with the basics of detective work: divorce investigations. There was certainly plenty of work to be had in this area, with all the new opportunities for infidelity, not to mention the number of hasty, ill-conceived marriages, and the dearth of male detectives. The annual number of divorces in England and Wales nearly doubled between 1914 and 1918.[19] By the end of 1920, it was over five times as high, as were the number of prosecutions for bigamy.[20]

The most obvious target for these services was the military man abroad. He had served Maud well in the past, and now his numbers were growing by the day. Furthermore, life in the trenches, surrounded by mud and the stench of rotting feet, gave him plenty of time to wonder about the temptations on offer to his wife or girlfriend in the topsy-turvy world back home.

Kate Easton apparently had the same idea and had taken out adverts in the *Army and Navy Gazette*.[21] Maud, however, adopted a more targeted approach. Her adverts appeared in a more niche publication, the *Sportsman's Gazette*. It was a smart place to advertise if one wanted to attract the attention of the nation's wealthiest soldiers – and it also introduced me to a formidable woman called Emma Cunliffe-Owen, who had wheeled herself into the hearts of thousands of men by taking on the War Office from the comfort of her bath chair.

In the first eighteen months of the war, before the Military Service Act brought in conscription starting in March 1916, the British Army was heavily reliant on voluntary recruits. After the initial flurry began to dwindle, it was suggested that men might be more willing to join up if they could serve alongside men they knew. The Earl of Derby started things off in Liverpool on 28 August 1914, saying in a stirring speech, 'This should be a battalion of pals, a battalion in which friends from the same office will fight shoulder to shoulder for the honour of Britain and the credit of Liverpool.' Within days, he had raised four such 'pals' battalions, and soon groups of men were enlisting all over the country. They came not only from local communities, such as the Accrington Pals and Grimsby Chums, but also through shared professions and interests, forming whole battalions of stockbrokers, miners, artists and bankers.

Watching some of these new recruits drilling in Hyde Park near her home was the fifty-one-year-old Emma Cunliffe-Owen. Although largely confined to a bath chair due to rheumatoid arthritis, she had once been a keen sportswoman and thought the War Office had missed a trick by imposing an upper age limit of thirty-eight: her wide circle of ageing, sporty friends could do just as well on the parade ground.

She had never been one to be constrained by rules. Even her entry into the world had been unorthodox, occurring as it did in the Kensington Museum where her father was the director. When she was nineteen, she had married her barrister cousin Edward and had four children. By the First World War, however, the pair were amicably separated and Emma was enjoying a relationship with a surgeon nine years her junior.

In this spirit of living life on her own terms, she wired the War Office to request permission to raise a special battalion of men up to the age of forty-five, signing the telegram with the gender-neutral 'E. Cunliffe Owen'. With Lord Kitchener's go-ahead, she called her new endeavour the Sportsman's Battalion, hired a large room at the Hotel Cecil on the Strand and began recruiting in earnest.

Her advertisements made clear the type of man she was

looking for: 'Only those used to shooting, hunting, riding and outdoor sport, who are thoroughly sound and physically fit, need apply . . .'[22] Some specifically stated 'upper and middle class only'.[23] As chief recruiting officer, Mrs Cunliffe-Owen personally interviewed each applicant herself. She also ensured her men were well cared for. One recruit noted that 'the toothbrushes especially were the best in the army.'[24]

This approach was enormously successful. Within weeks, she had raised one battalion of 1,300 soldiers and was soon recruiting for another. The Sportsmen were a formidable bunch, standing literally head and shoulders above the average army recruit; even the lowest ranks were filled with well-fed public- and grammar-school boys and varsity men. As well as the general hunting-shooting-fishing brigade, there were explorers, golfers, boxers and cricketers (including Matilda Mitchell's new husband, the Surrey batsman Tom Hayward), a Wimbledon umpire and an Olympic archery champion.

As the war went on, the original class and age restrictions were relaxed for those with the right attitude, from the chauffeur who enlisted alongside his aristocratic employer to the sixty-four-year-old big-game hunter and close friend of Theodore Roosevelt, Frederick Selous. Eventually, as one recruit recalled, 'Practically every grade of life was represented, from the peer to the peasant . . .'[25]

Still, in terms of a concentration of wealthy soldiers, Maud couldn't have found a better market for her services. The subscribers to the *Sportsman's Gazette* included not only current members of the battalions and those who had been transferred elsewhere but their friends and families. In terms of reaching society's finest, it was arguably more effective than a full-page spread in *The Times*.

It was an entertaining read, too. Alongside biographies of famous recruits, sporting banter and spoof letters, there were adverts for Burberry and Aquascutum, luxury hotels and, for those missing the peaks of the Himalayas, mango chutney. From May 1915, taking up a quarter of a page in each issue, was Maud's contribution:[26]

MAUD WEST, "The Lady Detective,"

Is entrusted by the nobility and gentry with

Divorce Shadowings and Secret Inquiries

in all parts of the world. She is assisted by a permanent staff of male and female detectives, who have been skilfully trained in all matters of a delicate and complicated nature, and whose integrity is unimpeachable.

All Languages spoken.   Terms very moderate.

Old Established. References to Leading Solicitors.
'Phone : 8561 Gerrard.

MAUD WEST, Albion House, 59 New Oxford St., London.

MAUD WEST.—It is of the greatest importance that a client should know, when engaging a private detective, that confidence is being reposed in the right person. A visit to Miss Maud West will immediately inspire this confidence. After a consultation with her, one leaves her presence with a light heart, and settled conviction that their case will be handled dexterously and with that skill and forensic judgement so rarely found in a woman and never in a man. She is a striking personality, and her successes are phenomenal (vide Press).

MAUD WEST is entrusted with the most delicate matters, and her clients include members of the nobility and gentry, besides many of the
LEADING LONDON LAWYERS.

MAUD WEST, Albion House, 59 New OxfordSt., London, W.C.

It was a far cry from her usual two-line adverts in regional and national newspapers and was shameless in its emotional manipulation. By its very presence, it planted the suggestion that all might not be well at home, whilst the text promised a soothing maternal touch, so absent in the trenches, and a deft and discreet service to put things right. It may as well have read, *There, there. Let Nanny sort it out.*

When the copy of Harry Elliot's war record arrived from the National Archives, I discovered that Maud had a fair amount of coddling to do at home, too. The document outlined how Harry had been called up in June 1918, just days after his thirty-ninth birthday.[27] In his initial medical examination, he was classed as A2, or fit for service with further training. Had he left it there, his secret would have been safe. But he decided to appeal and, in doing so, managed to leave behind a historical record of his most intimate problems. This was not his intention. He only wanted the Middlesex Appeal Tribunal to understand how very unsuitable he was for military service:

> I have pain under my heart, & have suffered from neuritos [sic] so badly that I have been unable to sleep. The impediment in my speech is sometimes so bad that I am unable to speak.

Nor did he have high hopes for the future, adding forlornly, 'The Pearl Assurance Co. will not grant me a full insurance on my life.'

In a supporting (if not very supportive) letter, his local doctor suggested that there was little wrong with Harry's heart and pointed out that his patient was 'highly neurotic as seen in the stammering, blushing, etc.' Dr Moran did, however, list everything physically amiss, namely:

(1) Varicocele of left testicle
(2) Hernia (inguinal) left side
(3) Hypermetropic Astigmatism
(4) Stricture of Urethra

Translation: Harry Elliott was a hypochondriac bundle of nerves with a dodgy testicle, a hernia in his groin, psychosomatic aches and pains, poor eyesight and had difficulty peeing. The latter, the doctor helpfully explained, was 'a complication after gonorrhoea 21 years ago.'

I grabbed my calculator. That would have been in 1897, when Harry was about eighteen. If he was indeed Edith's only husband, the one she had secretly wed when she was nineteen, they would have run away to get married not long afterwards. So when she wrote that her new husband 'was not at all strong', that was no lie. No wonder she didn't elucidate. Furthermore, the trouble had apparently continued: Dr Moran mentioned that he had treated Harry during a relapse in 1917 that had caused a severe haemorrhage and had got his patient 'greatly down'.

The British Army, however, was unmoved. They had become adept at sniffing out malingerers, and they counted the stammering and blushing Harry Elliott amongst that number. After granting him a second medical examination in August, the appeals board upgraded his fitness ranking from A2 to A1 and packed him off for basic training. By that time, however, the war was all but over and, with no army service or pension records to suggest otherwise, it seemed that he returned home to Edith after the Armistice was declared in November in more or less the same pitiful condition as when he left.

The partnership intrigued me. How did they meet? Given the evidence so far, Harry Elliott was hardly a prime catch, so how did he end up with a go-getting lawyer's daughter like Edith? When I started digging into his background, it only added to the mystery.

According to census reports, Harry and his eight siblings grew up in Hoxton in the East End. Their father was a carpenter. When the social reformer Charles Booth drew up his meticulous, colour-coded *Descriptive Map of London Poverty* in 1889, the colour he chose for Harry's street was light blue. This wasn't the worst of Booth's categories – there was also dark blue before one descended into the living hell of black – but it still wasn't somewhere to hang about. 'Rough', 'criminal' and 'vicious' were just some of the words Booth and his team of researchers used to describe the area.[28]

Even Harry himself had brief experience of life behind bars. In the summer of 1893, when he was fourteen and working as an errand boy for a chemist in the City, he was caught filching coins to fund a trip to the seaside along with his eleven-year-old brother Alfred and a fourteen-year-old friend. It was Alfred who got caught with his hand in the till, and it didn't take him long to confess to the whole scheme. All three boys were subsequently arrested, hauled into court and sentenced to a week in prison. They only escaped the 'good whipping' the judge said they deserved because 'unfortunately two of them were over age.'[29]

All in all, Harry's historical record was a sparse but sorry catalogue of indignity and embarrassment. Still, the juvenile crime, the venereal disease, the nervous tics, the class difference – apparently none of this mattered to Edith. As far as I could tell, she loved Harry Elliott and that was that.

A Lady's Folly

BY MAUD WEST

A well-known lady in society, whom I shall call Lady Alice – she was the daughter of a Peer – during the war, took up work as a V.A.D. nurse in a hospital. One of her patients was a corporal in an infantry regiment; the two fell deeply in love with one another.

The corporal, before the war, had been a clerk in a city office, and the difference between himself and his nurse as regards rank and wealth would have made it difficult if not impossible for the lady to have obtained her family's consent to a marriage between them. They decided to get married secretly; as soon as the corporal was able to leave hospital he married his titled nurse at a registry office; there was no honeymoon; the evening of the day of the marriage the corporal returned to France, and a few weeks later he was killed in action. Nobody knew or even suspected that the titled lady who had been the corporal's nurse was his widow; everybody thought her to be a single girl.

Shortly after the Armistice she became engaged to a gentleman in the Diplomatic Service. After the announcement of the engagement had appeared in the papers the blackmailer got to work immediately. A notice appeared in several of the London papers to the effect that if

'Alice—' would come to the Charing Cross Post-office at noon any day during the week she would hear something about her husband; the initial letters of the husband's Christian and surname were given.

Lady Alice saw the notice and she at once came to the conclusion that it was intended for her. She went to the Charing Cross Post-office, where she met one of the men in the blackmailing gang who were working this particular business. I must explain that Lady Alice had not divulged even to the man to whom she was engaged the fact that she was a widow. She was terribly and most foolishly afraid of this fact becoming known, and she was precisely the type of person who falls very readily a victim to the professional blackmailer. She paid five thousand pounds in blackmail; if the blackmailing gang had not been too greedy they might have got off safely with their money; but they tried to get another five thousand pounds out of their victim, and this made her desperate, for she could not have found the money except with very great difficulty.

Then she came to me; there was only one thing to be done. Lady Alice had an appointment the following day to meet one of the blackmailers at Charing Cross. I went in her place. From the description Lady Alice had given me of the blackmailer I was sure I would recognise him; in any case I had an idea that I had come across this gentleman before in the course of my work on the continent. He was a short, thick-set individual, with a dark moustache and a fat, pale face. We arrived at the meeting place almost simultaneously, and I recognised the man at once.

I went up to him immediately and told him that Lady Alice was unable to come, and that I had come in her place. He looked extremely nervous and very suspicious.

'Well,' he inquired, 'what have you to say?'

I did not waste time. 'Not very much,' I replied. 'I am a detective and I want back that five thousand pounds that you got from Lady Alice; no, don't go away. If you stir I shall have you given into charge of the police at once.'

We were standing by the kerb at a crossing. He looked very wicked and rather frightened; to tell the truth, I thought he would be sure to make a bolt from me, and if he had I might have been placed in a difficulty, for as a matter of fact I was to a great extent bluffing when I threatened that I would give him in charge of the police. My plan was what we call a 'try-on,' but it succeeded. The man didn't stir.

'Lady Alice,' I went on, 'behaved like a fool. You see she has told the man she is going to marry about her former marriage, so there is no use in her paying you thousands of pounds to keep the matter dark, is there?'

I proved to him who I was and convinced him that he was as near to prison as perhaps he'd ever been. Then the man offered to give me back two thousand pounds.

'No use,' I said.

Finally he offered to give me back four thousand pounds. If I didn't take that I might do as I liked. I believe it was all the money he could give back; most probably his confederates had taken the other thousand pounds. Anyway I thought it better to take the money. We went into a teashop and he paid me the money then and there in notes whilst we were sitting at the table. It is nearly always the case that a person blackmailed for the first time gets frightened and usually pays.[30]

Chapter Eight

The Secret Adversary

The ways of the blackmailer are manifold. Like the tentacles of an octopus his fingers stretch out in all directions seeking fresh victims.

Maud West, 1929[1]

In 1918, Maud's list of services – *divorce shadowings, secret inquiries, etc.* – began to include an extra word: *blackmail*. As a crime, it was nothing new. Blackmail had emerged in its modern form in England during the late eighteenth century, when criminals first sensed the opportunities that lay in the disconnect between private sexual behaviour and what society and the law deemed acceptable. Initially, they targeted gay men, sodomy at the time being punishable by death, but expanded their operations in the hyper-moral Victorian age to include adulterers. By the time Maud was in business, anyone with a secret, sexual or otherwise, was fair game.

Private detectives had been dealing with blackmailers for years, as had Maud, although they only made an entrance in her pre-war stories after she had defeated their schemes, by which time they were boiling with anger and bent on revenge. Their primary purpose seemed to be to give her the opportunity to deliver some of her best lines:

'I am fortunate in finding you alone, Miss West . . .'

I picked up a loaded revolver from my writing table. 'Oh, not quite alone,' I answered, with a laugh.[2]

But now she was on a crusade. After the social and sexual upheavals of the First World War, blackmail was entering its heyday, and she started to write articles in which the crimes and methods of these 'parasites' were at the fore.[3] The majority of blackmailers operating in post-war Britain, she said, were members of foreign gangs who, acting on information gathered by local agents, would swoop in and out of the country to torment their victims.[4] In 1919, she had one particular gang in her sights:

> Since the signing of the Armistice the elite of the Continental blackmailers, known as the Black Hundred, have been extremely active. During the four years of war there were few cases of blackmail in this country of any importance or even on the Continent. But the cessation of hostilities opened up new fields of enterprise which the professional blackmailers have been quick to exploit.[5]

She claimed that members of the Black Hundred had been gathering details of court martials held during the war and using them to blackmail the soldiers concerned, once they had returned to civvy street.

One example she gave involved a young engineer who had enlisted in the early days of the war and served through to the end, being wounded three times in the process. 'His army record was of the highest kind,' Maud wrote. But on one occasion at the Somme, he was court-martialled for leaving a front-line trench without permission: 'It was a terribly hot day, and he went out of the trench to fetch some water for a comrade who was suffering from heat stroke and badly in want of a drink.' He had been sentenced to ten years penal servitude, although this was later remitted.

Shortly after the Armistice, the engineer returned to his home town to rebuild his life. He was walking home one evening when, according to Maud, 'he was roughly hustled by a man of the working class; the man seemed to be the worse for drink. He began abusing the engineer, and then to threaten him . . .' Exasperated, the engineer eventually marched him to the police station. As he was leaving, a well-dressed man approached and asked to speak to him for a few minutes. The conversation quickly took a menacing turn:

'You have just given a man in charge of the police for being drunk and molesting you,' said the man.

'I have,' replied the engineer.

'Well,' replied the other, 'when that man is charged at the police court tomorrow he will tell the story of how you were court-martialled in France for cowardice, and how you narrowly escaped being shot for the offence; the story will get into the papers unless—'

The man stopped speaking.

'Unless what?' asked the engineer.

'Unless you pay me five hundred pounds tonight. Of course, you can charge me for blackmailing if you wish, I am content to run my risk of your doing that.'

The risk to the engineer's reputation, however, was too high and so he paid the money and withdrew the charge against his 'drunken' street hustler. As Maud explained, the whole thing had been a set-up from start to finish.

The scheme reminded me of something Robert Graves had written in *The Long Weekend*. The Great War, he argued, had prompted an equally great shift in British society. By 1918, there were still 'two distinct Britains', but these were no longer based rigidly on class; the camaraderie necessary to survive life in the trenches had all but eliminated that old order between men. Instead, Britain had polarized into 'the Fighting Forces' and 'the Rest' – and the Fighting Forces 'had reduced morality to the single virtue of loyalty'. Even the seven deadly sins could be forgiven, he said, 'so long as a man was courageous and a reasonably trustworthy comrade.'[6]

This new emphasis on gallantry and service to King and Country meant anyone hiding some failing in their war record would have been a ripe target for blackmail. As I discovered, even the suggestion that an officer hadn't spent the entire war as a model of stoic heroism was enough to extract money from his family. In 1916, for example, *The Times* reported the case of a man who was found guilty of obtaining ten pounds by false pretences from the estate of an officer killed at Gallipoli. The crime, it transpired, was just one of a series of frauds on the families of fallen soldiers, 'which he sometimes accompanied by innuendoes on their reputations which were nothing short of blackmail.'[7]

Others took a more hands-on approach. In 1924, during the trial of Edith Bassett, who was accused of blinding her lover in one eye with acid, it emerged that she had married dozens of young officers during the war as a means to blackmail their families. That scam had only ended in the summer of 1918 after one family employed private detectives to investigate her background, leading to her brief imprisonment for bigamy.[8]

But these were individual rogues. What about the Black Hundred and other gangs that Maud wrote about? Had they really existed? Beyond what I had read in fiction and seen in films, I realized I knew very little about blackmail. It was undeniably a convenient plot device and gave work to the furtive bass sections of Hollywood orchestras, but had it ever really been a viable career option that could keep a man in moustache oil *and* offer the opportunity to work with like-minded colleagues? It was time to return to London to find out.

*

I took a book by Basil Tozer to read on the train. For a man who was primarily a sports journalist, he was proving curiously helpful in my research: first writing about the methods of private detectives, then interviewing Maud in 1914 and now with his 1929 book, *Confidence Crooks and Blackmailers: Their Ways and Methods.* Still, the blurb looked promising: 'This book will, if read carefully, enable even simpletons to avoid being duped by rogues.' It was even delivered in large, simpleton-friendly print, so, by the time I arrived at Euston station, I was an expert on short cons and the blackmailing opportunities on offer in 1920s London.

Like Maud, Tozer portrayed blackmail as a team sport which required at least two players: one to dupe the victim and one to extort the money. The majority of his scenarios centred around sex in one form or another: his blackmailers posed as psychoanalysts to mine their wealthy clients' sexual secrets or as police officers to patrol the shrubbery in London parks. And he seemed to know what he was talking about. When it came to the illicit nude dancing shows, or 'fig-leaf performances', staged purely to blackmail the audience, Tozer was oddly specific about their location: 'If not Gooch Street [sic], then Maddox Street, W.1.'[9]

He also wrote about nursing homes in which patients were seduced by nurses and then caught *in flagrante* by the matron in scenes that wouldn't have been out of place in a 1920s *Carry On Blackmailing.* But Tozer's cast didn't just include buxom nurses and pyjama-clad men. 'In the same way,' he wrote, 'well-to-do women patients have been blackmailed when of peculiar temperament and nursed by an exceptionally attractive nursing sister.'[10]

In the cafe of the British Library, I looked over Maud's own accounts of blackmail cases. Disgraced officers aside, the majority also revolved around sex, although in her stories it was strictly heterosexual and mostly hidden deep in people's pasts. There was the elderly Colonel George, for example, who had 'fallen victim to the wiles of a woman far beneath him in social life' whilst serving abroad as a young soldier;[11] Lady V— who had written some indiscreet letters to an Austrian gigolo; and a 'well known and respected gentleman' who was spotted making regular visits to a woman 'who was not too particular as to how she made her income.'[12]

It was clear that a significant number of these victims had either fallen prey to individual conmen or opportunistic amateurs. So what of the Black Hundred, that elite gang of continental blackmailers? For all Tozer's undercover work in Maddox Street W1 and elsewhere, he hadn't mentioned them – and when I moved on to the library's newsroom, I struggled to locate them there, either.

There were the late Tsar's Black Hundreds in Russia, originally founded to protect the monarchy but who quickly became anti-Semitic armed mobs, organizers of pogroms and torturers extraordinaire. But, following the October Revolution, surely they were far too busy facing Bolshevik firing squads to be scouring Britain for disgraced officers? The name had also been subsequently applied to Unionist gangs in Belfast who were evicting Catholics from their homes, but rain-sodden Ireland was hardly 'continental'.[13]

Or was 'Black Hundred' a typo? The Black Hand, part of the New York Mafia, included blackmail amongst their activities. But, again, I could find no evidence of their work in Europe outside Sicily. Besides, Maud mentioned the Black Hundred again in *Answers* magazine later in 1919:

> It is safe to say that ninety per cent of professional blackmailers carrying on operations in this country are foreigners, and most of them belong to the Continental gang known as the 'Black Hundred'.[14]

She seemed adamant that they existed, and I soon had to admit that the idea wasn't as far-fetched as it first seemed. I came across some very colourful gangs in the press, both continental and home-grown. In 1923, for example, the French police and Scotland Yard were on the trail of a pan-European band of conmen headed by a one-legged Australian and a Scot with a cauliflower ear.[15] Another outfit seemed to have pre-empted the 1960s vogue for heist capers by a good forty years when, on one summer's day in 1928, its members had fanned out across London armed with false letters of credit, which they used to extract £30,000 from various banks before escaping to Brussels by plane from the Croydon Aerodrome.[16]

There were also the London gangs slugging it out for control of the underworld: the Red Hands of Deptford, the Silver Hatchets in Islington, the Sabinis and Cortesis of Clerkenwell, the nightclub queen Mrs Meyrick and her confederates in Soho. These and dozens of other London gangs dabbled in blackmail on top of their usual thuggery and thieving, but it wasn't their raison d'être. When it came to pure blackmail, there didn't seem to be anyone operating on the scale that Maud described. I had brief yet high hopes of the League of the Crimson Triangle, a society devoted to 'terminating and punishing the existing immorality in the United States of America and in the British Isles', but that turned out to have only one member, a seventeen-year-old railway clerk from Lincoln who was trying his luck with a local businessman over the deflowering of a girl on the city's West Common.[17]

Then, suddenly, there they were, the Black Hundred, hidden away on page eighteen of the *Era* in March 1919:

" MILLION DOLLAR MYSTERY."
THE VENGEANCE OF THE " BLACK HUNDRED."

The piece described the ordeal of a woman named Florence Hargreaves, who had been kidnapped by the Black Hundred but managed to escape by leaping from the upper deck of a steamer into the sea before being rescued by a hydroplane which arrived just in the nick of time. It was thrilling stuff. The only problem was that it was the plot of a film, *The Million Dollar Mystery* of the headline, which had premiered on 4 March at a cinema in Piccadilly.[18] Suspiciously, this was just a month before *Pearson's Weekly* ran Maud's exposé of the activities of the crack European blackmailing gang that went by exactly the same name.

Still, Maud can't have got all her ideas from the cinema; there had to be some truth in her tales of blackmail. By all accounts, it was a core part of a private detective's work. On reading press reports of blackmail cases that had ended up in court, however, it soon became clear that another of her claims – that ninety per cent of professional blackmailers were foreigners – was also unlikely to be accurate. Britain didn't need to import moustachioed villains from the continent. Her citizens were perfectly capable of extorting money from each other themselves.

Indeed, writing in 1908, Kate Easton had suggested that the most common threat came from within the home: 'The blackmailing of their masters and mistresses by servants is practised to an extent that would open the eyes of a man in the street.' In an age when even modest households relied on hired help to keep up with the daily chores, there was certainly little privacy to be had. But it wasn't just maids and valets:

> Cabmen have been known to make the lives of indiscreet lady passengers almost unendurable by their constant demands for 'hush money,' and hotel servants, who have recognised men and women visitors as being other than 'Mr and Mrs Brown,' as indicated on the register, have, from time to time, joined the growing ranks of this class of criminal.[19]

By the 1920s, however, it seemed to have descended into a free-for-all. Amongst the hundreds of examples I found, there were named individuals bled dry for visiting prostitutes, a barrister held to ransom over some letters written to him by a 'Lady Clarence', a former tax inspector blackmailed over his frauds on the Inland Revenue, and the widow of an army major ensnared after taking out an advertisement for companionship.[20] None would have been out of place in Maud's tales.

The blackmailers, too, were often colourful characters, happy to use a bit of drama to enhance their efforts. One, a telephone operator who overheard an incriminating conversation, sent his victim letters signed 'B. Ware.'[21] Another disguised himself as a clergyman to collect money from a businessman who had been compromised in Piccadilly by a young clerk.[22] Others were simply inept. The ex-lover of a baronet, for example, made the rookie error of sending her threats and demands straight to his solicitor.[23]

As always, there were also corrupt private detectives using information gathered in the course of their work to make some extra money on the side. One, for example, had extracted thirty pounds from a young domestic servant under the threat of exposing her relationship with a man he was shadowing for a divorce investigation.[24] Another tried to blackmail Lord Terrington in 1925 over 'several items of interest' that might harm the political career of his wife Vera Woodhouse, one of the first female Members of Parliament.[25] There were even suggestions that some detective agencies had been set up purely for the purpose of blackmail.[26]

If caught, the penalties were severe, ranging from three years to life imprisonment, and the authorities took the crime very seriously: one judge in 1924 called it 'one of the worst cancers of civilisation', another 'moral murder'.[27] It was such a blight on society that even private detectives, who could earn good money from blackmail investigations, urged victims to go straight to the police. As Maud wrote in 1929:

> If only people would take this advice and act upon it, then the handsome emoluments which many professional and amateur blackmailers are drawing to-day would be cut off at the base, and one of the most despicable types of crime of modern days would be a thing of the past, because it is on the fear of publicity that the blackmailer thrives.[28]

Kate Easton was of the same mind, but, as she pointed out in 1908, this fear of publicity worked both ways. Prosecution meant that the victims' names would appear in the press, leading to gossip and speculation even if the finer details were suppressed. Nine times out of ten, she said, victims went straight to private detectives for the matter to be dealt with discreetly and efficiently.[29] Even after 1925, when blackmail victims were finally awarded anonymity in the newspapers, there was widespread reluctance to press charges as cases were still discussed in open court with spectators in the gallery.

Besides, there were those who would never go to the police, whether or not they had to appear in court. Significantly absent from the witness box, for example, were those arguably most likely to be targeted by professional blackmailers: gay men. How could they go to the police when the root of their trouble – their sexual identity – was itself a crime? The press skirted around the issue. They might report on 'effeminate' male blackmailers, but the victims were invariably portrayed as naive and heterosexual dupes. In 1927, for example, the barrister Helena Normanton raised the subject in *Good Housekeeping*, saying, 'Probably thousands of innocent men have paid blackmail under a threat of being accused of unnatural vice . . .' but made no mention of those victims who actually *were* gay.[30] Nobody did. Even Basil Tozer, for all his candour in writing about the nation's sexual proclivities, made only oblique references to night-time 'irregularities' in Hyde Park.[31]

But they were out there and in trouble. Take the flamboyant Willy Clarkson, for example. In the permissive world of the theatre, his homosexuality was an open secret. There was even a public urinal named after him: 'Clarkson's Cottage', situated around the corner from the Wardour Street wiggery, was a grim, solid grey iron building, but its West End location promised good times to be had. Indeed, the toilet's international reputation was such that after the Second World War it was bought by a wealthy American as a folly for the grounds of his country mansion in New York state – allegedly on the basis of its architectural merit.[32]

But Willy was also a public figure whose livelihood and reputation, not to mention his prized royal warrant, could be destroyed should his personal life ever come under wider scrutiny. The tangled mess he created in protecting himself only came to light after his death in 1934, when various court cases regarding his estate suggested that not only was he acquainted with William Hobbs, one of the most infamous inter-war blackmailers (who had relieved the soon-to-be Maharajah of Kashmir of £150,000 in 1919), but over a thirty-year period had made a string of fraudulent insurance claims for fires at his shop. This secondary career as an arsonist was attributed by some to the need for hush money relating to his sexuality.[33]

So what did private detectives do when their clients wouldn't, or couldn't, go to the police? How did they make the problem go away?

The first step, of course, was to identify the blackmailer, a task often easier said than done. Kate Easton told of one case in which she and a female assistant had moved into a brothel near Soho Square for a few days for this purpose.[34] Maud also hinted at a secret code used by blackmailers to identify one another, which she employed after trailing one suspect to a Parisian hotel. She knew he was a blackmailer; she just wasn't sure that he was the right one:

> The plan I adopted was to pretend I was, to use professional parlance, 'in the same lay' as himself ... I have learnt at great risk and trouble something of the secret methods by which a professional blackmailer can often ascertain when he is in the company of a brother (or sister) practitioner. In a short while we were on terms of tolerable intimacy, and the man was fully convinced that I was in the same business . . .[35]

Over a champagne-laden dinner, he let slip enough details for her to know she was on the right track.

Having identified the criminal, the detective would next try to recover the evidence they held against the client. This was often in the form of letters. A common trick of female blackmailers was to get married men to send them a note confirming the date and time of an agreed tryst; others used personal correspondence stolen by household staff. The incriminating letters in Maud's stories generally ended up in hotel rooms, which made them easy to retrieve either through subterfuge or, as in one case she told in 1919, sheer bluff:

> 'I am a detective,' I said, 'and I want you to give me back the letters Lady V— wrote you. I can give you a few seconds to make up your mind. I have two Scotland Yard men downstairs.'
> I put my hand on the electric bell, and began to count.[36]

Another option was to buy the evidence, although, as one detective discovered, this could have unforeseen consequences. At the inquest into the death of a young woman called Madeleine

Wiltshire in 1927, it was found that she had been involved with her husband Henry in blackmailing a number of men she had seduced for the purpose. An inquiry agent named Gerald Lewis, acting on behalf of a vicar who had been caught in their web, had been meeting the Wiltshires individually to persuade one of them to sell the correspondence. Henry refused, but Madeleine showed willing. When Lewis went to the handover, however, he found Henry in her place. Madeleine's cyanide-infused body was later discovered in a rented room in Soho. The coroner was convinced that Henry had killed her, but there was insufficient evidence to send him to trial.[37]

If retrieving the evidence by fair means or foul didn't work, the next move was to obtain evidence of other crimes that would see the blackmailer in prison for an unrelated offence. As Maud said:

> The blackmailer is ever a blackguard; almost invariably other crimes can be laid against him. Nor is this surprising. A man so despicable that he will stoop to blackmail can never be conscience-stricken about mere theft, fraud, or forgery – and these other crimes frequently cause his undoing.[38]

She gave by way of example her case of the elderly colonel who she said was being blackmailed over an affair from his youth, describing how she had trailed the blackmailer to Paris and watched the house he shared with his confederates: 'Instinctively I felt that I was about to find the weak spot in his armour.' When the house was empty, she broke in and found equipment used to forge bank notes. The gang were arrested on that basis, and the blackmail stopped.[39]

A similar technique involved, in Kate Easton's words, 'what some detectives might call blackmailing the blackmailer' – and that was exactly what it was. She explained how she had successfully dispatched the 'Terror of the Tea Rooms' (a professional seductress who picked up her victims over afternoon tea) by writing a polite note offering her the choice between leaving the country or being shadowed constantly by detectives who would warn everyone of her true intentions. The woman left by the next boat.[40]

By her own admission, Maud relished blackmail cases, calling them 'extraordinarily interesting because you do get some real insight into the curious workings of people's minds.'[41] I could see why. Of all the work private detectives undertook, this type of crime highlighted the very worst in people. Maud's interest lay in the psychology of the perpetrators ('It is really astonishing what the blackmailer will think and do'), but I found the victims even more interesting. Did they curl up and allow themselves to be bled dry or put up a fight?

Some fought back in extraordinary ways, as was demonstrated by a case that had bounced around the courts in Belfast for a number of years. It started in the hands of an unnamed private detective who was hired in 1921 to investigate some threatening letters sent to various members of the wealthy Walker family. The letters had come from a middle-aged woman called Ellen Whan, who had given birth to Mr Walker's child when she was a young maidservant and was now seeking payment in exchange for her silence.

The letters were disturbing enough – one was a drawing of a coffin with details of Mrs Walker's impending funeral, another said, 'I will shoot you' – but then the chocolates began to arrive. The first box was laced with oxalic acid, the second with phosphoric match heads, the third with broken glass.[42] The matter was handed over to the police, and Ellen Whan was charged with attempted murder. In 1928, however, the case returned to the courts with new evidence that she had been framed by Mrs Walker, who had sent many of the letters and bought the oxalic acid herself.[43]

This was an extreme example, but amateur blackmail cases were rarely clear cut. Was Ellen Whan justified in her original demand? In a world where many struggled to feed their families whilst others breakfasted on champagne, who could blame the poor and downtrodden for attempting to extract their due from those who had wronged them? Maud didn't, if her statement in 1924 was anything to go by:

> Some of the cases are sad, as, for instance, when the offender does not start with the idea of blackmail, but is pushed into it by force of circumstances. It may be that he is almost destitute and has lost everything of value except this one piece of information which he threatens to use.[44]

How else could one expect to attain any measure of meaningful justice from a system tipped so heavily in favour of the rich and the male?

*

One Harrods tennis outfit (cheap)

Lady's bicycle in good condition (£3 10s.)

One large easy chair (£5)

Harley-Davidson and sidecar, late 1919, in perfect condition (£120)

Two Aylesbury ducks, five Runners, and twelve hens in full lay (12s. 6d. each)

There were no dark secrets or menaces there, just a jumble of things that the residents of Pearley, Finchley Avenue were attempting to offload through the *Hendon and Finchley Times* between 1918 and 1921. They were also seeking a housekeeper ('good home, wages and outings – Apply after 7 pm') and, for some reason, frequently looking to buy gentlemen's tricycles.[45]

Using a mishmash of electoral rolls, old census reports and army records, I had established that the house in Finchley Avenue was more crowded than I had thought – and not just with poultry. There was Edith, of course, and Harry, who had clung on to life despite the misgivings of the Pearl Assurance Company; the house-keeper appeared to be a woman called Helen Barber, but also in residence was the youngest of Harry's eight siblings, Charles Lawrence Elliott, and his wife Mollie. At some point, there was also a puppy, although whether it survived into doghood was unclear:[46]

£5 REWARD.
SPRINGER SPANIEL DOG, BLUE-GREY
AND BLACK. AGE 5 MONTHS. NAMED
" PRINCE."—C. ELLIOTT. " PEARLEY,"
FINCHLEY AVENUE, FINCHLEY, N.3.

Tennis, ducks, lost dogs: it was all very suburban. The Harley-Davidson added an edgy touch, but it was still far removed from the picture of the Elliotts' home life that I'd imagined. It soon became apparent, however, that life at Pearley was not all it seemed.

The mystery started to emerge as I tried to find out more about Charles. Less than robust health seemed to run in the family. According to his First World War record, Charles had left the family home in Hackney to report for duty in the Army Cyclist Corps in July 1915. He was nineteen years old. His recurrent piles weren't ideal for a cyclist, but neither was his club foot encased in its special boot, which the medical examiners appeared to have missed. As such, he undertook only light duties and was eventually sent to work in the Labour Corps storerooms. In March 1918, he was finally discharged as permanently unfit due to his disability, but he'd given it his best, as a note by his commanding officer made clear: 'A very good man – honest & trustworthy.'[47]

After moving in with Edith and Harry at Pearley, however, he

appeared to have made a remarkable recovery, to such an extent
that the Sportsman's Battalions would have welcomed him with
open arms. In October 1920, for example, he took silver in the
Gentleman's Championship Medal at the Finchley Swimming
Gala.[48] In 1926, he was fined twenty shillings for haring around in
a noisy motor car.[49] Ancestry even had his aviator's certificate,
which he'd gained in a de Havilland Gipsy Moth at the Cotswold
Aero Club in August 1934.[50] In the accompanying photograph, he
looked quite the debonair flying ace:

He had a completely different build to the weedy eight-and-a-
half stone he had presented to the army at nineteen. His occupation
was given as 'Dentist' and his address at that point was the flat in
Great Russell Mansions.

A club foot or haemorrhoids didn't preclude any of this, of
course, although the type of fitness regime required to transform
him into a strapping pilot would have been challenging. What was
more suspicious was that whilst married to Mollie, trading as a
Harley Street dentist and performing weekend aerobatics over
the Cotswolds, Charles also appeared to have another wife in
Clapham and a thriving business manufacturing radios.

I went back over everything and double checked. Had I got confused, or missed something? Was it just coincidence that Edith and Harry knew two men with identical names who had been born on the same day? But, no, the evidence was clear. Only one such man existed. Harry's brother, the *real* Charles Lawrence Elliott, lived in Queen's Road, Clapham with his wife Kate. He built radios for a living, and had followed his father into being a Freeman of the City of London. Whoever was living with Edith and Harry was an imposter.

What was going on? Were the Elliott boys' criminal roots stronger than I thought? Were they running some kind of scam? Or were Edith and Harry somehow beholden to this man and his wife? Maybe I'd been reading too many of Maud's stories, but life in suburbia suddenly looked a lot more interesting.

The Clairvoyante Case

BY MAUD WEST

One day a well-known lawyer came to my office and asked me to handle a case which, from the beginning, interested me greatly. He represented an extremely wealthy family, which possessed a closely guarded secret. This secret, shared only by three senior members of the family, had somehow become known, and an unknown individual was making excellent capital out of his knowledge, and had already secured several handsome money 'presents' from the family as the price of his silence.

His method of getting this money paid over was so clever that there was not the slightest clue as to his identity, and therefore it was impossible to interview this impudent blackmailer and to discover how he had obtained possession of the secret.

I asked the solicitor if the three members of the family had discussed the secret at any time, and he elicited from his clients that they had done so, but only on occasions when they were alone, so they thought it impossible for it to leak out in this direction. However, the idea occurred to me that it was very possible that someone employed in the house had overheard one of these conversations and communicated the information to some individual outside, and I decided to start my investigations from this basis.

Altogether there were eight servants of both sexes employed in and about the house, and I puzzled my brains as to the best method by which I could get into the confidence of each of these servants and discover whether a conversation had been overheard and the secret divulged that way.

Eventually I formed a plan. I sent off an operative post haste and engaged a room over some business premises in a small town which was situated near the house. We furnished this room with dark hangings and crystal globes, and after a great deal of trouble secured the atmosphere usually associated with palmists and fortune-tellers. Then I had a wonderful robe made, covered with black cats and moons, and all the rest of the paraphernalia of the 'seeress.'

Shortly afterwards all the servants at the house received a printed circular which informed them that 'Madame—, the celebrated clairvoyante,' had taken a branch office in the nearby town, and that she would be glad to give one free reading to the recipient of the circular.

The plot worked, although results did not happen as quickly as I had hoped, and it was some three weeks before the first maid-servant from the house appeared. I told her fortune (I made it a very good one), and, by some cleverly planned questions, managed to elicit from her quite a little information about the other maids in the house. She went off very pleased with her 'free reading,' and promised that she would send the other servants.

One by one, they came, usually on their afternoon off, and it was quite obvious to me after I had seen and talked with each one, that they were innocent of any complicity in the blackmail. But there was one maid-servant who had not taken advantage of my free offer, and it was only after a great deal of scheming in which I used two of the other maid-servants as my unconscious aids – they having told her how marvellous my readings and advice were – that I managed to get this particular girl to come for a reading.

Directly I saw this girl and talked to her I was struck by her astuteness and intelligence, and I made up my mind that I would endeavour to use the scheme which I had worked out might be successful if I suspected one of the servants.

I had previously interviewed the members of the family, and discovered as nearly as possible the circumstances under which the conversations between themselves had taken place; the time of night or day, and the exact descriptions of the different rooms in which they had talked.

With these facts in my mind, after I had turned the lights down to a glimmer and produced my crystal globe, which I placed on the table between us, I began to describe a scene which was a vague description of one of the rooms where the discussion had taken place. Then I described the members of the family seated together talking, and, as I noticed the girl's face growing whiter and whiter, it became obvious to me that I was on the right track, and that this was the girl who had listened and overheard the conversation.

I next began to describe a personality like that of the girl on the opposite side of the table. Then I said that I saw her in my crystal listening to the grave secret being discussed.

I was watching the girl out of the corners of my eyes, and I could see that she was thoroughly frightened. I began to advise her that her connection with some outside person, with reference to the secret she had overheard, was a very dangerous thing, and might bring very great difficulties into her life.

Suddenly the girl gave an exclamation and burst into tears, and almost before I realised the absolute success of my scheme she was letting out the truth.

She had overheard the conversation, and had told her sweetheart. He was the unknown individual who had, by means of anonymous letters, so cleverly blackmailed the family, and, although for certain reasons no proceedings were taken against him, an interview which he had shortly afterwards with a male member of my staff convinced him that any further lapse on his part would quickly end him in gaol.[51]

Chapter Nine

Wanted: Someone Innocent

Experience has to be earned,
but it is fine capital.

Maud West, 1928[1]

'HOW'S YOUR LIVER? . . . Do you feel tired and drowsy? Do you feel depressed?' What about chilblains, biliousness or brain fog? Do you have a Strange Fear of People, Places and Things? *Dandruff?* Judging by the advertisements pouring out of Albion House after the war, the people of Britain had been left in an itchy and twitchy state after four years of conflict.[2] But, as ever, its residents were on hand to provide relief through dubious patent remedies. One new enterprise had taken the quackery to a new level, however. Run by a former mining engineer called Frederick Turquand, the Albion Electric Company was hawking a High Frequency Electricity machine for the home treatment of everything from lacklustre hair to shell shock.[3]

Curious as to what this marvellous contraption looked like – was it more akin to a cattle prod or an electric chair? – I'd searched patent records to see if Turquand had submitted an application with the necessary drawings. He hadn't. But, whilst looking, I found that a Henry Elliott of Pearley, Finchley Avenue was also something of an inventor. In 1927, he'd taken out a patent for a hat and coat hook that could be affixed to the wall using a suction cup:[4]

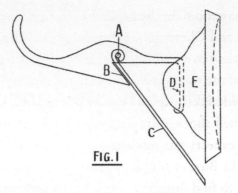

FIG. I

It was the perfect gift for a roving lady detective in need of somewhere to park a rakish cap, but it also got me thinking about Harry's involvement in the Maud West agency. Although he cropped up in the press occasionally as an assistant detective and was named as the manager in one advert, he'd also been described as 'a husband of independent means.' Was he just a silent partner, fully hands on, or somewhere in between? The coat hook suggested that he spent a fair amount of time tinkering in a shed, which in turn possibly explained the obsession at Pearley for purchasing gentlemen's tricycles. There was also evidence that he had business interests elsewhere: in 1925, he'd been sued for debt by a man from Friern Barnet and had told the judge, whether truthfully or not, that he had lost £500 on some financial speculation and was only earning £4 a week.[5] If he had independent means, they weren't very reliable.

Curious inventions aside, Albion House was as colourful as ever, largely thanks to an influx of theatrical agents. Given the building's proximity to London's theatreland, there had always been a few rattling around, but now agencies and production companies were spread throughout the building. Many specialized in variety and music hall and summoned performers to their offices for auditions, ensuring a steady flow of chorus girls, acrobats and pantomime dames clattering up the stairs.[6] Another noticeable change was that the car showroom on the ground floor now displayed rows of Buicks, Fords and Chevrolets, all made by American manufacturers who had taken over redundant wartime production plants.[7]

The effect of the war was also evident in the activities of another newcomer, Frederick Turquand's wife: whilst Mr T was jolting men out of their shell shock, Mrs T (a 'splendidly energetic woman', as one would expect) was tending to casualties of a different sort. Mrs Turquand's Bureau for the Aristocratic Poor had opened its doors in 1921 to find domestic work for society women who had been driven to 'stark, staring ruin' after losing their menfolk in the war. As the London social correspondent of the *Queenslander* reported:

> In one country mansion there are three of her clients, two holding titles, who undertake the entire domestic work. No one can know better than a born gentlewoman how another gentlewoman's house should be kept, and I feel sure these mistresses who employ such find they have treasures.[8]

It was a noble effort, but such women represented only a tiny proportion of those who found themselves unexpectedly having to make their own way in life, with all the challenges that presented.

There had been more women than men in Britain for decades, but the slaughter of nearly three-quarters of a million soldiers had made the gender imbalance perceptibly worse. As young officers were represented disproportionately in this figure, middle-class women in their twenties and thirties were particularly affected. Whereas they might have had expectations of marriage and motherhood, many now had little choice but to go it alone. For some, the opportunities they forged in business and public life would be their salvation, but, as Maud pointed out, there were also plenty of traps in this brave new world for the unwary.

There were, of course, the ever-present bounders, gigolos and love rats to lead them astray, and blackmailers to pounce on any indiscretions, but in 1919 she identified a new threat, one that had emerged as a direct result of the war. The victims, she said, were young women who had worked in munitions factories and other wartime enterprises. Having laboured around the clock for four years with little opportunity to spend their wages, many had substantial savings and no idea what to do with them. Circulars and advertisements promised all manner of business and investment opportunities. As Maud wrote:

> I don't say that all of them are fraudulent, but many of them are – the 'partnership' fraud is being worked now for all it is worth by alert but entirely unscrupulous people. Their victims are, for the most part, girls who are not very well educated, and who are inexperienced and quite ignorant of the world. It is simply astounding how readily some of these girls have been induced to part with their savings.[9]

She told of one client who had fallen prey to a gang who haunted tea shops and restaurants looking for young women with money to spare. 'She was a pretty girl of about twenty-three who had been working, I believe, at Gretna during the war,' Maud wrote. She had saved over £400 and was staying in London with her aunt, enjoying her new-found financial freedom. One night, whilst dining alone at a West End restaurant, she fell into conversation with a young man. Romance blossomed. At a concert one afternoon, they bumped into one of his friends, 'a genial, prosperous-looking gentleman of about sixty', who took them to tea and persuaded them to become managing partners in his new photographic business. The price of each partnership was £400. It was to be a joyous adventure with people she liked. After Maud's client had handed over her portion of the money, however, both men disappeared.

'No girl should part with a farthing of her money to anyone offering her a partnership of any kind without the fullest and most complete investigation of the character, both of the business and the people who make the offer,' Maud wrote.[10]

The painful innocence of many young women was highlighted by another of Maud's warnings: 'Girls should be particularly careful about partnership offers in massage establishments.' She explained that such businesses had enjoyed a resurgence since the end of the war and many women believed they were investing in reputable health parlours, no doubt happy to do their bit for the rehabilitation of the war-weary populace. By the time they discovered exactly what was involved, however, they were trapped. Any attempt to extract themselves, by legal action or otherwise, was met with the threat of their association with the sex trade being exposed. They either had to stick it out or walk away penniless. One girl, Maud said, having been cheated out of all her war savings in this way and unable to find another job, had killed herself.

Throughout the 1920s and 1930s, the papers were full of examples of fraudsters taking advantage of the paucity of women's education in business and financial matters. Some stalked war widows with pensions, others targeted the surplus women earning their own living for the first time. Bogus stockbrokers seemed particularly common, with one even managing to ply his trade from his sickbed at the Greenwich Infirmary by persuading one of his nurses to part with £857.[11] Others created elaborate back stories. One man, for example, posed as a shipwreck victim awaiting $35,000 compensation from the Canadian Pacific Company to defraud over twenty women.[12] Another duped a woman out of £3,000 by claiming not only to be the heir to a Scottish estate but also the owner of a valuable scientific patent for creating synthetic nitrogen.[13]

These men were imaginative; I had to give them that. But the reach of their operations was nothing compared to that of what was arguably the most pernicious racket of the time. Maud had a story to tell about that, too. It was set during the war, and she had been approached by a client whose sister had repeatedly been writing large cheques to someone he could not identify. Nothing would induce his sister to reveal the reason and, although he didn't think she was being blackmailed, there was patently something wrong. She was in a particularly vulnerable state, still in shock and struggling with the grief of losing her husband in the trenches. Could Maud find out what was going on?

By shadowing the woman, Maud discovered that she had been meeting an unsavoury character who lived in a squalid East End street. 'At one time he had been a bookmaker,' she reported, 'but his clientele having left to attend a little affair in Flanders, his crooked mind saw a chance to obtain an easy living by posing as a spiritualist and robbing war widows.'[14]

It was a problem that would become all too common in the post-war years. Throughout the 1920s, millions of widows, mothers, fathers, brothers and sisters would turn to spiritualism for answers as they tried to come to terms with the loss of male relatives so brutally cut down in their prime.

Not all spiritualists were out to defraud, however. Many saw it as a science, no less venerable than that of electricity and radio waves. The leading proponents of spiritualism often came from rational, science-based backgrounds. The most famous, Sir Arthur Conan Doyle, was a medical man by training. Another, Sir Oliver Lodge, was an eminent physicist who specialized in electromagnetism. Both had been involved in psychic research since the 1880s, and both had lost sons during the war.

In 1916, Sir Oliver had published a book called *Raymond, or Life and Death*, which detailed the conversations he'd had with his recently deceased son across the great divide – and this, he said, was not so great as people feared. The book became an immediate bestseller, and in the tenth edition Lodge added an addendum in which he described the bonds between the fallen soldiers now in the paradise of 'Summerland' and those who mourned:

> There they find themselves still in touch with earth, not really separated from those left behind, still able actively to help and serve. There is nothing supine about the rest and joy into which they have entered. Under their young energy, strengthened by the love which rises towards them like a blessing, the traditional barrier between the two states is suffering violence, is being taken by force. A band of eager workers is constructing a bridge, is opening a way for us across the chasm; communication is already easier and more frequent than ever before; and in the long run we may feel assured that all this present suffering and bereavement will have a beneficent outcome from humanity.[15]

The tender picture he painted of noble young men in Summerland fighting on for a better future was just what people needed to hear: that the slaughter had not been in vain and they, too, might receive a few personal words of solace floating down from paradise.

From a legal point of view, however, those who delivered these messages, whether they held seances, gazed into crystal balls, read palms or used telepathy, were open to prosecution. If money had changed hands, this could be a simple charge of fraud, although both the Witchcraft Act of 1735 and the 1824 Vagrancy Act were also used to drive home the point that superstition had no place in an enlightened society.

When it came to gathering evidence for such cases, female

detectives came into their own. It was easy work. All the detective had to do was make an appointment, have her fortune told and then describe the inaccuracies of the reading in court. Rarely was the real reason of their visit suspected, although one was reportedly told in 1934, 'I have a turbulent feeling about you. I feel uneasy inside, as though I had something to fear.'[16]

One of the earliest examples I found came from 1904, when Amy Betts and Dorothy Hempest, along with their employer, the former Scotland Yard inspector Charles Richards, had visited three fortune tellers operating in the West End under the names of Yoga, Professor and Madame Keiro. The detectives had been hired, through solicitors, by the *Daily Mail* as part of an exposé of 'Bond Street fortune tellers'.[17] The owner of the *Mail*, Sir Alfred Harmsworth, had followed this up in court to see whether smart society palmists would be treated with the same severity by the law as their shabbier counterparts who, as the *Morning Post* put it, 'extracted sixpences and shillings from servant girls.'[18]

At the trial, Amy Betts was described as 'an aristocratic looking lady in a big black hat' who had been working as a store detective for the Army & Navy Stores.[19] She gave an entertaining account of the reading she had received from Madame Keiro; Dorothy Hempest did the same for the Professor. Dorothy's headgear was not mentioned, although a clue was given as to how much money these early assistant detectives had to spend on such things when the defence produced an apologetic letter about the case that Dorothy had sent to a friend who was a palmist. 'I have been starving for months,' she had written, 'and then this case comes along. I did not start it. When I had instructions to go to these people I could not very well refuse.' When cross-examined about the letter, she fainted.[20]

I could find no evidence of Dorothy Hempest's fate, but Amy Betts had carried on working for department stores and detective agencies for a number of years. She was back in court in 1916 to test-ify against another fortune teller, a 'Professor Melini', whose pros-ecution also seemed to be the result of a *Daily Mail* investigation.[21]

The subject undoubtedly sold papers, which brought me back to the headline I had come across early on in my investigation: 'Revolver Shot at Seance – Lady Detective to Shoot Spirit'.[22] That had appeared in March 1926, in the midst, I discovered, of one of the regular scandals that had convulsed the world of psychic research in the inter-war years.

That spring, a new anti-spiritualism movement had been launched: the grandly titled Catholic Crusade Against Spiritism. Supported by two archbishops, eight bishops and a cardinal, along-side prominent individuals from the lay population, its objections ranged from the theological to the social. One neurologist linked the practice of mediumship to an increase in the number of 'luna-cies' over the past fifteen years, and alleged that spiritualists were placing advertisements in the papers seeking the care of patients who were mentally unsound ('Permanency preferred') in order to train them as mediums.[23] (Was that, I wondered, what the strange doctor was up to in *The Times* next to Maud's advert in 1909?)

At the same time, Sir Arthur Conan Doyle and a group of fellow spiritualists were trying to clean up their image by denouncing the celebrated 'trumpet medium' (and part-time burglar) Frederick Munnings, whose seances were enlivened by the use of a silver horn suspended in mid-air to amplify messages from the spirit world.[24] Their letter in the journal of the London Spiritualist Alli-ance, *Light*, on 13 March did not deny Munnings' 'intermittent psychic powers', but criticized the 'cold-blooded and deliberate artifice' he employed during his seances. This had recently been quite literally illuminated at a private house party: whilst Mun-nings was exuding ectoplasm in the darkened drawing room, a servant fixing a fuse below stairs had unwittingly caused a standard lamp to turn on at an inopportune moment. There, for all to see, was the apparatus that held the trumpet in place and allowed Munnings to manoeuvre it from his seat.[25]

The press leapt upon both stories, printing details of how people like Munnings engineered their deceptions, along with expert opinions on how they might be unmasked. Many of the proposed tests required complex scientific instruments, but Maud had a better idea. As the *Sunday Post* reported:

> A revolver shot will ring out at a spiritualist seance shortly to be held in a part of London which for obvious reasons is not indicated. The firer will be Miss Maud West, London's intrepid lady detective. She has been invited to attend the seance, the time and place of which are as yet unknown to her, in order to test in this dramatic fashion whether or not the ghostly figure is in reality a spirit.[26]

Maud explained that she would not shoot to kill, 'but my shot will be accurate enough to prove the point at issue. I can shoot straight. I have proved that on more than one occasion during many years of detective work in all parts of the world. I am glad to say that I have never fired with fatal effect, though this does not mean I have missed my aim.' For good measure she added, 'This experience will be the most remarkable in the whole of my career, and there can be few women who have packed more excitement and adventure into their lives.'

As the article was accompanied by a photograph of Maud dressed as Charlie Chaplin and there were no follow-up reports, I could only assume – and hope – that it was a joke.

How seriously Maud took the idea of clairvoyance as a whole was more difficult to gauge. I'd noticed that she referred to 'bogus' spiritualists, leaving open the possibility that there were genuine ones to be found. Did she share the views of Arthur Conan Doyle, who defended authentic psychic activity as fiercely as he denounced its fakery, or was she keeping her options open to ingratiate herself with her readers, a good proportion of whom would have been believers themselves?

She recounted one instance when she had a visitor one morning whilst she was trying to piece together various clues in a missing-persons case. The woman was seeking Maud's help, but there was little Maud could offer. The woman's difficulties seemed to stem from the fact that she was 'highly strung' and suffering from 'an inferiority complex'. She did, however, claim the gift of second sight. To humour her, Maud suggested that this might be put to good use:

> ... I folded the papers lying under my hands relating to the case I had in hand, and asked her to convey to me the impressions they created in her mind.
>
> Closing her eyes, she appeared to relax. After a few minutes' silence she began to describe a certain street, the details of which were so vivid that I conjured in my mind an impression of the East End of London. As I listened I sketched on paper a map of the street as I visualised it from her description. By some strange chance I immediately identified the map as corresponding to a certain locality in East India Dock-road. I was impressed, in spite of myself.[27]

That afternoon, Maud headed to the docks. As the woman had said, one of the houses on that road was higher than the others. 'It is almost incredibly true,' Maud wrote, 'that I picked up a trail of the missing girl at this house.'

More often, however, detectives preferred to use only the trappings of spiritualism, rather than actual messages from beyond, to assist their work. Maud had claimed a significant victory by setting herself up as an itinerant fortune teller to test the honesty of the housemaids in 'The Clairvoyante Case', and she also related an instance in which two female detectives had used similar means when tracking down a runaway wife. They had established that the wife had a very close friend who lived on the Continent. One detective had travelled to Europe to befriend this woman, who spilled all sorts of details about the missing wife, including the address of the private hotel in England where she was staying as 'Mrs Smith'. The other booked into the hotel and amused her fellow guests with tarot readings: 'When Mrs Smith's turn came she listened in amazement to secrets which only one woman knew – fresh from the agency's card filing index system.'

I wasn't entirely sure how this would have helped restore Mrs Smith to her family – maybe something had got lost in the retelling – but the *New York Tribune* was convinced: 'Quite obviously no man could have proceeded by this simple and direct route,' it concluded. 'Instead, acting on scientific principles, and proceeding by clews, he would have had to follow Mrs Smith from hotel to hotel, city to city, employing an army of watchers and spies who would have been constantly exposed to physical danger, heat and cold.'[28]

The raw years following the war had also seen a resurgence in frauds relating to matters of the heart. In 1919, Maud issued a warning to her readers about bogus matrimonial agencies, which, she said, were enjoying a revival since demobilisation had begun.[29] Usually operating by post, these swindlers would promise introductions in exchange for money – the going price being around £25 (£1,000 today) – and then play the role of suitor themselves. If a meeting was arranged, the bureau owner would go in person or send their wife or daughter.

One example she gave was that of a German matrimonial agent whom she called 'Eisner', who targeted people who had dreams of marrying into money. The fees he charged were often ten times the going rate, an expense many were willing to pay to achieve a life free of financial woe. The men and women he matched, however, were generally equally poor: each was told that the other was keen to keep their fortune a secret to avoid gold-diggers. That particular tale had come to a typically Maud-like dramatic end with the help of an irate Portuguese client whom she accompanied to Eisner's office:

> The Portuguese demanded his money back. Eisner affected to be very angry, and he requested the Portuguese to clear out of his office at once. Then the Portuguese rather startled me. He whipped out a revolver, and, pointing it at Eisner's head, swore he would blow his brains out if he didn't refund him his money at once . . . After that adventure Eisner closed down his business and cleared out of the country.[30]

Maud said that few such cases came to court due to the victims' desire for privacy. However, I did find some prosecutions for cases remarkably similar to those she described. When reminiscing about his career in the *People* in 1939, for example, the ex-Scotland Yard chief inspector William Gough confirmed that matrimonial agencies were often run by German immigrants. He gave the example of Jacob Kuppers, who had been arrested in 1911 for obtaining money by false pretences. Kuppers had written fake love letters to his clients and shared the task of attending face-to-face meetings with his wife.[31]

Elsewhere, I found the case of a sixty-four-year-old Irishman who added a dash of extortion to his frauds on the lonely hearted. When he was arrested in 1925, the police found a box of 5,000 letters from women he had duped over the years. His modus operandi was to take out advertisements via matrimonial agencies,

presenting himself as a wealthy widower in search of companionship. He would then invite women to stay at his home in North
London and blackmail them over their lack of propriety.[32]

Yet, whilst women were the target of many of these financial
swindles, they also had a particular game of their own they could
play: 'damage hunting'. This involved using the law to extract
money from men who had been tricked into offering, and then
withdrawing, proposals of marriage.

Breach of promise to marry had been part of English contract
law for centuries. As a legal remedy, it was open to either sex, but
it had traditionally been used to compensate women for being left
on the shelf after a lengthy engagement. By the 1920s, however,
the concept was looking increasingly old-fashioned and out of step
with the new freedoms women could enjoy.

An anonymous lawyer, writing in *Answers* magazine in 1919,
made it clear that the legal profession viewed most breach of promise cases as 'vulgar', 'petty' and a waste of court time. In one recent
case, he said, 455 love letters, 152 postcards and 52 telegrams had
been presented as evidence: 'The reading of silly effusions brings
giggles from the gallery, but the Bench is frankly bored and unsym-
pathetic to all parties.' Nor, he said, should a jury be expected to
assess the value of a broken heart: 'The contract to marry cannot be
compared to a commercial bargain, so overlaid is it with sentiment
and psychology.'[33]

The barrister Helena Normanton, however, argued in 1928 that
there were still circumstances in which breach of promise suits
were appropriate:

> Whenever a woman has been very deeply wronged by the cir-
> cumstances of her engagement, such as that she has been
> withheld from the matrimonial market for a considerable
> number of years, or her chastity has been filched from her, or

the fact of her expected marriage has prevented her fitting herself for the labour market, then the defendant should compensate her up to the measure of her financial wrongs.[34]

She did concede, however, that breach of promise law was increasingly being used either out of spite or for commercial gain. Some cases, she said, were little more than 'blackmail by litigation'. As for repeat offenders, these were common in America, but could not flourish in England due to the legal system: '. . . the fact that a lady had recovered damages in one action would make a jury here reluctant to encourage her in the next.'

Maud would have disagreed. As one who dealt with matters often unseen by the courts, she had pointed out in 1919 that British damage hunters used only the *threat* of legal action to extract payment. As an example, she shared a case brought to her by an artist who was being pursued for breach of promise. When he had received the first request for compensation, he'd written back, admitting everything and enclosing ten shillings by way of settlement. The damage hunter responded with an action for £1,000. Maud and her client waited. As expected, the case was withdrawn the day before it was due to be heard. 'She dared not have gone into court,' Maud explained. 'I had ascertained that she already had had damages from at least three other victims, whom I could have produced.'[35]

None of my research into the frauds perpetrated on the vulnerable or naive had shed any light on what the Elliott brothers were up to. But, whilst researching the variety of business opportunities – genuine or otherwise – that might have tempted women with war savings, I'd made another unexpected discovery about Maud's personal life.

It was contained in a short *Daily Mail* piece about an exhibition that had been held at the American Women's Club in Grosvenor Street in 1937. Organized by the Alpha Club, a women's business network which welcomed one representative from each profession into its membership, the exhibition had showcased the variety of businesses run by women in London, from tea merchants to property developers and silver fox farmers.[36] It was, the *Daily Mail* said, 'a revelation of what women are doing in every sphere of life.' The article itself, however, contained a revelation of a very different kind. One of the accompanying photographs was of a young, dark-haired woman wearing a jaunty hat and a tight, guarded smile.

The caption read: 'Miss Maud West jun., a lover of detective work – "sometimes a chic West End butterfly, sometimes a newsboy."'[37]

Maud West *junior*? Surely not. The journalist must have misheard in the clamour of the exhibition. The woman in the photograph had to be one of Maud's staff. But no, the reporter was adamant that she was indeed the 'daughter of Maud West, woman detective' and was tipped to take over the agency at some point.

A child. I had assumed that Maud had been too busy to be a mother. She was hardly ever at home. Besides, what about Harry? Was he even the father? His medical report hadn't sounded particularly promising in that regard.

Coverage of the exhibition elsewhere suggested that Maud West junior was very much her mother's daughter, at least. For a start, she was keen on disguise, although she advised against the 'old-fashioned' sort. That was rarely necessary, she said: 'New eyebrows and make-up and a different style of dressing can change a girl so much that her friends won't recognise her.' That's not to say she eschewed all her mother's tricks; she had once 'acted as a male chauffeur for a week without being detected.'[38]

At the time the photograph was taken in 1937, Maud junior was twenty-five years old, so she would have been born sometime around 1912 – and there would be a record of her birth to prove it. Having nothing else to go on, I started with the assumption, unlikely as it seemed, that Harry was her father. The civil register listed quite a few female Elliotts born in the London area during that period, but I struck lucky early on. Before long I had a copy of her birth certificate in my hands.[39]

Her name was Evelyn, and Harry was indeed her father. She had been born on 6 May 1913 in a terraced house in Willesden, north-west London. Maud would have been in her early- to mid-thirties at the time, Harry thirty-three. Interestingly, Harry hadn't been working as a detective at the time; he gave his occupation as 'advertising agent'. Was this his main career? If so, he must have had connections in the press. Was his the invisible hand behind Maud's success in terms of self-promotion?

Looking closer at the dates, I realized that Evelyn had been born just three days after Maud's first set of articles concluded in *Pearson's Weekly*. She would have been heavily pregnant whilst writing and presumably unable to undertake her usual work. Sleep deprivation after the birth could also explain her strange, rambling piece in the *Pittsburgh Press* later that summer. As for her statement that she was close to a breakdown during the First World War, not only was she short-staffed and looking after haemorrhaging Harry, but she had a toddler to contend with. No wonder she was exhausted.

Evelyn's arrival on the scene had been a surprise – perhaps as much to Maud as to me – but it also held the key to unlocking the mystery of Maud's past, because there on the birth certificate was the name I'd been seeking for months:

*Edith
Maria
Elliott
formerly
Barber*

Barber. I'd come across that name before. It was the surname of the housekeeper at Pearley – or, as now seemed more likely, not the housekeeper but a relative of some sort. A maiden aunt, or an unmarried sister? It wouldn't be difficult to find out. I could now track down all of Edith's family. I'd be able to find her relatives in the legal profession who'd got her started in the detective business – her father, her brothers, her uncle – and the mother she never mentioned.

As for her marriage to Harry Elliott, the boy from the wrong side of the tracks, just when had that taken place? They seemed a curiously mismatched couple. Had they really eloped when Edith was nineteen, or had the wedding taken place later – say, in the nine months before Evelyn's birth?

I cleared my desk, ready for the next influx of paper.

The Countess and the Snowman

BY MAUD WEST

One day a client who appeared by special appointment under the name of Mr. Smith went straight to the point by saying: 'Miss West, I have had strict inquiries made about you, and I am satisfied that I can trust you on an important matter. I am now going to relieve myself of a mental burden.'

An odd way of expressing himself, I thought, yet his demeanour was so serious that I refrained from smiling.

My client was a foreign nobleman whose daughter, an only child, had left home. According to all reports she had become associated with people of the underworld. As she was now known to be in London, he instructed me to find out her associates and how they were obtaining the drugs to which she had fallen victim.

The case was not a simple one, but I did not anticipate that it would take me into places where cocaine is made or that I should see it in the process of manufacture.

To establish the identification of the girl was rather difficult because it was imperative that no open inquiries about her should be made. My only course was to haunt the hotel lounges and clubs night after night, and even make friends with women of questionable character.

After several nights, my patience was rewarded. I was sitting smoking in a night club, having previously heard some talk about a 'countess', when a beautiful girl entered. Tall and slender, she spoke with a slight foreign accent. Immediately I recognised her as the nobleman's daughter. A full description of her appearance had been supplied to me, and a thin, almost unnoticeable, blue line on her lower lip completed the identification.

I obtained an introduction to her, and we became quite friendly. Even at this time she was under the influence of drink or drugs. To obtain her address I offered her a lift home in my car. She not only accepted but invited me inside. We had been talking for about ten minutes when the phone rang, and I heard her say to the caller, 'No, don't come to-night. I have a friend here. In any case, I could not get the money.'

As she replaced the receiver, I expressed regret for inconveniencing her.

'Oh! don't you worry,' she replied. 'It is only Tom wanting money for the "snow" which I sold for him.'

Several weeks went by. The girl was watched day by day, and I met her every evening. I spent my client's money lavishly in trying to create the impression that money was no object to a fool.

One evening, I called at the flat only to learn that the 'countess' was packing and could not see anyone. Making my way in as an old friend, I learned that she was going to Paris next morning. I could not get any address out of her, so next morning I, too, was bound for Paris, disguised as an old lady.

On arrival at the Gare du Nord, the 'countess' entered a waiting car with a man. Luckily, I got a sporting taxi-driver who took up the chase of the car with delight. How we drove! I was tossed from one side of the cab to the other round the corners all the way to Porte d'Orléans. Then a wheel of the cab came off. Hastily giving the man some money, I grabbed my case and jumped on a tram-way car to the bewilderment of the driver and occupants. However, the tram, having got me across the circus in which direction the other car had gone, was now held up in a traffic block.

There was not an empty taxi to be had. I was becoming really agitated when I noticed that the driver of a car was evidently watching me. Taking the bull by the horns, I asked him to follow the car in front which was just moving off. 'It is a matter of great importance,' I told him.

'Yes, I expect it is,' he replied, 'or you would not be disguised as you are. Old ladies, you know, can't run and jump on trams as you did. Jump in.'

I admitted my disguise and mistake in being too active, and found a really good friend who helped me considerably, first by tracking the car and its occupants to their destination, and afterwards loaning me his car until I could arrange to hire one.

The block of flats the 'countess' and her companion had entered were typical of most flats or apartments in Paris. I kept observation until one o'clock the next morning – without any sign of the 'countess' or the man.

Early next day inquiries by my Paris agent about the occupants of the flats revealed that the only likely one was rented by a man named Brozan. He was something of a mystery to the concierge. Apparently he had no occupation, and was in the habit of being away for weeks at a time, never saying where he was going or where he had been. This information was not much use to me. However, early in the afternoon the man Brozan left the flat and, hailing a taxi, drove to a travel agency where I saw him book two tickets to Rio de Janeiro. I likewise booked a ticket.

At this point I let the man go, as I had to make a few purchases and send cables. In fact, I did not attempt to go near the flat at all, but simply took the train the next morning for Boulogne, and lay in wait for them. When they in due course arrived, I was alarmed at the appearance of the 'countess'. She looked desperately ill and on the verge of collapse.

We sailed on one of the Blue Star Line boats, the journey taking about 15 days, during which time I was in disguise the whole time as a nurse. The purchase of that uniform was a happy inspiration. Two days' journey from Rio I was approached by Brozan, who asked whether I could do anything for his wife, as she was seriously ill. I jumped at the opportunity.

In the 'countess's' cabin I found her in such a terrible state that she did not know me. I was able to help her a little, and finally I learned the extraordinary story of her life. It appeared that during girlhood she had always been wild and restless, with an insatiable desire for adventure. In a round of the night clubs she had met Brozan and married him without her parents' knowledge. She expressed great sorrow about her father's anguish, but declared that she was not fit to go back to him. At Rio de Janeiro my offer to accompany Mrs. Brozan to her hotel was gratefully accepted.

The next day I tracked him to a house in a low quarter of the town. After waiting a long time until he had left, I determined to investigate. Going down the back steps of the house I made my way cautiously along a narrow passage. As I turned a corner I suddenly found myself facing an automatic revolver, held by a heavily bearded, dirty-looking man, who made one grab at me and pushed me into a small room. I think he was a Portuguese. I did not understand his language, and he could not speak English. He left me in the room, having locked the door as he went. By this time I had a chance to look round the room, which had all the appearance of a laboratory.

The man returned in a few minutes accompanied by an American who asked me what I was doing there. I explained to him that I had evidently mistaken the place, for I was a journalist seeking 'local colour'. He just smiled and looked at me intently. Then I called bluff to my aid, and calmly asked: 'What are you weird people doing here?'

His reply was like a shot from a gun. 'Jane,' he said, in boastful innocence. 'We make all kinds of poisonous drugs. Would you like to try some?'

Airing a little knowledge of chemistry, I soon got the man talking. Eventually he showed me how cocaine was made. He told me that the extract was got from coca leaves, mixed with lead acetate, that it was filtered and rendered alkaline, and then purified by crystallisation from alcohol.

So, this was what my man Brozan was up to – a maker of deadly drugs. I apologised for intruding, and thanked the American for his 'local colour'. Unfortunately he was so pleased with our little acquaintance that he offered to show me back to my hotel. As I had given him a fictitious name and the wrong hotel, I hardly knew what to do. However, I suggested that we should take wine at one of the cafés, and there I managed to lose him.

From further inquiries I learned that Brozan had various agents who made friends in hotels and night clubs with people who might be persuaded to carry parcels through the French and Belgian ports and post them to other agents in various parts of the Continent and the British Isles. I immediately informed my client of my discoveries, and received instructions that I should do everything possible to persuade the girl to leave the wretched life she had been leading and return to her own country.

I was very doubtful about this because, for one thing, his daughter was too ill to be moved. However, I went straight back to my hotel, and again adopting the uniform of a nurse, called on her. She was unconscious. I explained to the doctors in confidence that I had been sent by her father and was allowed to stay by her bedside.

I shall never forget that scene as long as I live. The genuine grief of Brozan – for he really loved his wife, scoundrel though he was – was pitiful to see. For several hours I stayed there. The 'countess' never recovered consciousness but died that night as I sat stroking her poor, bloodless hand on the coverlet.

Matters moved quickly after Brozan's wife was buried. He and his confederates were arrested. Though he got his deserts as a scoundrel, I shall always think that his love for that wilful, misguided girl was a beautiful thing.[40]

Chapter Ten

Tracks in the Snow

You must have something of the
primitive hunting instincts to enjoy
being a detective.

Maud West, 1938[1]

'There is no more interesting department of detective work than the tracing of missing people.'[2] So said my new book, a hefty manual called *Crime Detection*, which had been published in 1928 for private detectives in the United States. I'd had it shipped over from a rare-book dealer in Long Island and whilst much of the content, such as the sections on the Mafia and tips on using bloodhounds, was particular to the work of American detectives, it was the best resource I'd found yet on the practicalities of inter-war investigative work.

Reading the chapter about missing people, I could see why such cases might brighten a detective's day. This was real sleuthing, starting with the slenderest of clues – a list of books borrowed from the library, a cryptic postcard, an empty bank account – and heading off into the unknown in search of answers. Who knew what might turn up? Elopement? Fraud? Insanity? *Murder?*

More often than not, however, the hunt had a different purpose. America, it seemed, was scattered with unsuspecting heirs to European fortunes who had emigrated to the land of freedom and opportunity. Following the trail from immigration records to house-to-house inquiries, the book said, may have lacked excitement, but the romance! From the vast prairies of the Midwest to the gold-speckled shores of California, ordinary folk were toiling away unaware of the good news heading in their direction.

The same applied on the other side of the pond, although the hunting ground for British detectives was even more extensive, taking in not just the New World, but the whole of the British Empire and beyond. In *Crook Pie*, John Goodwin said that this aspect of detective work was arguably the best part of the job:

> It often entails travelling in comfort in strange and fascinating countries, with no risks or anxieties, and as the missing heir or relative is almost invariably the recipient of 'something to his advantage' such journeys do not terminate in any of the unpleasantness that attends other kinds of searches.[3]

The words 'missing persons traced' appeared in almost every detective's advertisements at one point or another, so it was clear that this kind of work formed a core part of the job. Foreign travel, too, seemed a given. When Charlotte Antonia Williamson, aka Antonia Moser of Moser's Ladies Detective Agency, was divorced by her husband in 1890, for example, he cited as one of the death knells for the marriage a work trip she had wanted to take to Constantinople with her boss (and suspected lover) Maurice Moser.[4] In 1926, Maud herself said:

> . . . to dash to Holland, France, Spain, Italy at an hour's notice means no more than a trip from London to Brighton to most people. The longest journeys I have made so far, in connection with cases, took me to South Africa and the British East Indies. On both occasions I travelled with my own maid bearing copious letters of introduction, and had the most wonderful time.[5]

In general, however, I suspected that most missing persons inquiries played out closer to home and with much less glamour. In 1921, the *Illustrated Police News* had reported that the number of missing people was on the rise, with the list of lost souls issued nightly by Scotland Yard being 'more marked' than ever. An anonymous private detective added, 'Women form a large proportion of those who, as far as their own world is concerned, vanish utterly.' Many of these, they said, were 'young and obscure actresses' who had been lured away on the promise of marriage, only to be abandoned. 'The real mystery is the question of their ultimate fate. We have often been able to trace a girl up to the point of her disappearance, only to lose all clue to her further movements. We know that she does not leave the country, but no more.'[6]

Over the coming years, commentators would not be short of suggestions as to what became of such women, the majority of theories revolving around three things guaranteed to induce moral panic in the inter-war period: nightclubs, drugs and foreigners.

Nightclubs had their roots in the smarter London drinking dens of the war, whose owners had sidestepped the ban on serving alcohol without a meal after 10 p.m. by sending out a sorry sandwich or two with every bottle of champagne. Few cared about the catering, however, as under the tables toes were beginning to tap to a new rhythm that would soon erupt into a rambunctious blaze of joy and abandon, transforming the city's nightlife for ever.

Jazz had first arrived in Britain along with the American heiresses who had propped up the aristocracy in its hour of need. The alarm caused at the time by the 'monkey cage' dance floors at debutante balls was demonstrated by a letter written by an anonymous peeress to *The Times* in 1913. 'May I ask the powerful aid of *The Times* in a matter of grave perplexity?' it began, before its author unleashed her quivering pen on 'the various horrors of American and South American negroid origin' she had witnessed in the ballroom:

> My grandmother has often told me of the shock she experienced on first beholding the polka, but I wonder what she would have said had she been asked to introduce a well-brought-up girl of 18 to the scandalous travesties of dancing which are, for the first time in my recollection, bringing more young men to parties than are needed . . . I would only ask hostesses to let one know what houses to avoid by indicating in some way on their invitation cards whether the 'Turkey Trot,' the 'Boston' (the beginner of the evil), and the 'Tango' will be permitted.[7]

Presumably this wasn't the same anonymous peeress who, six years later, Maud reported, was being paid sixty pounds a night to shimmy across a West End dance floor, a fact that had emerged during a routine investigation into the woman's finances. By then, the dance boom was in full swing. New enterprises were springing up all over the city, and a spot of 'celebrity' endorsement from cash-strapped society women could make all the difference to a club's success. So could attractive youngsters, as Maud explained in 1919:

> Sometimes even girls of no social position, but who are exceptionally pretty, get paid to attend dances. I know of two girls, the daughters of a solicitor's clerk, who were paid £5 5s a week each to attend the dances at rooms in a northern suburb; but they were of course, more than ordinarily pretty. Their presence was a good advertisement to the rooms, and brought a number of young men to them, which of course, was just what the management wanted.

When Maud penned this article for *Answers* magazine, she struggled to find much dirt on the new 'jazz rooms'. She said she was brought in occasionally by the management of such places to shadow individuals of dubious character. One of these, she claimed, turned out to be a Parisian jewel thief, but he was exposed before he could cause any trouble. She also told of a country vicar who had invested in one London enterprise and was collecting a hundred pounds a week in return until his sister hired Maud to put a stop to it.[8] But that was as much scandal as she – or anyone else – could muster.

As nightclub culture took hold, however, the stories became darker. Attention turned to the West End, where the clubs attracted everyone from chorus girls to members of the aristocracy and paid little heed to the usual boundaries of class or race. Their patrons applauded black musicians and mingled with Chinatown dandies, prompting dark mutterings about the pernicious influence of the 'black devil' and the 'yellow peril'.

Some clubs were permanent fixtures, such as the Silver Slipper, the Joker and the Manhattan. Many more sprang up and shut down in the blink of an eye. They were notorious for excess. If an activity could carry the word 'illicit', it was to be found in one of these clubs: illicit drinking, illicit gambling, illicit sex, illicit drugs. London's mob bosses adopted them as part of their territory and fought over the rights to fleece their customers, but they also offered a conducive atmosphere for those with more modest criminal ambitions.

One ruse Maud warned her readers about was that played by a new breed of gigolo-cum-blackmailer who would offer his services as a dancing partner to married women whose husbands, for whatever reason, preferred to stay at home:

One of his most popular schemes is as follows: After securing by some means an introduction to a lady who is fond of dancing, he acts as her partner for some months and behaves in a perfectly normal manner. Having, more or less, obtained her confidence, under some pretext or other he takes her for a drive in a private car, which is probably hired one evening, and which breaks down in some lonely spot . . .[9]

This would be conveniently situated near a country inn, where the blackmailer would treat the woman to supper whilst the car was being 'repaired'. A few days later, an anonymous note would arrive, warning the woman that she had been spotted with a man in suspicious circumstances and, unless payment was forthcoming, her husband would be informed. When shown the note, her dancing partner would, of course, advise her to pay up – and so the blackmail cycle would begin.

Female criminals, according to the newspapers, were just as dangerous, stalking West End clubs in search of young men they could lure away to a wallet-emptying card game or seduce for the purposes of blackmail or breach of promise.[10] Maud had her own story about a run-in with one such woman, which she told a number of times. The woman, she said, had been blackmailing the younger son of a well-known London family, claiming that she had been 'compromised'. It was a familiar situation, but when Maud visited one of the woman's regular haunts and attempted to gain her confidence, she was rebuffed.

'Evidently,' Maud wrote, 'she did not care for the society of women . . .' So, after rummaging through her box of disguises, she returned to the nightclub as a man of seemingly unlimited wealth. The woman soon latched on to her as a potential new victim. Maud played along. 'One night, after having had a lot to drink, I kissed her,' she confessed in one version. 'Being a detective has its dark side!'[11]

Another version merely involved flirting, but both ended with Maud back at the woman's flat, whipping off her wig and retrieving the evidence against her client. 'The last glimpse I had of her,' she recalled, 'was that of a dejected figure seated on the bed, her furious glances in amusing contrast to the "vamping" I had to undergo in the taxi.'[12]

That story, however, was nothing compared to some of the tales she told about her work rescuing young 'dope fiends' from their dealers and from themselves.

'Some of the most pathetic stories I have ever heard of young lives being ruined were revealed to me while tracing drug traffickers,' Maud wrote in 1931. 'The methods of pests who deal in dope are many; the work of thwarting them frequently involves great personal risk; and the human wreckage which they leave behind is pitifully large.'[13]

Until 1916, psychoactive drugs had been freely available in Britain. A shot of cocaine was often just what the dentist ordered, whilst over-the-counter medicines for coughs and other common ailments were laced with morphine and heroin. When the first soldiers had marched off to the front, many had in their pockets small packets of morphine and cocaine, bought by loved ones from their local pharmacy. Before long, the high-end stores had started to sell more upmarket versions of these as luxury gifts: Harrods offered a cocaine kit complete with a syringe and spare needles, whilst jewellers created silver matchboxes containing tiny tubes of morphine.[14]

As the war went on, concerns grew as to the effect this was having on the troops. The *Times* medical correspondent, writing in February 1916 about the rise in 'cocainomaniacs' in the army, described the drug as 'more deadly than bullets'. He warned, 'It will, for the hour, charm away all [the soldier's] trouble, his fatigue, his anxiety; it will give him fictitious strength and vigour. But it will also, in the end, render him worthless as a soldier and a man.'[15]

The authorities agreed. In the summer of 1916, the sale of any product containing cocaine and opium to soldiers was banned under Defence of the Realm Act (DORA) regulations. This would later be expanded to include all citizens and be enshrined in the Dangerous Drugs Act of 1920, which prohibited the sale without prescription of almost all psychoactive drugs.

The first post-war drugs scandal, however, arrived just two weeks after the Armistice, with the death of the actress Billie Carleton in November 1918. Billie was starring in the patriotic play *The Freedom of the Seas* at the Theatre Royal at the time, her difficult reputation and long-standing opium habit having done nothing to prevent her becoming the West End's youngest leading lady at the age of twenty-two. After the curtain fell on 27 November, she slipped into a dress of transparent black georgette and, fuelled by cocaine, attended the Victory Ball at the Royal Albert Hall.

It was a grand and emotional affair. The dancing lasted into the small hours and, afterwards, Billie invited a few friends back to her apartment at the Savoy. When she finally fell into bed, she took her usual dose of the barbiturate veronal to knock her out. The next afternoon, her maid became suspicious when the loud snoring coming from Billie's room suddenly stopped. Billie was dead, the drugs scattered about the flat a clue to the cause.

At the inquest, details of her lifestyle came to light: the decadent opium parties, the sugar daddies who kept her in luxury and her close friendship with the married costume designer Reggie de Veulle, who trailed rumours of homosexual blackmail and cross-dressing in his wake. Reggie had been the one to supply the drugs. He, in turn, had got them from a dealer in Chinatown.

The perils of drugs were cemented in the public mind a few years later with the death of twenty-one-year-old Freda Kempton. Freda had been scraping a living as one of the hundreds of dancers who worked in West End nightclubs, teaching patrons the steps to new dances and keeping the dance floors buzzing with energetic displays of the latest moves. Such women were paid a tiny salary by each club, which they had to make up through tips and fees for dancing with wealthy men. In some of the seedier establishments, men were encouraged to 'book out' dancers for more private entertainment.[16]

Accordingly, Freda spent her nights tumbling in and out of taxis between different venues, keeping going by regular boosts of 'snow'. This was provided by Brilliant 'Billy' Chang, the so-called Dope King of London, who ran his drugs empire out of the Chinese restaurant he owned in Regent Street.

But when Freda died of cocaine poisoning in March 1922 in her rented rooms in Bayswater, it wasn't an accidental overdose. The autopsy showed she had over six grains of the drug in her stomach. One would have been enough to finish her off. At the inquest into her death, the jury returned a verdict of suicide. The coroner added that Freda had been depressed and short of money, and blamed in part the 'precarious' lifestyle she led as 'one of those who tried to turn night into day.' A charge of manslaughter against Billy Chang was mooted, but abandoned for lack of evidence.

Freda's tragic death became a defining landmark for those charting the moral degeneration of British society. Stories circulated of young women, estranged from their families and stripped of autonomy through drink and drugs, lost in a downward spiral of hedonistic destruction.

In 1926, Maud related the case of an eighteen-year-old who had fallen under the influence of 'a notorious and unscrupulous woman' at a West End club: '. . . when I saw her she was in a pitiable state. She had been induced to part with about £300 under threat of betrayal to her parents. Her money gone, her self-respect vanished, she had become the plaything of the men who frequented the place.'[17]

The toxic friendship seemed unbreakable, but she managed to extract the girl by inviting the pair to a fictitious opium party at her flat, where she exposed the unscrupulous woman's true nature. The story ended with the older woman attacking Maud with a hat pin ('And hat pins are dangerous weapons in the hands of an incensed woman') and the young girl returning to her family only to die a few months later ('her health was ruined').[18]

Some years later, Maud would also hint that an amnesiac she had retrieved from a farm in South Africa was Freda Kempton's secret lover, driven mad by news of her death,[19] and claim Billy Chang as an old acquaintance.[20] But then, she claimed a lot of things. In one case, she said she had been given a free hand, with unlimited money, to stem the supply of cocaine to a young heiress, only to hit a seemingly insurmountable wall of her own making: 'After one or two arrests had been made through my instrumentality, I found that the drug-dealers were becoming so cautious that any new purchasers were being looked on with suspicion.'[21]

What to do? She consulted a friend in the medical profession who supposedly furnished her with 'an almost innocuous preparation', the effects of which mimicked the jitters of a genuine drug addict. 'The success of this ruse was instantaneous,' she reported. '. . . After taking the preparation I was offered cocaine three times within two hours, and I was able to go from den to den unchallenged, even welcomed.'

After identifying a number of dealers, she had them shadowed and then handed over their details and a summary of their activities to the police. The biggest coup in the 'wholesale and wholesome clean-up' that followed, she said, was the arrest of one of the leading importers of cocaine, who was using a small East End sweet factory to receive his wares. The drugs, Maud said, had reached the sweet factory from the Continent 'by a roundabout route', first going to Africa, where they were secreted in shipments of ingredients, and then shipped on to Britain: 'A code arrangement enabled the factory proprietor to locate the precious consignments amongst the bulk parcels.' That proprietor, she added, 'was a man of excellent repute. He was a churchwarden and a member of the local borough council, whom the breath of suspicion had never touched.'

It was, of course, completely untrue. There was no evidence of any such raid: although the newspapers reported significant coups on the part of European police in catching drug smugglers, British victories seemed limited to the arrests of individual dealers. Maud *was* right about the way illegal drugs entered the country, but that information was available to anyone who took a morning paper.

Work by the newly formed League of Nations and international customs authorities had established that most cocaine in Britain originated in Germany, Holland and Switzerland, where chemical factories processed raw materials from Asia and South America before shipping the finished product back whence it came. A small proportion of that was then smuggled back into Europe. In one raid on a drugs ring operating out of Berlin and Copenhagen, cocaine was found disguised as boot polish, shaving soap and sealing wax;[22] in France, customs officials found two coffins crammed with the same.[23] I could find no definitive evidence of how it arrived in Britain, although hearsay had it that drugs were hidden in artificial eyes, false teeth, table legs and walnut shells.[24] A sweet factory, therefore, seemed a reasonable invention.

But where did the truth lie? I doubted that Maud had ever been tasked by a wealthy client to shut down the international drugs trade single-handedly, as was her excuse for some of her less believable adventures in South America, but addiction was a fact of life and its effects would undoubtedly have fed into a fair number of cases that landed on Maud's desk. To what extent might she, or her staff, have needed to ferret around in the underworld in the course of their work?

It was a question, I suspected, that would never be answered. The evidence was scant to non-existent. The only verifiable instance I could find of a private detective being involved in a drug-related case came from 1926, when a detective had been hired to shadow the French actress Régine Flory, a highly strung cocaine and opium addict, on a visit to London. His task was to prevent her from coming to any harm. As this only came to light after Mlle Flory unexpectedly shot herself in the middle of a conversation with the managing director of the Drury Lane Theatre, I figured it was possible that other detectives were engaged on similar – and more successful – missions.[25]

It was easier to establish the truth about the other popular scenario in which young women went missing. An example of this was a case Maud related to a journalist in 1938 in which the daughter of an upper-class family had fallen in love with a man from Chile. Her parents were against the match, so the couple had eloped. They were halfway across the Atlantic before one of Maud's detectives, who had discreetly joined them on the journey, was able to creep into the man's cabin to rifle through his papers:

> It turned out he had business relations with one of those houses in Valparaíso where, despite all the measures taken by the police, white girls were still being trafficked. Usually, the inexperienced young things don't find a way out after the doors of such an establishment have closed behind them. This time, however, the set-up failed – a brief conversation between the detective and the captain was sufficient and the impostor was

arrested by the police in Valparaíso, while the detective returned the young girl to her happy parents.[26]

The idea of innocent white women being duped by swarthy foreigners into a life of 'white slavery' in South American brothels had been a common trope for many years. Enforced prostitution undoubtedly existed: the first international treaty to tackle the problem had been ratified in 1904, the second in 1910, and the League of Nations had taken on the issue in 1921 (changing the term from 'white slavery' to 'traffic in women and children' to remove the element of race). But Western fears about the scale and nature of the situation, fed as they were by xenophobia and fear of 'the other', remained disproportionate.

In Britain in 1913, Teresa Billington-Greig of the Women's Freedom League had decided to investigate the disturbing stories that had led to the passing of the controversial Criminal Law Amendment (White Slave Traffic) Act the previous year. There had been widespread claims of girls being trapped or seduced, bundled into cars, drugged and taken to 'flats and houses of ill-fame, there outraged and beaten, and finally transported abroad to foreign brothels under the control of large vice syndicates.'[27]

Despite thorough and persistent questioning, however, she had found no evidence for any of the stories that had informed the legislation, and suggested that the 'ridiculous scandal-mongering' detracted from the very real necessity of addressing the social and welfare issues surrounding prostitution. She also took issue with the depiction of women as 'impotent and imbecilic weaklings' that these stories promoted, asking why there had been no reports of the men involved being 'brained with fenders, or injured with chairs, pictures or other articles of furniture; why doors are not barricaded, windows smashed, and the night rent with screams.'[28]

Hers, however, was a rare voice of reason. The idea of white slavery touched upon so many issues – the politics of sex work, immigration, 'moral hygiene', women's emancipation and so on – that there was always someone ready to fuel the fire with fresh stories to serve their own ends.

Margaret Damer Dawson, to give one example, claimed to have been inspired to set up the WPS during the First World War following the attempted abduction of two female Belgian refugees under her care – a convenient excuse for one seeking to disguise more naked ambitions.[29] Tales of white slavery also proved a useful tool for those seeking to 'protect' the virtue of young women, a task that was getting increasingly difficult as more and more women chose to live life on their own terms.

But as an explanation for the reported rise in missing women? As Teresa Billington-Greig, who herself had run away from stifling family expectations at seventeen, put it: '. . . there are hundreds of feasible reasons why girls and women should desire to leave their homes, and dozens that will explain why, having left home, they may desire to remain undiscovered.'[30]

Maud knew this. Not only had she also supposedly run away at nineteen, but she had years of professional experience dealing with the difficulties and disappointments of family life. In all probability, the bulk of her missing persons work would have involved locating those who had chosen to disappear – both male and female – with the occasional spot of heir hunting on the side. But where was the drama in that?

Meanwhile, I had a missing-persons case of my own that was proving surprisingly taxing. The man in question was dead, but how – or where or when – he came to be that way was a mystery. All I had to go on were four words:

Robert Barber (deceased), sailor. This, according to Edith and Harry's marriage certificate, was Edith's father. Not a barrister, then – not even a solicitor or a solicitor's clerk – but one of the great mass of men who kept the British Empire afloat through their sweaty and rum-sodden devotion to life on the ocean wave. At least, that's what Edith told the vicar, and who would lie to a man of the cloth?

The ceremony had taken place on a quiet Thursday in May 1901 at St Saviour's Church in Forest Hill, south-east London. Edith said she was a twenty-year-old spinster who'd been working as a drapery assistant. Harry, twenty-one, gave his occupation as 'manager'.[31] But there was something a bit cloak-and-dagger about the whole affair, something a bit *off*.

The couple were staying in rented rooms for a start, and they hadn't been there seven weeks earlier when the census was taken. The two witnesses were a local laundress, possibly plucked off the street for the occasion, and the son of a scaffold builder from Hackney, presumably a friend of Harry's. None of the family members who would typically act as witnesses were anywhere to be seen; not Harry's parents, nor any of his eight siblings. Robert Barber (deceased) couldn't have been expected to attend, but Edith must have had other relatives. A mother, at least. Where were they?

An internet search revealed that there was indeed a sailor called Robert Barber who had produced a daughter called Edith Maria – and, according to the General Register Office, he was the only man by that name to have done so in Britain for many years. Furthermore, he came from Deptford in the clanking heart of London's docklands, just three miles from Forest Hill where Edith and Harry had made their vows.

It all looked very promising, apart from a few details. The first was that Robert Barber's daughter had been born in November 1884, which would have made her sixteen, not twenty, when she got married.[32] Knowing Maud's ambivalent relationship with the truth, that wasn't necessarily a problem. Nor was the fact that Robert Barber was very much alive and kicking in 1901: claiming otherwise would have helped to ease Edith's way to the altar without the parental consent required by anyone under twenty-one. Of more concern was that, when she stood at that altar, Edith Maria Barber was dead and had been for some time. She'd been lowered into a tiny grave in May 1887 after succumbing to measles and pneumonia at the age of two.[33]

I'd have thought I had the wrong man, were it not for my next discovery: Edith and Harry had been in Deptford on the evening of the census just before their wedding. They weren't staying with the Robert Barber I'd found, but they were with his elderly parents – Robert Barber senior and his wife Mary – three streets away. Edith was listed as their granddaughter; Harry as a visitor.

What was Maud up to now? The public records were clear: there was only one child called Edith Maria Barber who had a father named Robert, and she was dead. Yet there she was, tucking into supper with Robert's parents in 1901. There is almost always a simple answer to genealogical conundrums, but none of the theories I could come up with qualified as simple.

Had reports of the two-year-old's death been mistaken? A clerical error, perhaps, or a medical one? But there was a death certificate *and* a burial record, which meant either inconceivable incompetence on the part of the authorities or that little Edith had somehow gasped back to life and clawed her way out of the grave.

Besides, there was no sign of her in the 1891 census or anywhere else between her death in 1887 and reappearance in 1901.

Maybe Maud had used her family's wealth to bribe this poor, bereaved family to pretend she was one of their own? She'd admitted that she had run away to get married in secret; had she left out the part where she had done so using a false identity? But why bother? The neurotic, gonorrhoea-ridden Harry Elliott wasn't *that* much of a catch. No, it had to be something more serious, something about her past that she was keen to sweep under the carpet even then. A criminal record, perhaps? I thought of the sassy diamond thief I'd come across early in my research. What had become of that Maud West after she left prison? What if Maud had been using her real name all along?

It was a delicious proposition, but also utterly absurd. Of course it wasn't the answer; Maud wasn't living out the plot of a Wilkie Collins novel. Still, she was hiding *something*, I was sure of it. But what – and why?

An Unusual Pastime

AS RELATED BY
THE *SAN FRANCISCO EXAMINER*

Detective work, like newspaper work, will not wait upon convenience. What must be done must often be done instantly . . . If the telephone rings and she must catch the boat train leaving for a Channel steamer for India or one of the great American liners, Miss West is ready for an immediate start.

She received instructions from a firm of solicitors in London one day, acting on behalf of a young American woman who wished her husband kept under observation, she related. He was very wealthy, but apparently he had 'a bee in his bonnet and wanted to do things he shouldn't.'

The trail began in Paris, city of strange romances . . . She disguised best of all as a man, and with different facial make-up each time she dogged him all over the French capital. Then he made for London and the woman shadower followed him across. He carried with him one particular bag of odd shape, and when he got to Dover he entered a hotel and left this part of his luggage, saying he would call for it on his return journey to France.

Maud West was determined to get that bag. From Dover to London is about a hundred miles. She got into the train to London, and halfway on the journey she got out and sent a wire from the station telegraph office to the Dover hotel. She said she wished the bag sent to a particular address in London immediately and she signed the American's name to the message.

Not long after her, the bag arrived. She took possession of it and went to the man's wife for permission to open it. This was given and the grip was opened.

'Great heavens!' the wife exclaimed. 'What's he up to now?'

The bag contained an imposing array of surgeon's knives and implements.

'Oh, dear; oh, dear,' she cried. 'Don't lose sight of him! Follow him wherever he goes.'

The bag was returned to Dover with appropriate explanations. In due course the husband collected it and made for New York. The woman detective booked a berth on the same ship, and during the voyage she spent her time shadowing the eccentric passenger about the decks. Whenever he went to his stateroom she kept watch in the alleyway, like a thief in the night. He met her several times, but never knew it was the same person.

One day she would be an elderly woman, another she would appear as a heavily moustached man. So the comedy went on until New York was reached. She trailed her man across town to the East side and she saw him enter a tumble-down building. She followed and listened at the door.

'Well,' said the visitor, 'got everything ready?'

'Yes,' a man's voice replied. 'I paid fifty dollars for a body that was fished from the river. It's downstairs in my laboratory.'

The woman detective drew closer to the door.

'Good for you, Doc,' said the other. 'Say, I brought my implements. I bought them in Paris, at the Pasteur Clinic.'

The woman detective waited only a little while longer until her suspicions were confirmed. As she had gathered, the strange American's eccentricity had turned to medical surgery, and he had entered into a compact with this doctor of shady reputation to assist in the dissection of a human body. The detective went and cabled the wife, received a reply giving instructions, and the result was that the would-be amateur surgeon found himself in the hands of an alienist and later removed to a private mental home.[34]

Chapter Eleven

Partners in Crime

I love detective novels.
They are so entirely unlike
the real thing . . .

Maud West, 1931[1]

On Monday, 6 March 1922, news broke of a brutal murder that had taken place over the weekend in Berkshire. The setting was a lonely inn at Gallows Tree Common, a place as bleak and isolated as it sounded. The victim, the Crown and Anchor's fifty-two-year-old landlady Sarah Blake, had been found lying in a pool of blood that Saturday morning. Two dirty glasses had been left on a dresser, signs of a shared tipple preceding the frenzied attack that left her with over sixty bruises and stab wounds. On Sunday evening, working by the light of an oil lamp, the Home Office pathologist Bernard Spilsbury established that although her skull had been fractured four times, it was the four-inch gash on the back of her neck that killed her.

The murderer had locked the door to the inn when he left and tossed the key into the garden, and a bloodied knife with a single strand of hair was found in a hedge nearby. The motive, however, was unclear. Mrs Blake, a widow, had no enemies and nearly £500 lay untouched in her private quarters. Rumours abounded of a strange cyclist with a Roman nose, excitable manner and stutter who had been spotted in the vicinity asking for refreshments. It was too much for the local police to handle, so Scotland Yard had been brought in.[2]

A few days later, Maud was also at the scene. She wasn't there in any official capacity, just rubbernecking on behalf of the readers of *Lloyd's Sunday News*, a commission that probably looked better on paper than it did in reality.[3] There was little to see. Scotland Yard had been and gone. The body was in the mortuary, the inn locked up, and the only person Maud could find to talk to was the taxi driver who had driven her the seven miles from the railway station at Henley-on-Thames – and he'd barely been able to find the inn, let alone add any local insight. Besides, murder wasn't really her game. Nor, it seemed, was country life ('I saw few signs of civilisation'), but work was work, so Maud gamely stomped around in the mud for a while, then got back in the taxi and went home. There, she used the information already published in the press to string out a 500-word opinion on the case.

Forget about the mysterious stuttering cyclist, she said. He's a red herring. This was the work of a local; a stranger would have taken the latch-key with him to dispose of far away, not thrown it down on the path. The motive was robbery – Sarah Blake had told a number of people about her savings – but the intruder had been startled by something ('the sound of a mouse running across the floor would be sufficient') and panicked. He was obviously an amateur; a professional would have stopped well short of sixty blows before he made his escape.

As it happened, she was right on all fronts, except for the mouse. In due course, the bloodied knife was traced back to its owner, a skinny, fifteen-year-old farmhand called Jack Hewett who had testified at the inquest as the last person to have seen Sarah Blake alive. He confessed to the murder, explaining that he'd heard about the money she kept at the inn but had startled himself by his own capacity for violence. Beyond that, his only defence was the cinema: 'I wish I had never seen the pictures,' he allegedly said to a police sergeant. 'They are the cause of this.'[4]

Still, I wondered what Scotland Yard had thought of Maud sticking her oar in mid-investigation. In fact, what did the police think of Maud in general?

On the face of it, detective work in London – both public and private – was one big old boys' network. Many inquiry agencies were run by retired Scotland Yard detectives, who in turn employed other ex-officers on their staff. They retained their titles and plastered them all over their letterheads as a sign that they were the real deal:[5]

Charles Richards,
Pensioned Inspector
Criminal Investigation Department,
New Scotland Yard.

PRIVATE AND CONFIDENTIAL REPORT

TELEGRAPHIC ADDRESS, EYESERVICE, LONDON.
TELEPHONE Nº 1212 BATTERSEA.

Informal visits to and from the Yard, cosy out-of-hours chats, a swift pint after work: such things kept this network alive. So where did this leave Maud and Kate and all the other women who tried their hand in this testosterone-heavy profession? Shut out in the cold? Not necessarily. When Kate Easton was asked in 1907 about her relationship with Scotland Yard, she replied, 'They are very good to me. I employ on my own staff more than one pensioned police officer.'[6] This, no doubt, made it easier for her to develop relationships with those still working as policemen.

Maud, too, found the police helpful, as she explained in 1914:

Do I find much jealousy or hindrance on the part of the regular police force or the C.I.D. Department? Oh no! Not at all. On the contrary, they are always very good to me, but in return I am always careful never to bring up a police officer as a witness, or drag his name into a case.[7]

Based on all the crime novels I had read, I'd expected more animosity. But Maud and Kate, like all private detectives, were sitting on a wealth of information that could prove useful to the police, and vice versa. In real life, a good reciprocal relationship made everyone's work easier. Besides, most of the time they were pursuing different aims. As Maud pointed out in 1930, 'The main difference between a private detective and a Yard man mainly consists of the fact that the latter, because of the nature of a case, will always try to make arrests . . . whereas this is usually the last thing we want to do.'[8]

If anything, the services provided by private detective agencies were useful for taking the pressure off the authorities when official resources had been exhausted. The *Policewoman's Review* said of Maud in 1931 that 'In certain cases where relatives, etc., have not been satisfied with the evidence the police have collected, she has been called in to supply more, and she cannot speak too highly of the willing help which the police have always afforded her.'[9] I'd also found evidence of Scotland Yard and private detectives working cases concurrently. When Viscount Tredegar's daughter, the Hon. Gwyneth Morgan, disappeared in December 1924, for example, it was an inquiry agent who was summoned to identify her body when it was fished out of the Thames by the police five months later.[10]

The key to the relationship was discretion. This was especially important, I discovered, when it came to London's lady detectives. By the 1920s it was fine for Maud to say that she helped the police with criminal matters, even that she had been instrumental in securing a few arrests, but that hadn't always been the case. The relationship between female detectives and Scotland Yard had once been a matter of utmost secrecy – even, some might say, of paranoia.

The official version of women's involvement in the police was that it had started in the First World War, with the WPS and the WPV slugging it out over the morals of young women. The work they did during those difficult years convinced Commissioner of the Metropolitan Police Sir Nevil Macready that the 'lady in blue' was needed on the streets of London. In November 1918, he started sending women out on the beat for the first time. Clothed by Harrods and fuelled with pride, these women were striding into the pages of history, but they weren't the first women to work for Scotland Yard.

As early as 1899, for example, *Cassell's Saturday Journal* had revealed that the Yard was employing private lady detectives on the sly:

> More than one . . . is working fairly regularly for the department, but who they are none but the authorities know. They are paid by fees, and frequently receive as much as £10 for a single case. Such secrecy, however, is used in their employment that even their receipts are signed in fictitious names.[11]

They were still there, unofficial and unseen, in February 1914, according to the London correspondent of the *Leicester Daily Post*: '. . . there has lately been a considerable addition to the number of trained women employed by Scotland Yard on detective work in various directions,' he wrote. 'Although these lady detectives seldom come into the limelight in big cases they form a very valued part of the organisation at Scotland Yard.'[12] The article mentioned their work with West End palmists, which seemed to extend beyond the case I had found, and said they were also doing 'splendid service' with regard to prosecutions under the new white slave traffic legislation and in keeping an eye on militant suffragettes.

The same year, the *Daily Mirror* had reported that Scotland Yard was using female private detectives at the House of Commons. They would sit in the ladies' gallery during contentious debates, ready to pounce on any suffragette intruders before they could make a scene. 'They are so fashionably attired,' the paper reported, 'as to be quite indistinguishable from the usual gathering.'[13]

Just like male private detectives before them, Scotland Yard had discovered that there were some situations in which employing a smart woman was the only way to go. But why keep it so hush-hush? Perhaps the furore that erupted after Sir Nevil Macready introduced his women's patrols in 1918 offered a clue.

In line with the bulk of work that women police volunteers had done during the war, the primary purpose of Macready's women's patrols (he objected to the term 'women police') was to control prostitution. They had no powers of arrest, and their terms of employment were extremely poor: short contracts, a wage which could only be accepted by those with private incomes, and no pension. This was justified in part by the fact that one of the prerequisites for these early recruits was that they came from reasonably refined – and wealthy – families, the assumption being that they would have to rely on class and character to assert authority rather than physical presence.

Even with these limitations, eyebrows were raised. The real row, however, began after various political manoeuvrings in 1919 resulted in an unexpectedly forward-thinking piece of legislation achieving royal assent that December: the Sex Disqualification (Removal) Act gave women the right to enter professions from

which they had previously been barred. They could now qualify as solicitors, barristers, accountants and veterinary surgeons, serve as jurors and gain university degrees. Some exceptions were outlined in the legislation (women could not, for example, work in the diplomatic service), but what about the police? Should an exception be made there, too?

A committee was convened in 1920 to consider the matter. Led by Sir John Baird of the Home Office, the committee took evidence from police forces throughout the country, whilst others piled into the debate in the press.

Many of the arguments were well worn and predictable. Could women's dainty feet withstand eight hours or more on the beat? How would they protect themselves? They couldn't be armed, surely? What if their weapons were snatched from their hands and used against them? What effect would they have on their male colleagues? It was a given that female recruits could never give orders to men,[14] but might their presence cause trouble of a different kind? As one magistrate pointed out, male and female officers out on the beat together would be 'sufficiently youthful for the ordinary human passions to be in full play . . .'[15]

And what about male criminals? How would *they* feel? One faction argued, perfectly seriously, in 1924:

> Of course, nobody worth calling a man would allow himself to be forcibly conveyed to a police station by a woman; if she attempted to use force, he would be morally bound to restrain her until the arrival of a male constable.[16]

Underlying all this, whilst also contradicting many of the arguments about women's inability to withstand a bit of a scuffle, were concerns that many of the voluntary wartime patrols had their roots in the suffragette movement. Sir Nevil Macready warned that recruitment into the official police force had to be carefully managed so as to avoid women with extreme views, such as 'the vinegary spinster or blighted middle-aged fanatic.'[17] He had already declared war on Margaret Damer Dawson of the WPS and was trying to get her military-inspired voluntary patrols off his patch.

But many of these women were vinegary for good reason, having witnessed first-hand how the criminal justice system treated their sex. Force-feeding and sexual assault aside, Nina Boyle, one of the founders of the WPV, had been campaigning for segregated police vans ever since a fellow Women's Freedom League member had to endure an 'orgy of indecency' between a male prisoner and a prostitute en route to Holloway.[18] Between 1913 and 1918, the League's journal, the *Vote*, had employed a court reporter to provide a running commentary on the respective 'justice' meted out to male and female prisoners, which was enough to make any woman, spinster or not, pickled with vinegary rage.[19] Women were treated with disrespect whether they were appearing in the dock or the witness box. Sentencing, too, was discriminatory: grievous bodily harm against a woman might get a man three months imprisonment, but a woman convicted of soliciting could receive nine months plus hard labour.[20]

To its credit, Sir John Baird's committee was unmoved by the more alarmist opinions swirling around. In August 1920, after hearing all the evidence, it recommended that women aged between twenty-five and thirty should be recruited to the police, albeit in a limited capacity, and that good training and pay were essential if they were to be effective. It added that they should be sworn in and given powers of arrest, but should not have to perform duties that might expose them to physical danger.[21] As for the work they *could* do, it was agreed that this should be restricted to issues concerning women and children. When the Home Office circulated the report to constabularies around the country, however, it included a note suggesting that the recommendations regarding pay and powers of arrest were best ignored.[22]

The debate was far from over. Whilst the Baird Committee was still taking evidence, Sir Nevil Macready had left Scotland Yard to take command of the British troops in the Irish War of Independence. In 1922, his successor ordered the immediate disbandment of the women's patrols (or 'Macready's Monsters', as some preferred), ostensibly as a cost-cutting measure. After a huge row, they clung on in diminished numbers, but the mithering continued. At the same time, however, others were wondering whether the time had come for women to be included in other areas of police work – as detectives, for example.

In a letter to the Baird Committee in 1920, Sir Nevil had presented a shopping list of women he wanted for specialist investigative work at Scotland Yard:

> I want to have the woman I can put into an evening dress, with some diamonds or whatever she wears, and send to a place to mix with other people, and also I want women at the other end of the scale. Then some nurses are excellent. It is very good to have women with nursing experience.[23]

Sir Nevil wasn't alone. The Lancashire Constabulary had also been experimenting with female detectives. The chief constable explained that they assisted with all manner of cases, including murder, and had proved invaluable when eliciting more sensitive, personal information from female witnesses, especially when it came to dealing with Sinn Fein in the area. Whether they were truly the equals of their male counterparts, however, was open to question. The police historian Joan Lock, having spoken to veterans of these early years, concluded in 1979 that their work was 'largely clerical and secretarial with the occasional decency statement, pickpocket observation . . . and decoy duty during spates of sexual attacks.'[24]

All the evidence from Lancashire and Sir Nevil was brought before another inquiry into the use of women in the police that took place in 1924. When the Bridgeman Committee issued its report that August, it reinforced the Baird conclusions and made the additional recommendation that women be admitted as plain-clothes detectives at the discretion of each force.

Inevitably, as London's most high-profile female detective, Maud was approached by the press for her opinion on this particular development. 'I think that some women are admirably fitted for detective work,' she told the *Manchester Guardian* in 1924, '. . . they would be a great asset to the country.'[25] This wasn't just because they could slip into an evening dress or wheedle information out of female suspects. In some ways, she said, they were better suited to the work than men, echoing what she had said a few years earlier in the *New York Tribune*:

I employ women in every investigation requiring subtlety, craft, guesswork, diplomatic conversation, or plain common sense . . . For the finer and more delicate work I invariably find that a woman is able to clear up the case in much less time than a man. She has more tact, quicker perception, and an equally vivid imagination.[26]

This, in turn, reminded me of something Antonia Moser had said in 1901 about working with Maurice Moser: 'One thing is very curious, that we both attack the same case in entirely different ways, and arrive at our results sometimes from opposite poles.'[27]

Britain's lady detectives had always known that they brought a unique perspective to investigative work, and now the authorities were listening. But when Maud said that some women made good detectives, she meant just that: *some* women. Following the Bridgeman report, Scotland Yard had been inundated with letters from prospective recruits, something Maud had been dealing with for years:

> Never a day passes without my getting letters from people who tell me that they have a special gift for this work, and that all their lives they have wanted to do it ... They send me their photographs, and when they do not write they telephone. Why do they do it? They have been to the pictures and they are fascinated with the view of a detective's life.[28]

Even if they hadn't gone to the pictures, I suspected women might have seen Maud as an attractive employer. She was fair to her staff, paying for telephones to be installed at their homes so she could summon them when needed or call early in the morning to tell them not to come in: 'Then the day is their own; but their salary comes in at the end of the week just the same,' she explained. 'In that way we are able to make up for the terribly hard work we do at other times.'[29] When things were slack in the office, they could read a book or knit or sew, as long as they were ready to act as soon as a call came in.

As for pay, they could expect to start on around five pounds a week – a shop assistant might earn two pounds – but, as Maud pointed out, 'This salary represents more than £5, really, as a detective lives for many weeks in each year either in hotels or private houses, entirely free of cost.'[30]

To enjoy these perks, however, her staff had to pass a strict vetting and training programme. The majority of letters she received from potential recruits went straight in the bin. 'Most of them are unsuitable for the work,' she had written in 1913,[31] and her opinion had not changed by 1924.

Looking at the list of attributes she sought, it wasn't surprising that few measured up to her standards. Anyone with a limp, lisp or other outstanding characteristic was rejected out of hand; redheads were directed towards the nearest hairdresser for a colour change. The remaining candidates had to demonstrate a natural ability and liking for the work as well as 'great tact, great strength, great perseverance and, of course, courage.'[32] Then there was intuition, patience, acting skills, the ability to make quick decisions and a willingness to work uncertain hours in all weathers – although whether all her female staff had also been to university, could speak four languages and were 'as good at handling a revolver as a lipstick', as one foreign newspaper reported in 1931, was more doubtful.[33]

Should a woman – or man – meet these requirements, they were admitted for training. Maud said her own training had been a self-directed affair:

> For many months I set myself to study law, often attending the courts to watch the procedure, reading books by celebrated criminologists, learning languages, and dabbling in the art of disguise and make up.[34]

Her own detectives, however, were offered more assistance – for a price. She charged a training fee, although this was returned minus expenses if things didn't work out: 'I give them a couple of weeks' trial. Then, if I consider they are unsuitable or unfitted for the game, I frankly tell them so.'[35] There was another cull at the end of the first month.[36] The full probationary period lasted three, with Maud's beady eye on their every move.

'One of the tests I give a pupil is to tell her I shall be at a certain big store at a given time, on a given day,' she explained in 1926. 'She is told to describe exactly what I have done and where I have been before arriving there. In other words, to "shadow" me. If she reports accurately all my movements (of which I am perfectly well aware) it is a big point in her favour.'[37]

Maud also placed great emphasis on observation skills and trained her recruits using methods similar to those employed by Scotland Yard.[38] She would begin by pointing to a man in the street and asking her student to tell her of someone else with a similar nose or brow line. Faces came first, followed by the way people stood and moved. Each student was different, with some quick to recognize facial features, others mannerisms – Maud herself was drawn to mouths and teeth – but these skills could be expanded over time. 'Whereas you might see one point,' she explained, 'because I am trained to it, and because I have certain attributes that have become highly developed, I can see 100 points.'[39]

A trickier prospect was identifying people from their descriptions. She knew one man who had an intuitive gift for this, she said, but most people struggled:

It is surprising how many people resemble each other in certain particulars. You may so often be told you cannot possibly mistake him: he turns his foot in, or he hunches one shoulder, or one eyebrow is shorter than another; and when you begin to look about you find there are ten people of the same height, size and general appearance who turn their foot in, or hunch a shoulder, or have one eyebrow shorter than another.

'It is remarkable, too, how many people have doubles,' she added.[40]

Tell me about it, I thought.

Two Edith Barbers, two Charles Lawrence Elliotts, and a shifting number of barristers and solicitors: there were altogether too many people in Maud's family tree. In one of her articles about detective careers, she had muddied the water even further by adding another lawyer (her grandfather), removing the brothers she had mentioned to Basil Tozer in 1914, and introducing her mother for the first time:

> My grandfather and my uncles were lawyers ... I had not thought of any special career for myself, perhaps because it wasn't essential for me to work at all. My mother, who had studied medicine, wanted me to follow in her footsteps, but the notion didn't appeal to me. I was very boyish in those days, although I had no brothers to back me up. In fact, I was always called 'Jack' by the family.[41]

More lies, or more clues? I'd never known anyone to be so inconsistent.

The only way forward was to ignore everything she'd ever said about her family and focus instead on the hard evidence available, such as where she and Harry had spent the night of the census, just before their wedding.

The house in Staunton Street, Deptford, which belonged to Maud's alleged grandparents, was a standard three-up, three-down terrace with creeping damp and soot-stained windows. On his

map of London poverty in 1889, Charles Booth had coloured the
street purple.[42] In Booth's cheerless world, purple was a middling
place to dwell, not exactly comfortable, but not slovenly, either:
the curtains got washed occasionally and the doorsteps scrubbed.
This was where Robert Barber senior and his wife Mary had raised
their five children – four sons and one daughter – after moving to
London from Norfolk thirty-five years earlier. Robert senior was,
like Robert junior, a merchant seaman, so if there was a family of
lawyers to be found, it didn't now seem likely it would be on the
paternal side.

By the time of the 1901 census, the only one of Robert and Mary's
five children left at home was their forty-two-year-old spinster
daughter Mary Ann, a ladies' nurse who looked after new mothers
and their babies in the weeks following birth. At the time, she was
in bed herself, suffering from some unspecified illness. Apart from
Harry and Edith, the only other occupants of the house that night
were two lodgers and a fifteen-year-old girl called Alice, who was
listed as another of Robert and Mary's grandchildren.

Looking at all the evidence, it occurred to me that there *was*
a simple explanation for Edith's presence in the house that night.
Like most families at the time, the Barbers were keen on recycling
names: Robert, Mary, Alfred and Elizabeth all appeared multiple
times in their family tree. *It is remarkable, too, how many people
have doubles.* I had a feeling that the name Edith Maria had also
been used more than once.

The theory I was forming didn't involve Edith's so-called father,
Robert junior. At least, I hoped not, because my eyes were focused
on his sister Mary Ann, the ladies' nurse languishing on her sick
bed in Staunton Street. *My mother, who had studied medicine,
wanted me to follow in her footsteps.* Mary Ann had never married,
but that didn't mean she didn't have any children.

When a batch of birth certificates I had ordered arrived from the General Register Office my suspicions were confirmed:

Name: Edith Maria Barber

When and where born: Fifteenth September 1880,
2 Staunton Street

Mother: Mary Ann Barber, a domestic servant

Father: _____

There *were* two Edith Maria Barbers – and this one, who would grow up to become Maud West, was illegitimate.[43] The birth hadn't been registered for five weeks, so there had been time for the father to step forward, but no one had. The same thing happened six years later when Alice, evidently Edith's sister, was born.[44]

To be caught out once was one thing, but twice? That smacked of the kind of wilful abandon that, decades later, policewomen would be hired to crack down on. Maybe Mary Ann was a modern woman who wanted children but not a man; maybe she didn't want children but liked the way they were made; maybe she'd had a couple of run-ins with over-entitled employers. There was, however, another possibility. It was well known that the common-law wives of London mariners often supplemented their incomes by attending to the needs of sex-starved sailors when their own menfolk were away at sea.[45] There was no evidence of a common-law husband in Mary Ann's case, but Deptford offered plenty of opportunities for a quick and lucrative fumble in the dark alleys and rowdy taverns that littered the cramped, dockside streets.

As such, the chances of identifying Edith's father were slim to non-existent – the likelihood was that she didn't know herself – but the reality remained that, in Victorian eyes, she had arrived into the world stained with sin, doomed to spend her life marked by a stigma that was not of her making. In the eyes of the law, she had no father, so who could blame her for making one up, whether that was the sailor who would give her legitimacy at the altar or the solicitor/barrister with all his attendant relatives, who would provide the intellectual and social cachet she required to succeed as a detective?

The Fatal Letter

BY MAUD WEST

One December evening I was about to leave my office. I was, in fact, closing the door behind me when a grey-haired, silk-hatted gentleman ran from the lift almost into my arms.

'Can I do something?' I asked.

'I want Miss West,' he said. 'And at once. There is not a moment to be lost!'

'I am Miss West,' I said. 'Come in, but remember,' I added with a smile, 'more haste, less speed.'

Seated in my office he made me acquainted with these rather startling facts:

He was a solicitor, and acted for a well-known city gentleman, for whose wife he also did certain business. About a month before, the gentleman had informed him that he suspected his wife of carrying on an *affaire* with another man, and had instructed the solicitor to obtain the necessary evidence of misconduct, and, when this was secured, to write him at once in order that divorce proceedings might be immediately taken.

In the meantime, the gentleman, after giving some excuse to his wife to cover his absence, had left his home and was living just outside London.

The solicitor had obtained the necessary evidence, and

had written, on this very day, a letter to the husband setting out in detail exactly what his wife had been doing, and making suggestions for the best means of obtaining definite evidence of the misconduct.

Strangely enough, on the same day, it had become necessary for the solicitor to write to the wife with regard to certain securities which he was negotiating for her, and, at six o'clock that evening, to his horror the lawyer had discovered that the letter written to the husband had been sealed up in the envelope addressed to the wife and posted! Delivery of this letter would mean that the wife would know exactly what was happening and could take steps to cover her tracks and stop the necessary evidence being secured.

'Delivery of that letter must be stopped somehow,' said the solicitor, wiping the perspiration from his brow. 'I don't care how you do it but it must be done. I will pay anything if you can stop that letter from reaching the hands of Mrs—'

I promised nothing, but I informed him that I would do my utmost. It seemed hopeless in the short time at my disposal, but I said that I thought there was a chance.

He went off despairingly; then, sitting at my desk, I tried to formulate some plan by which I might achieve my object.

Eventually I got an idea. I sat down at the telephone and summoned every operative that I had in London.

An hour afterwards twelve of them met me in my office, and I instructed them that somehow, within the next two hours, they must obtain for me the names and addresses of three servants employed in the wife's house, and also the names and addresses of their mothers or fathers or nearest relative.

At nine o'clock that night one of my men rang up. He had been successful in obtaining the name and address of the parlourmaid, and also that of her mother, who lived at Ealing. Twenty minutes later I was on my way to Ealing, and one hour later, after a banknote had changed hands, the parlourmaid's mother had sent a wire to her daughter saying that she must return home immediately without fail.

At ten o'clock the parlourmaid arrived, who, after another conversation, agreed to my request.

Next morning, at 7.30, I presented myself at the wife's house armed with a letter from the parlourmaid, informing the housekeeper that she could not return for a few days owing to her mother's severe illness, but was sending a deputy, who was, of course, myself.

I can be very ingratiating when I choose, and after I had arrived I immediately got on the right side of the housekeeper, and then proceeded to tell her that I believed that I had worked for her mistress (the wife) years before in Shropshire. The housekeeper argued that this could not be so, and after some talk she agreed that I might take up Mrs—'s early morning tea and letters, so that I could see if I was right!

I had hoped that I should have the opportunity of removing the letter – which bore the name of the firm of solicitors on the back of the envelope – on my way upstairs, but, unfortunately, the housekeeper accompanied me to show me Mrs—'s room. As she opened the bedroom door for me – for I was carrying the tray – I saw my one chance. There was a fire burning in the bedroom.

I put down the tray on a table, said good morning to Mrs—, who was awake, drew the curtains, and then, taking up the pile of letters walked towards the bed. As I passed the fireplace I slipped, and shoved the top letter – the fatal letter – into the fire. The thousand to one chance had come off!

And I think that the first-class 'telling off' which I got from Mrs—, and secondly from the housekeeper, and the burn – the mark of which I still have on my arm – were well worthwhile when I remember the sigh of relief of the solicitor when I was able to telephone him that the 'fatal letter' had been burned – unread.[46]

Chapter Twelve

The Wrong Man

To know how to watch, to know
how to wait – these are the
corner-stones of our work.

Maud West, 1926[1]

Maud might have enjoyed a long and successful marriage, but her business was largely dependent on the failure of others to do the same. For all the blackmail, missing people and scam artists, a good part of her work would always be divorce investigations. Much of this work would have come via family solicitors, but some of her advertising efforts were clearly designed to attract the unhappily married direct to her door, as her details appeared in theatre programmes and hotel brochures – the kind of places one might find oneself either on an outing with a tedious spouse or dallying with a more exciting prospect.[2]

Although Maud actively pursued divorce clients, she didn't take the subject lightly. As she wrote in 1930:

Each case of divorce is a tragedy. Behind the formalities of the law lies a human story; human suffering and doubt, and possibly much loneliness in someone's future life.[3]

The article was called 'Who is to blame in divorce?' Having witnessed the fallout from so many broken relationships, she was in a good position to offer an opinion on the matter. Although wary of being too simplistic, she nevertheless placed most of the blame on the shoulders of men:

> Sometimes I am amazed at man! He will, for the most obscure reasons, prefer the light attractions of some will-o-the-wisp of love against the deep and constant devotion of a charming and trustful wife.

Yet she also believed that men were often biologically incapable of resisting the impulse to stray. Man bore, she said, a heavy cross:

> A cross which consists of an indefinable weakness in his sex make-up; a failing which, in a great majority of cases absolutely prevents him from treading the narrow path where happiness lies.

As for women? 'An infinitesimal minority' struck her 'as being persons from whom any man would seek to escape', but the majority of her criticism was aimed at those who failed to take into account their husbands' propensity for will-o-the-wisps:

> These women, often egotistical and selfish, fail as wives, for they have not learned the rule of adapting the home life to the needs of a man and of making him reliant and dependent upon them – as wives, as homemakers – for happiness.

Considering her own situation, it was a curious attitude to take, but she was adamant that such women deserved everything they got when their husbands turned to 'a more feminine and sympathetic type' for the comforts lacking at home. She reserved further scorn for women who pushed gender equality too far. This, she said, could give their husbands 'a repressed complex against women generally' leading to resentment and hostility.

In 1919, she had sent a dispatch from the front line of the sex war to prove her point. Under the heading 'Why Sex Hate Is Growing', she described instances in which female clients' infuriation and frustration over gender inequality had spilled over into uncontrolled rage aimed at their bemused and confused husbands. One had nursed mounting resentment week after week as her husband hosted Sunday evening gatherings for his male friends, until one evening she rushed into the room to hurl abuse and a good number of ornaments at the group. Her husband agreed to a separation, but she told Maud she wanted more: '. . . cannot I do anything to get rid of the beast altogether? It drives me mad to think that I am tied to him. I don't want to be any man's property!'[4]

Maud also reported a lecture she had heard whilst on kleptomania watch at a private house. The speaker was a furious French 'advocate of the sex war' who felt that the granting of votes to women was no more than a placatory measure by the patriarchy:

> 'We women are like hungry wolves following a travelling sleigh on the snow!' she shrieked. 'The people in the sleigh fling out whatever food they have to stay the onrush of the wolves, but that only keeps the wolves off for a time. When there is nothing more to fling to them they overwhelm the travellers, and that is what we shall do. We shall overwhelm the men and they shall occupy in the future social structures of the world an even lower place than they have given us, their slaves.'

Maud was not impressed.

Perhaps she preferred her feminism more grounded in reality. After all, her job involved problem solving, seeking solutions, and working with what was in front of her – and what she must have seen was that, although a great shift in women's lives was afoot, the ones who benefited most were those who could afford to take risks. The economic and social reality for the majority of married women was that they relied on male breadwinners to provide for them and their children. As such, it was best not to rock the boat *too* much.

That didn't mean that she was against divorce. 'There can be no question, in my mind,' she wrote, 'that divorce is a good thing . . . [It] is usually the *only* remedy which enables some unhappy people to hope.'[5]

She must have welcomed, therefore, the two pieces of legislation passed during the 1920s that made divorce more accessible to those unhappy folk. The first was the Matrimonial Causes Act of 1923, which allowed women to pursue divorce on the basis of their husband's adultery alone. No longer were they required to prove additional causes such as rape or domestic violence. Due to the trauma of testifying about such matters (if they were true) or the bother of fabricating them (if they were blessedly absent), there had always been fewer women than men petitioning for divorce. In 1924, however, the figure hit fifty per cent for the first time and continued to gradually rise until it reached a peak of sixty per cent in 1927 and 1928. From that point on, with a few exceptional years mostly during the Second World War, wives would remain the most common party to instigate divorce proceedings.[6]

The second change in the law came with the Judicial Proceedings (Regulation of Reports) Act 1926, which attempted to curtail the prurience of the press by prohibiting the publication of evidence from any divorce trial or other marital dispute, other than the basic details of the petition and the judge's summary.

It was still a flawed system. As the writer and parliamentarian A. P. Herbert said in his satirical novel *Holy Deadlock* in 1934:

> If you violently knock your wife about every night the ordinary person will conclude that you have not much affection for her; but the law requires you to prove it by sleeping with another woman . . . It would be the same if you were certified a

lunatic: or became a habitual and besotted drunkard: or were sentenced for embezzlement ... or were found guilty of murder ... Such trifles mean nothing to the divorce laws of this Christian country. Adultery, misconduct, intimacy or nothing – that's the rule.[7]

One solicitor pointed out in the *Sphere* in 1932 that this absurd situation was unique to Britain: 'Disease, habitual drunkenness, and cruelty are considered good and sufficient reasons for divorce in other countries.'[8] But Britain was peculiarly hung up on sex and couldn't bring itself to entirely abandon its ancient ecclesiastical ideas about divorce ('Thou *shalt* break the Seventh Commandment')[9] in favour of something more fitting to modern lives. Many, such as A. P. Herbert, were campaigning for further reform, but, for the time being, the rules were set and everyone had to abide by them.

Some people tried to play the system, by spending an awkward night at a hotel with a friend of the opposite sex before directing their spouse's solicitor towards the establishment's visitor book, for example. But, unless handled carefully, this could lead to charges of collusion or perjury. It was much easier to hire a professional who knew how to gain, or manufacture, evidence that would satisfy the courts whilst avoiding any legal pitfalls. Private detectives not only knew how to spin innocent situations into scenes of debauchery, but, as John Goodwin reported, also had co-respondents on their books ready to go: 'Should a husband wish to give his wife the usual evidence, the detective will undertake to "find the lady." She (bless her!) is a professional co-respondent and her alias is "a woman unknown."'[10]

Maud was aggrieved by such slurs on her profession. 'So long as private detectives are engaged in bringing criminals to justice they are regarded as public servants,' she wrote. 'The moment their inquiries relate to divorce or other matrimonial troubles there is a tendency in some quarters to label them as despicable hirelings.' The job of the private detective, she said, was to establish the facts and nothing more:

> He is not 'paid to get evidence.' His investigations often prove happily the innocence rather than the guilt of the suspected party. Personally I always find pleasure in removing any unwarranted suspicions which might threaten to break up family life. At the same time, though it is no part of my duty to act as a censor of morals, I am still frail enough to find satisfaction in bringing to justice either men or women who aggravate their matrimonial offence by calculated cruelty.[11]

How this insistence on truthfulness worked in practice was hard to see. Although a few of her clients may have been thrilled to discover their partners were models of fidelity, most surely had their minds set on divorce and merely needed a detective to provide the evidence required by the courts.

Gathering such evidence, Maud said, was 'particularly arduous and exacting': not only did it involve persistent shadowing, which I was beginning to realize was her least favourite part of the job, but such surveillance was frequently unproductive. Tellingly, she didn't say what she did when shadowing failed to provide results.

Occasionally, matters resolved themselves in unexpected ways. In 1937, *The Times* reported a case in which a detective named Richard Rogers, having failed to get evidence against a woman in her native Belgium, returned to London and withdrew from the case. He immediately returned to Zeebrugge, introduced himself to the wife and 'made violent love to her'. It was the beginning of a torrid affair. In the end, a fresh set of detectives was hired and Rogers was named as the co-defendant in the divorce case for which he had initially been hired.[12]

Most detectives, however, preferred to retain their fees and looked for more reliable ways of getting results. One such method came to light in 1905, when one of Henry Slater's lady detectives had befriended the stubbornly faithful wife of a prospective divorce client in order to persuade her to loosen her morals. The pair had travelled to Lausanne together, where the detective had introduced the wife to a young Italian medical student and positively pushed them towards a dirty weekend in Paris.[13]

Another option was to stitch up a random acquaintance, as happened in the case of Percy and Alice Richards, which reached court in November 1919. The two detectives involved were given a severe dressing down by the judge for their underhand behaviour. Both worked for Maud, and one was her husband. For all her fine words, it seemed that Maud wasn't entirely innocent of the more grubby tactics employed in divorce inquiries.

Percy and Alice Richards lived in a large semi-detached house in Grosvenor Road, Church End, just around the corner from the Elliott family home. They had been married since 1906 and had one daughter. Percy had spent most of his career as a commercial traveller, but now, at forty, he had a desk job at the Admiralty, having recently received a commission in the Royal Naval Reserve.

The marriage had been a happy one for the first two years. But, reading between the lines of their testimony in court, it had quickly slid into an uncomfortable mix of resentment and indifference. Percy had abandoned Alice briefly in 1910. He had only been away for three weeks, but during that time had enjoyed an affair at an Eastbourne hotel with a wealthy widow. Alice had forgiven him, but Percy still craved freedom. He eventually left for good at the beginning of 1916. To get a divorce, however, which Alice did not want, Percy needed evidence of his wife's adultery. This he found – or manufactured – with the help of his local lady detective.

Their patsy was a local chimney sweep called Charles Bryant, who had worked for the Richards for six years. By all accounts, he was a happily married man. In court, the first insinuation came from one of the Richards' neighbours, who claimed that Bryant's cart was frequently parked outside the house in Grosvenor Road ('We were very sorry for the horse . . . It was very cold standing there all day.').[14] In response, Bryant pointed out that he swept between fourteen and fifteen chimneys a day on top of other work, and didn't have time for dalliances.

One of those chimneys, incidentally, was at Pearley in nearby Finchley Avenue, which made for an awkward moment when Harry appeared as a witness to describe what he had seen at the Richards' house on 22 February 1916. He and his colleague Leslie Howard had been smuggled into the house through a window by Percy, after which they concealed themselves in the attic. According to Harry, Bryant arrived shortly after eleven. Incriminating snippets of conversation floated up the stairs, including the statement by Alice, 'I told Percy to sling his b— hook.' In the late afternoon, they crept downstairs and looked through a crack in the dining room door. There, Harry testified, they saw Alice sitting on a chair with Charles Bryant kneeling beside her, his arm draped around her neck. They were professing their devotion to one another in a scene that wouldn't have been out of place in a two-bit melodrama:

WOMAN: You are my own true darling, aren't you, Charlie? Are you always true to me?

SWEEP: Of course I am, darling. Are you always true to me?

The judge, Sir Thomas Horridge, rarely hid his contempt for private detectives. On one occasion, he declared that 'There is nobody in the world whose opinion I have so little respect for as a private detective',[15] so it was no surprise that after hearing from all parties in the Richards case, he said:

I am quite satisfied that this woman never committed adultery at all, and I am perfectly shocked at the lies of these two assistants of the woman who keeps a detective agency. They have come here and both of them lied to me about what took place on that occasion.[16]

He dismissed Percy's petition and awarded costs and a decree nisi to Alice, along with custody of their daughter. Thanks to the sensational mix of an officer's wife, a chimney sweep and unreliable testimony from private detectives, the judge's comments were widely reported – no doubt much to everyone's embarrassment.

Maud's most high-profile case, however, came some years later, in 1933. It involved the Scottish baronet Lord Inverclyde and his second wife June, an actress. This was high society at its most glamorous and, from a research point of view, it was perfect: not only did the case attract extensive coverage in the press, but June had also written about the experience in her memoirs. Between the two, it was possible to build a comprehensive picture of how Maud and her team went about gathering evidence and what it was like to be on the receiving end of that attention and the public scrutiny at the subsequent trial.

Alan Inverclyde was the grandson of the founder of the Cunard shipping line, although he only took a nominal interest in the family business. He was an adventurer at heart, taking his steam yacht *Sapphire* to India and Malaya in the mid-1920s, and then the *Beryl* on an exhaustive tour of the crumbling ruins of the Mediterranean a few years later.

His wife was born June Tripp, but by the late 1920s she was famous enough to be known simply by her screen name, *June*. Her parents were both actors, and she had been on the stage since childhood. At the age of ten, she had danced alongside the Russian prima ballerina Anna Pavlova;[17] as an adult, she split her time between the theatre and silent films. Her most famous role was as Daisy Bunting, the original Hitchcock blonde, hamming it up in a wig opposite Ivor Novello in Hitchcock's first thriller, *The Lodger: A Story of the London Fog,* in 1927.

The pair had met in the summer of 1928 at a party on board the *Beryl* at Antibes, where Inverclyde was broodily licking his wounds after the break-up of his marriage to the young and glamorous Olive Sainsbury. By the following spring, they were married and living at Inverclyde's family home, Castle Wemyss, on the shore of the Firth of Clyde.

It was clear from the start that it had been a mistake. Alan disliked June's theatre friends and complained that she talked about being a chorus girl in front of the servants; June discovered that Alan's broodiness was not due to a broken heart but an irredeemable part of his character.[18] Barely a year after the wedding, June asked for a divorce: 'I want my freedom to earn my own living again. *Please.* All you have to do is go away with a woman for a few days. Is this too much to ask?'

It was. Alan replied, 'You will never have any reason to divorce me. I shall bide my time until I obtain grounds for divorcing you. And I do not think I shall have long to wait.'[19]

He did wait, however. For over two years. In the meantime, June left Castle Wemyss and attempted to get the marriage annulled. Her petition stated that Alan was incapable of consummating the marriage and, in the legal terminology of the time, that this incapacity was 'incurable by art or skill.'[20] This was dismissed. She asked for an allowance of £5,000 unconditional on her behaviour. Inverclyde refused. She next obtained a divorce in Reno, Nevada in order to marry the Hollywood director Lothar Mendes, but the wedding was called off when she realized she would still be guilty of bigamy under English law. She returned to Europe.

In 1932, Inverclyde made his move. He instructed his solicitor, who, in turn, instructed Maud to set her watchers on to June. They started in Paris. In her memoir *The Glass Ladder*, June recalled dodging Inverclyde's detectives with her friend Pepé de Landa:

> Like children ringing doorbells and running away, Pepé and I would get out of a taxi at the Vendôme entrance to the Ritz, scoot through the hotel and out of the Rue Cambon door. In separate vehicles we would drive to out-of-the-way inns in the country, meet for a quick aperitif, leave together, and go to one or another *maison particulière* in the Avenue de la Grand Armée, and, having been admitted, peer through a crack in the high carved door until two men in a familiar black Citroën had lit cigarettes and settled back for a long wait. Then we would sally forth, hailing a cruising taxi, and take a circuitous route to the Meurice, where I was stopping, and there say goodbye.[21]

After six days of this, she said, the black Citroën was gone. The co-respondent in the case would not be Pepé, however, but Tony Paanakker, whom she described as 'a big, blond, exuberant Dutchman with a wealthy American wife, a house in Paris, and a burning desire to make his name as an impresario.'[22] At the time, this desire was focused on June as the actress he wanted to play the lead in a new play, *Ballerina*.

When June returned to London to appear in *Over the Page* at the Alhambra theatre, Paanakker followed. Whilst the *Ballerina* script was being developed, she said, he would pick her up from her dressing room after the evening performance, 'rush me into his green, foreign car and drive me to my flat, talking shop all the way.' There, after supper, they would 'light cigarettes, make drinks and settle down to read, discuss, and sometimes battle over the script.'[23]

Maud, however, had suspicions that there was more going on than business negotiations. Her staff were watching the pair's every move. June was quite aware of this:

> . . . if I were in a light enough mood I would pause beside a
> ratty-looking little man who stood beside a lamp-post reading
> a newspaper through dark glasses. 'Good morning, Alphonse,'
> I would smile . . . I could see his little eyes sliding towards me
> behind the glasses. He never answered me.

Perhaps that was because his name wasn't Alphonse, as would become evident at the trial. But Maud hadn't just posted a man under a street lamp. Every night, June wrote, 'there was always the same nondescript dark car posted on the corner almost opposite my front door with two men in the front seat.' If she was with Paanakker, it would remain there until he left. Otherwise, it would leave soon after she returned home.

June said that she was careful never to bring any actual lovers back to her flat for a nightcap, but was confident that her professional relationship with Paanakker would not be misconstrued, especially as she had a butler and maid on hand who could attest to the innocence of their meetings.

When June received copies of Maud's reports from her solicitor in the spring of 1933, however, she found a description of her passionately kissing Paanakker on her doorstep, after which he drove to a nearby garage to park his car, returned to the flat, and didn't reappear until daylight. Yet, June said, Paanakker was in Berlin at the time, and the man had been her brother Suthie, who had borrowed Paanakker's car to take her to the Café de Paris for a much-needed night out. When Suthie dropped her back home, she saw the detectives' car parked in its usual place. As she claimed to have written in her diary: 'The car was there again and suddenly my nerves gave way. I was awful, blubbering like an infant. S garaged P's car and I talked all night. Last memory: poor S nodding on the chaise-longue. Must apologise.'[24]

She also said that the house butler who served her set of flats was approached in a local pub by one of Maud's team, plied with beer and promised payment if he would testify against her. 'Another sleuth,' she wrote, 'paid court to one of the housemaids, perhaps with the same objective, but to quote the girl, "I wasn't 'aving any."'

The trial began on Tuesday, 14 November 1933 at Parliament House in Edinburgh. It was scheduled to last four days but spilled over into the following week. The public gallery was packed throughout. Maud was there, along with her team of detectives, ready to give evidence against June.

The first day opened with Baron Inverclyde's testimony, followed by that of the Parisian detective Charles Courtois, Harry and his colleague Henry Howard Stephens. On the Wednesday, Maud gave evidence herself alongside three more of her assistants and two garage attendants they had located in the course of their inquiries. The assistants were named as James Black, Mrs Langford and Cecil Elliott. I hadn't come across any of them before. Presumably, Cecil was one of Harry's many relatives from Hackney, interesting in itself, but what about the others? I made a note to check them out, along with Harry's co-conspirator in the Richards case, and Stephens and Courtois.

The Thursday and Friday were given over to June's defence, which, in her words, was delivered in front of 'row upon row of sensation-seekers'.[25] This was confirmed by the *Edinburgh Evening News*, which added that the crowd consisted mainly of women who 'assembled in force in the main corridor' when the court adjourned for lunch. There were so many hoping to gain access to the afternoon proceedings that the court police struggled to keep them under control. The scene, the paper reported, 'was one of the most extraordinary witnessed in Parliament House for many a day.'[26]

After testimony from her maid, her brother Suthie, her dresser at the Alhambra, the former steward of her block of flats and her solicitor, June was called to give evidence. Paanakker had declined to appear, claiming he was 'broke' and couldn't afford the journey from Paris.[27] As June made her way to the courtroom, she heard a young barrister call out to another, 'Let's go and watch the little Inverclyde being crucified!'[28]

It was unquestionably a long and painful ordeal. She was in the witness box for three and a half hours on the Friday morning and then cross-examined by Inverclyde's barrister for most of the afternoon. The closing speeches had to be postponed until the following week.

Many regional and national newspapers had sent special correspondents to cover the case. As they were prohibited from publishing any evidence from the ongoing trial under the Judicial Proceedings Act of 1926, their reports were initially limited to the basic details of the allegations and a list of each day's witnesses. The Act didn't, however, apply to judges' summaries, and the judge in the Inverclyde case, Lord Fleming, was particularly thorough in this respect. As soon as he delivered his verdict on 22 December, papers throughout the country produced pages of special reports.

There was widespread criticism of Paanakker's failure to attend the trial, leaving June to defend the case alone. No one believed his pleas of poverty. Maud had established that he had a flat in Piccadilly, often stayed at the Berkeley Hotel and his home in Paris was in one of the best residential districts. Furthermore, he usually travelled by air and dined at the most exclusive restaurants.

It also appeared that he had duped June as to how much he could help her career. They had met on a theatrical train from Manchester to London in the spring of 1932 and soon afterwards June had signed a contract authorizing him to negotiate film deals on her behalf. But, as emerged at the trial, his day job was as president of a French company dealing in Stetson hats and he had no contacts in the movie industry. Inverclyde's barristers had suggested that this contract, and the plans for *Ballerina*, 'were merely a "blind" to ingratiate himself with the defender and give him the opportunity of enjoying her society.'[29]

And enjoy it he did. Maud and her employees had followed Paanakker and June for seven often wet and miserable weeks in the autumn of 1932. They worked around the clock, with a minimum of two detectives on duty at all times, sometimes as many as five. When shadowing June from the theatre at night, it seemed they worked in a team of four, ready to follow on foot or by car as necessary. When watching the flat, they might stay outside from midnight to eight or nine o'clock in the morning. During the seven weeks, they witnessed the pair leave the theatre together on sixteen occasions, dine at a restaurant seven times and return to June's flat in Hertford Street eleven times. On five occasions, Paanakker spent 'practically the whole night' there. They noted that he had a key to the building.

Although there was some excitement when Paanakker and June had a row after June learned that she would not, after all, be cast in *Ballerina*, I was beginning to understand what Maud meant when she said shadowing was a tiresome business. Seven weeks of constant observation seemed excessive. But, as Lord Fleming explained, June's defence that on certain occasions the detectives had mistaken one of her neighbours for her, or her brother Suthie for Paanakker, or that Paanakker had left her flat at a reasonable

hour without the detectives noticing 'would have been a fatal criticism if the observations had been confined to one night . . .'[30]

As always, there was a question mark over the fact that private
detectives had been used at all. Harry had slipped up and claimed to
have witnessed something on a night his colleagues said he was not
on duty, which gave Lord Fleming 'some anxiety' about the amount
of collaboration that went into the detectives' reports.[31] As he said:

> It is obvious that a vitally important point in this case is whether
> the evidence of the detectives, generally speaking, can be relied
> on. It is a trite saying that such evidence must be carefully scru-
> tinised. On the other hand, it must be recognised that to lay
> down a rule that such evidence has to be disregarded would
> amount to a denial of justice in many cases.[32]

On balance, he decided Harry's blunder was not a vital matter,
and even went so far as to say, 'I was favourably impressed with
the way in which all the detectives gave their evidence.'[33]

Maud's team had done well. Inverclyde was granted his divorce,
but none of the parties emerged from the courtroom unscathed.
Inverclyde had shown himself to be vindictive in the way he pursued the matter, and June came across as a fame-obsessed strumpet.
As for Paanakker, it was generally agreed that he was the true vil-
lain of the piece. In his absence, he was ordered to pay the expenses
of both parties.

June, however, carried on like the trooper she was. On the evening of the verdict, she told the press that she did not intend to appeal: 'You can write "finis" to it,' she said before stepping onto the
stage as Cinderella at the Palace Theatre, Manchester. It was her very
first pantomime, and she received a standing ovation accompanied by
shouts of 'Good old June!' from the back of the circle.[34] Four years
later, she married an American millionaire and moved to Beverly Hills.

*

The Richards and Inverclyde cases had given me hope that I might find out more about the team Maud employed. It was unusual to have so many detectives named in court reports; usually, they were just anonymous figures tacked onto the end of news items with the words 'An inquiry agent also gave evidence.' But here I had six new names to investigate. Unfortunately, Mrs Langford seemed determined to stay in the shadows; likewise Henry Howard Stephens and Charles Courtois, and all I could establish about Leslie Howard was that he was unlikely to be the famous actor of the same name. I did find a James Black working as a constable in the Metropolitan Police in 1927, so it was possible that he, like so many other policemen, had moved into detective work after retirement.[35]

Cecil Elliott, however, was a different matter. I was sure he belonged to Harry's extended family somehow, so I pored through census data and vital registers, ordered birth certificates and generated mounds of notes and family trees. Most of it ended up in the bin, but what was left was astonishing.

Cecil *was* related to Harry, although in a more direct way than I had anticipated. He was Harry and Edith's son. Their daughter Evelyn may have been a relatively late-life baby, but she wasn't an only child. Cecil had been born on 7 March 1902, a respectable nine months and thirteen days after Edith and Harry got married. But that was just the beginning. There was also another daughter, Vera, born in 1904, then a son, Denis, in 1907; two more boys followed – Keith and Neville in 1908 and 1910 respectively – and that was all until Evelyn arrived in 1913.[36]

Six children. I'd been impressed that Maud had managed to raise one child whilst carrying on her work, but six? Just the thought was exhausting. In 1905, when she claimed to have started working as a detective full-time, she would have had two toddlers waiting for her at home. By the time her first 'Maud West' advertisements appeared in 1909, Cecil would have been seven, Vera five, Denis a terrible two and Keith a wobbly and curious ten months. And, as I had already noted, when her staff was depleted during the First World War and Harry's health disintegrated, Evelyn would have been at peak tantrum age.

None of this could have been made any easier by the fact that the Elliotts were always on the move. According to the addresses on the children's birth certificates, between 1902 and 1913 the family took in much of south London, before they settled at Pearley. After starting off in Brockley Rise, they moved to Forest Hill, Deptford, Putney, Twickenham, Fulham and Willesden. School records suggested stops in Lewisham and East Sheen as well. In total, I counted eleven addresses in as many years, and there were probably more.

There were also clues that money was tight. When I located the family in the 1911 census, they didn't seem to have any home at all. Harry was toiling as a pit hand at a colliery in County Durham where his brother and former partner-in-crime Alfred was an electrician; nine-year-old Cecil was with Harry's parents in Hackney, and Edith and the rest of the children were staying with her sister Alice and her husband Geoffrey Palmer in Ilford.

Curiously, there was another guest in Ilford that night: a thirteen-year-old girl called Nellie Barber. Was this the same person as Helen Barber, the housekeeper at Pearley? Another daughter, perhaps, born out of wedlock? Edith would have been around seventeen at the time Nellie was born. Also, thinking of Pearley, where did Fake Charles, the man masquerading as Harry's brother, fit into all this? Was he one of her children, too?

Six – seven? eight? – children, an enigmatic housekeeper, an imposter, an invalid husband and a sleuth with a hidden past? Maud West may not have been the spinster lady detective she claimed, but she was more than making up for it now. All I needed was a corpse, and I'd have the makings of a first-rate mystery novel.

A Poisonous Revenge

BY MAUD WEST

A woman client was ushered into my office one day obviously labouring under acute mental excitement. She said she had had a terrible morning and thought someone had been following her. Experience has taught me that one of the most common forms of delusion is the idea that the sufferer is being shadowed, but her intelligent recital of events caused me to find out whether she had actually been tracked to my office.

I changed into a somewhat loud plus-four suit, with a huge rakish cap, and leaving the office we went down a small side street, turned sharply to the left, and hid in a doorway. A few seconds later hurried footsteps approached and passed on. I took a glance at the individual and described him to my client. 'That's the man,' she exclaimed.

As we left the building I perceived the same fellow lounging against a lamp-post talking to a taxicab-driver. We there and then determined to have a little fun at his expense. Boarding an omnibus we went to a West End store. We spent the rest of the morning in a West End store, went to a restaurant for lunch, took a tube train and passed away the afternoon at a matinee. After the show I thought we should have no further use for our shadower – I had already studied him carefully – but by a trick of feminine cruelty I changed my mind and decided not to lose him. So we involved him in a taxicab drive to West Kensington to the flat of a friend with whom we took tea. Then we left by the back door. Three hours later I learned by telephone that the weary looking individual was still haunting the vicinity!

My client had warned me that the people we were dealing with would stick at nothing to gain their ends. Briefly, she had become an innocent victim to a huge scheme of distributing spurious notes. On learning the real facts, she had tried to break away from the gang but they had told her she was too far involved to back out and that if she 'squealed' her life would be forfeit. If the gang had definitely traced her to my office, my own life would not be worth much, either.

Eventually my client was able to substantiate her information in the proper quarter, and I take no credit for bringing the leading spirits of this dangerous gang to book. I learned, however, that two of the gang still at liberty had been charged with the duty of dealing severely with the 'squealer' and her inquiry agent.

I was soon to hear from them. About a week after the ringleaders had been sentenced I was in my office when a visitor was announced. Following my usual practice I scrutinised him through an aperture. Instantly I recognised – my shadower! He had shaved off his moustache and instead of his untidy clothing he was now immaculate. I told my secretary to inform him that I should not be back for some time.

Half an hour later a loudly dressed woman entered the office and asked for me in a fussy and important manner.

She was admitted, only to be followed by the immaculate one.

To my great surprise he made no attempt at violence. 'So we meet, Miss West,' he said in a cultured voice. 'Let me assure you I am delighted at the meeting.' Then, with a quick change of tone, he said sharply to his woman companion, 'Come on, let's go.'

Obviously, they had only wished to establish my identity for future reference. That they intended me harm was apparent. I realised I must walk warily and wait.

To this day I believe those crooks were responsible for the shock I received the next day. Reading my morning papers I was staggered to learn of my woman client's death. She had been a drug-taker for some time and was found dead in bed from an overdose of veronal.

Though a verdict of 'Accidental Death' was returned at the inquest, I am still certain that she was a victim of foul play. I had been with her on the evening before her death and she then spoke optimistically of the happy times ahead when we had secured the imprisonment of the rest of the gang.

Soon afterwards I had to go to Sheffield on another case. By some means, which I have never been able to discover, the news reached my enemies. All unknown to myself, they traced me to the hotel where I was staying. I had a slight cold at the time, and awakening during the night with a severe thirst, reached out for the electric light switch, intending to take a drink from the water bottle which stood at my bedside. As I did so the habit of close observation saved my life. Sleepy though I was, I noticed before retiring that the pattern on the inverted tumbler over the water bottle coincided with those at my own home. As I touched the tumbler now I saw that the pattern was different.

Immediately I became alert. A damp mark on the table showed that the water bottle had been moved half an inch since I had gone to bed, and the tumbler contained a smear of semi-transparent substance. On analysis later it revealed sufficient poison to have removed me very effectively.

Finger-prints on the glass and water bottle, which were photographed, enabled the police to identify the person responsible for the attempted murder. In fact the culprit, unaware of my discovery, was still staying at the hotel awaiting another opportunity to take my life. He proved to be an ex-convict who had apparently undertaken to remove me from this world in return for a sum of money.

Wondering whether the gang would leave me alone after this, I returned to London, but soon found them as determined as ever. One afternoon I received a telephone call from a woman who asked whether I could leave town at once with a male assistant. I replied that if the matter was urgent it could be managed. She gave me her name and address, a country house in Lincolnshire, and it was arranged that I should travel by car and be prepared, if necessary, to stay for a few days. Having confirmed the fact that a woman of that name did occupy the house mentioned, I left my office in a saloon car, accompanied by one of my assistants. As I wished to make a call at my home we went by way of Hampstead Heath.

Suddenly while passing over the Heath my driver accelerated and drew close to the curb. There was a terrific roar from the klaxon of a huge car as it attempted to pass us at top speed. Instinctively we glanced in its direction and as we did so the inside of our own car was lit up by a blinding flash. Before we had time to recover there was a loud, revolver-like report, followed by the shattering of both our windows.

The car raced on. I discovered that my hands and wrists were badly cut, while my assistant had a deep cut in his face, caused by a splinter of glass. I urged the driver to go in pursuit at all speed. We took such cover as we could on the floor of the car. I concluded as we raced along that the journey on which we were bent was another plan of the gangsters to lure us out to the open road. The stipulation that I should take a male assistant was simply a ruse to allay any suspicion.

As we approached the road junction where we were to branch off, the big car again loomed up alongside. Keeping abreast with us for a few yards, a passenger seated in front menaced my driver with a revolver and signalled him to stop. To gain time he slowed down. The other car did the same, and two men prepared to descend before the cars came to rest.

At that moment my driver seized his opportunity. Throwing the car into low gear he accelerated, and, changing up quickly, was away. Exactly what happened behind us I can only conjecture. Presumably the men were thrown into the road. We did not stop to inquire, but dashed on at top speed. Just as we were beginning to congratulate ourselves that we were clear at last, I saw through the back of the car two blinding headlights which were rapidly overhauling us.

At this moment, owing to a dip in the road, we found ourselves facing one of those rolling clouds of fog, so frequently found on the lower levels, while behind us the way was comparatively clear. My driver instinctively applied his brakes in order to take this dip at a safer speed.

The driver of the gangster's car, not realising the true reason for it, was apparently disconcerted by the sudden application of our brakes. He swerved quickly to the off-side, but, failing to pass between us and a lamp standard in the centre of the road, struck the standard with a terrific crash.

By this time we had had sufficient excitement for the evening, yet were bound to investigate what had happened. It was evident that we need have no further apprehension. The driver died before the ambulance arrived. The two men in the car presented a ghastly sight, although not seriously injured. By the time they had recovered sufficiently to attend court it was learned that they were wanted on a number of charges, and in the end, to my relief, they were put behind high walls for seven years.[37]

Chapter Thirteen

Sweet Danger

Always I have had the action, excitement, and
adventure which I craved. Without the risks and
pitfalls of my profession I could not have carried
on. They have made it worthwhile.

Maud West, 1931[1]

In 1926, Maud declared: 'To be shot at in the street is something
for which one must be prepared . . .'[2] But was it? *Really?* It was
evident that guns played a significant role in her public persona.
The piece announcing her unorthodox ghost-hunting trip in the
Sunday Post, for example, had said:

> Miss West's experiences have taught her to be prepared for any
> emergency, and she early discovered that an essential accom-
> plishment of a lady detective was to be a proficient revolver
> shot. By dint of much practice she has become one of the best
> lady shots in the country.[3]

Other detectives, too, made a point of flashing their weapons
at the press. Even Kate Easton had said in 1907, 'The last time I
used my revolver was to defend myself from a woman who tried to
throw vitriol at me. I pointed it at her and she fled!' She did, however, add a codicil: 'Between you and me, it was not loaded.'[4]

It was all good publicity, but how likely was it that Maud always
kept a little automatic pistol hidden in a drawer in her office and
a revolver about her person, as she claimed? Before 1920, as long

as one wasn't obviously drunk or insane, anyone over the age of eighteen could purchase a gun licence by handing over ten shillings at their local Post Office. In 1920, however, the law was tightened up, in part to deal with all the excess weapons in civilian hands after the war. If anyone wanted to keep their gun, they had to convince the police that they had good reason to do so. One of the legitimate reasons was self-defence, but did this extend to private detectives, loathed as they were?

I was attempting, unsuccessfully, to find out, when it occurred to me that the ranks of private detectives were filled with ex-policemen – and policemen issued the permits. Surely those connections came into play here? I couldn't see that Maud or Kate would have had any problem wangling a gun licence with the assistance of their male staff.

As for how and where they might have practised their aim, there were a surprising number of shooting ranges scattered about central London. As well as those run by rifle clubs and the facilities hidden away in government buildings and private institutions, there were places where members of the public could hire a revolver and shoot away to their heart's content. One such business in St James's appeared in the press twice in the 1920s due to fatalities on its premises. As the first casualty was an art dealer and the second a man whose identity remained a mystery despite extensive police inquiries, it seemed that anyone could walk off the street for a spot of target practice in their lunch hour.[5]

But what about those situations when drawing a revolver would be inappropriate? Considering store detectives' experience of violent customers, I was sure that female private detectives also arranged some form of self-defence training before they took to the streets. How else could they have dealt with the 'heaps of annoyances' from bounders and drunkards that Maud said forced her to hide her sex under male disguise?[6] Some of the places they visited – I thought of Kate hiding out in the brothel – must have put them at risk of sexual assault.

Maud seemed to have acquired a hefty right hook from somewhere. 'I did hit a man once, and in no less a place than a few yards from Bond Street,' she admitted in 1926. This display of unladylike behaviour had apparently arisen out of a routine bit of surveillance in which her prey had made a run for it and then grabbed her as she chased him around a corner:

> For a minute I stood panting, taken off my guard, then I did the only thing that seemed possible. I drew back a little, doubled my right arm and landed out with it, punching him as hard as I could in the middle of his somewhat portly figure. He gave a yell of anguish and fury that travelled after me as I ran – ran right across Oxford Street, through the traffic, and promptly lost myself in some of the small streets the other side of that thoroughfare.[7]

I still took most of her stories with a pinch of salt, but when it came to minor adventures like these, that pinch was getting smaller the more I learned about private detectives and their work. Yes, Maud had form when it came to stealing ideas from the cinema, but she must have undertaken thousands of inquiries over the course of her career. Although most of those would have turned up little more than minor indiscretions, statistically she must have wandered into dangerous territory enough times to cobble together at least some adventures based on real life.

Besides, when discussing her work in more serious settings, such as during the debate on women in the police, she downplayed the risks involved but did not deny that they existed. 'The work is not sensational, as people who get their ideas of a detective's life from the kinema imagine,' she said, somewhat hypocritically, in an interview in 1924. 'There would, of course, be danger in criminal work but very little in ordinary work . . .' When danger came, she added, it was 'rather a relief from monotonous investigations.'[8]

She also made it clear in some of her own articles that these brief respites from the dull slog were few and far between:

> Watching and waiting can become dreadfully wearisome, for such things must be very much the same day after day, case after case . . . And yet – well, it has its big thrills, I admit. I've been a detective for nearly twenty years now, and in those years there have been 'moments'. Moments in which life was hanging by a thread; moments in which quickness of brain might represent success for some big coup.[9]

When it came to looking for 'moments' that other detectives had experienced, the problem, as ever, lay in the clandestine nature of the work. Private detectives could have been held up at gunpoint every day for all anyone would know. Such cases rarely came to court and, if they did, it was debatable whether anyone could expect any redress. As the *Globe* commented in 1911 after a case broke down in which a detective had been assaulted by a man he was shadowing, 'To be followed about and spied upon is provocation greater than human nature can be expected patiently to endure, and only a very strict moralist would blame the victim who retaliates with personal violence.'[10]

Exasperation did seem to be the most common excuse for assaulting a detective. One soon-to-be divorcee, after finding two on her doorstep, had stabbed at the neck of one with her lit cigarette before slamming the door on his hand. 'I won't see you, you dirty snakes in the grass,' she had hissed before she struck. The court sympathized with her but agreed that she had gone 'a little too far.'[11]

Divorce could arouse violent passions. Even when they weren't annoying anyone, detectives undertaking divorce inquiries could find themselves caught in the crossfire between warring spouses.

In 1920, for example, one detective had accompanied her female client to pick up some clothes from the marital hotel suite and stood by helpless as the husband pulled out a revolver and shot his wife through the head.[12]

This led me to wonder if any private detectives had ever been killed on the job. A ghoulish day spent looking through *The Times* and the British Newspaper Archive using every grisly keyword I could think of, from strangulation to dismemberment, yielded no results. But it did introduce me to the case of Laetitia Toureaux, whose body had been found in a Métro carriage in Paris on 16 May 1937. Her murder had caused a sensation in France, and to a lesser extent in Britain, due to the nature of the crime: not only was the victim young and beautiful, but it was a classic locked-room mystery. Laetitia had stepped into an empty first-class carriage at the Porte de Charenton Métro station just before the train departed at 6.27 p.m. Less than a minute later, the train drew into its next stop at Porte Dorée, where passengers entering the carriage found Laetitia slumped forward, a nine-inch dagger sticking out of her neck.

The British press had reported the murder as that of a lady detective, but as I read further, there was much more to the case than first met the eye. According to the two historians who spent eight years unravelling Laetitia's story, she had indeed worked for a Parisian detective agency, undertaking surveillance in cases of adultery and doing routine background checks, but had also infiltrated a brutal fascist organization as a police informer. The Cagoule, as they were known, had been responsible for a number of atrocities in France, including two bombings, several murders and the attempted assassination of the prime minister. Crucially, Laetitia had been reporting on their activities not only to the French police but, it was rumoured, to Mussolini and his secret service as well. For complex political reasons, no one was ever charged with her murder, although suspicion fell heavily on the Cagoule's top assassin, Jean Filliol.[13]

It was a fascinating story and, although her situation was far removed from Maud's, it did highlight the dangers of messing with the underworld. Maud may not have been toying with continental terrorists, but, if my research into blackmail and the excesses of the West End was anything to go by, London had its fair share of vipers. On balance, I decided to allow her those occasional 'moments' when only quick wits and the reassurance of a revolver in her pocket could guarantee her safe return home.

One thing that set Maud apart from Laetitia Toureaux and Kate Easton, not to mention every male private detective in London and elsewhere, was what awaited her when she arrived home: maternal responsibilities. She wasn't the only female detective I had found who was also a mother – at the society palmists' trial, it had emerged that Amy Betts had a child – but she was certainly an unusual mother figure for the times.

With few exceptions, women from affluent middle-class families were expected to leave their employment when they got married, so the majority were far removed from the workplace by the time motherhood beckoned. There were many arguments against the employment of married women. Some were moral: marriage and motherhood went hand in hand, and the fabric of society would disintegrate if women neglected their primary duties of tending to the needs of their husbands and children. Others were economic: the country was in recession and they were stealing food from the mouths of unemployed men with families by unnecessarily crowding the job market and driving down wages.

Married women who ran their own businesses or worked in a freelance capacity had more of a choice whether to work or not, but rarely talked about their home lives. It was hard enough competing with men without opening themselves up to criticism about their domestic arrangements. Disapproval was always there, simmering away. A woman's place was in the home.

Occasionally, the disapproval erupted into an outright attack on their life choices. In 1922, for example, the bestselling author A. S. M. Hutchinson published a divisive novel called *This Freedom*. The story charted the life of Rosalie Aubyn from her Victorian childhood, in which men did 'mysterious and extraordinary things' and women 'ordinary and unexciting and generally rather tiresome things',[14] to her groundbreaking career as a banker and the 'mutually free and independent partnership' she enjoyed with her barrister husband.[15] Hutchinson gave a sympathetic view of the desire for equality and freedom which brought Rosalie to this point, and her capabilities as a businesswoman. But the final chapters of the book showed his real purpose, which was to paint a devastating picture of the consequences of a woman attempting to combine a professional career, marriage and motherhood.

Readers saw Rosalie give birth to three children and return to work after handing each one over to a nurse. 'I will not sacrifice myself for the children',[16] Rosalie says at one point, words by which she is damned as, one by one, her emotionally detached offspring fall by the wayside: her eldest son is expelled from school, court-martialled during the war, and imprisoned for fraud; her daughter dies from a backstreet abortion; and her youngest son commits suicide by throwing himself under a train. All this was blamed on her refusal to create a proper home for her family.

The book raised a storm of protest from within feminist circles, and the discussion spilled over into the mainstream press. That summer, the *Pall Mall Gazette* approached two professional women for their opinions.[17] The actress Sybil Thorndike, who had four children with her actor-director husband Lewis Casson, said:

If a woman is by nature a good mother, she will be a good mother, and her children will want for no impetus for good which she can impart. If she is endowed with a good business capacity she will be a good businesswoman; and there is no reason why she should not combine the two roles with the greatest success, provided she has sufficient vitality.

Helena Normanton, married but childless, gave a slightly different response:

Perhaps the motherhood of such women may be of a less fostering type than of the women devoted solely to maternity, but it may be much better from the point of giving a dual heritage of power, talent, and tradition to the children. What they lose in cotton wool they gain in courage and self-reliance . . .

How, I wondered, had Maud's children turned out?

I started with Vera and Evelyn. The evidence certainly suggested that they had inherited their mother's independence and spirit. For a start, they weren't afraid of the divorce courts. They had five marriages between them: Vera three and Evelyn two. Nor was Evelyn the only one to work as a detective. The Mrs Langford mentioned in the Inverclyde case in 1933 was, in fact, Vera. By then, she was twenty-nine and on her second marriage, but I had three articles in my files that suggested she'd been assisting her mother for some time. All were from the summer of 1921 and concerned 'a pretty fair-haired girl of 17' who had just started working for Maud West.[18] One said that she was actually *called* Miss West. At the time, I'd dismissed that as a mistake on the part of the reporter, but now I was sure this was Vera.

She'd been given a backstory designed to highlight her youth and glamour: as a keen cinema-goer, she'd been inspired by a film called *The Clutching Hand* to give up her job as a shorthand typist and move into detective work.[19] She was also keen to point out that she didn't *look* like a detective: 'If I did . . . half my effectiveness would be lost,' she said. 'I look upon it as a great compliment when people say to me: "Good gracious! Fancy you being a detective. I should never have imagined it."'[20]

Her mother's influence was also evident in her statement that 'I never disguise myself, except to wear old clothes, but I hope that will come later.'[21] She explained that she had only been in the job for a few months and was still in training. 'Most of the cases I have been engaged in so far have been thefts,' she said, before adding, without the benefit of hindsight, 'I have not had much to do with divorce, and I don't want to.'

She made another brief appearance in the introduction to an exclusive interview Maud gave to the *Sunday Chronicle* in 1926. Few writers of detective fiction, it began, had dared to pit a middle-aged woman and her daughter against the 'Moriartys of crime':

> Yet from a well-appointed office in New Oxford-street, London, there operates such a pair who are acknowledged experts in the unmasking of crime and the disentanglement of love intrigues. They are Maude West [sic], London's lady detective, and her daughter, who already has proved herself such a worthy antagonist of rogues and scoundrels that she has been dubbed 'Miss Sherlock Holmes'.[22]

How committed Vera was to this career in the long run was debatable. By 1937, it was Evelyn who was tipped to take over the agency. But, as I discovered on a trip to the National Archives in Kew, that never happened. The Second World War intervened, sweeping Evelyn into more clandestine work. Her personnel file had only recently been declassified and contained just five sheets of paper – but one of those was an extract of the Official Secrets Act that she had signed in September 1943.[23] That July, she'd been ordered to return to London from her postal-censorship job in Scotland for an interview with a top-secret organization based in Baker Street. She wouldn't have known who they were until she'd passed their strict vetting, but this was the Special Operations Executive (SOE), otherwise known as the 'Ministry of Ungentle-manly Warfare.'[24]

Any hopes I'd had of her being parachuted into Nazi-occupied France or hacking her way through the Burmese jungle were short-lived, however. As far as I could tell, she had never been more than a clerk: for the first year, she was based at the Baker Street HQ, but then was sent to the SOE mission in India where she stayed until she was signed-off in June 1946. Still, it said something that she'd been recruited at all. The SOE needed people they could trust and therefore relied upon personal recommendations, con-nections and pedigree, even for the lowliest positions. Evelyn's file said she'd been a 'confidential secretary' for Maud West. Although this brought into question how much actual detective work she'd done for her mother, it did resurrect the idea that the name Maud West held some sway in security circles: first the Thyssen pamphlet in the First World War, and now this.

Before leaving the National Archives, I decided to have a quick look at the documents they held relating to Vera's first divorce. I didn't expect to find anything of interest, but one small fragment leapt out at me:

> . . . and there is one child living issue of the said marriage namely
> Rea Eugene Axford born on the 5th day of September 1925.[25]

I hadn't even considered that there might be people still alive – traceable people – who had known Maud. But Vera's daughter Rea had been born in 1925, so it was within the bounds of possibility. I wasn't sure how I felt about that. I preferred my sources to be dead and buried, their lives scattered to the wind on yellowing scraps of paper. It was the whole point of the game. Besides, did I want to know the things they might tell me? I'd only ever wanted to find a nice, simple lady detective, and the story had got messy enough as it was. Bringing living people into the equation could only complicate matters further. Was I ready to finally let go of the narrative I'd been weaving for Maud West and allow Edith Elliott to come to the fore? Was I ready for the truth?

I peeked over my desk at the other researchers in the reading room. Nobody *knew* that I knew there was a grandchild – if I was honest, there was probably more than one – and, if this fact happened to come to light later on, I could always plead incompetence. *And they're all dead now, you say?* But this was the impulse that had led rogue historians to burn letters and misfile inconvenient evidence. I had to make *some* effort to find them.

Back at home, it didn't take long to trace Rea. She'd married a popular BBC newsreader, and both had been conveniently dead for over a decade. But she also had a half-brother, Vera's son from her second marriage, and he was very much alive and living in London. Furthermore, there was an address for him hiding in plain sight on the internet. Damn.

I put off writing at first, but soon the thought of one of Maud's grandchildren, infused with memories and just a phone call away, became too much to resist. What would he be able to tell me? Had tales of Maud's real adventures been passed down through the family? What would he recall of her and Harry? I wrote the letter.

Weeks rolled by. I'd given up all hope of hearing back when an email arrived from his daughter Silvia. Her father might once have been brimming with memories, she explained, but they were now lost in the depths of dementia. Even in his younger days, he had never spoken about his parents, let alone his grandparents. She thought there had been some sort of rift. But, she said, there was a cousin somewhere on the south coast who might be able to help. She gave me a phone number for a man called Brian.

I wasn't sure who Brian was or where he fitted into the family, but after a few missed phone calls, we were talking. I liked him immediately. He was in his eighties and enjoying retirement after a long career as an orthopaedic surgeon. Furthermore, he had a good sense of humour, which made the prospect of asking my list of weird and intrusive questions that much easier. Although slightly bemused that anyone would be interested in his family, he was happy to help. The only problem was his heart: he was due to undergo quadruple bypass surgery in a few days' time and tired easily. Nevertheless, he suggested that we talk briefly there and then: 'It's only plumbing, but you never know . . .'

We got the basics out of the way first. His father was Cecil, Edith and Harry's eldest son. He'd been born in 1934 and had lived with his grandparents on and off during his childhood. For a while in the 1930s, they were all packed into the flat opposite the British Museum until Brian's parents took a place of their own around the corner. I realized that he must have known Fake Charles: he, too, had lived in Great Russell Mansions at one point. Did Brian remember him? He laughed. Of course he remembered him. That was his father. Fake Charles – he of the swimming trophies and pilot's licence – and Cecil Elliott had been one and the same from the early twenties right up until Cecil's death in 1970.

I braced myself for some shocking revelation. Was there some great scandal in the family, after all? Was Cecil in hiding? Had he done, or witnessed, something so heinous that he lived in constant fear of discovery? But the reason concerned, of all things, dentistry.

New regulations under the Dentists Act 1921 had required all new entrants into the profession to pass an exam and then pay an annual fee for retention on the Dentist Register. Cecil had his heart set on a Harley Street career, but the new rules seemed somewhat bothersome. He was also too young to qualify. A plan was hatched. His uncle Charles was just a few years older than him and had no interest in teeth, so it was agreed that the most reasonable course of action was for Cecil to borrow Charles's identity in order to secure a place on the Dentist Register before the new regulations came into force. Cecil maintained this pretence for the rest of his life.

And Brian wondered why I found his family interesting.

We moved on to the other shape-shifter in the family. What could he tell me, briefly, about Edith? For a start, he said, everyone called her Edie. She was very much the matriarch, and always had the final say. He thought that she might have been the first female mayor of Holborn. (I checked. She wasn't.) As for how she earned her living, Brian had a vague idea that it involved 'a bit of investigating, I think. Something to do with divorce?' He had never heard of Maud West.

I could tell he was getting tired, so we whizzed through the family tree I'd drafted to check for any mistakes. Nellie Barber hovered uncertainly to one side of the chart. Where did she fit in? He explained that she was Edith's sister and, in Brian's words, 'a bit simple.' *Another sister. I'd missed that.* She'd never married, and he had no idea about their parents or any other members of that side of the family. I held my tongue. Illegitimacy could be a touchy subject and now was not the time.

As for his aunts and uncles, they all had 'ridiculous 1930s nicknames'. I had to agree. They weren't quite in Bertie Wooster territory, but edging that way. Neville, for example, was 'Boy-Boy' and Vera 'Girlie', whilst her third husband had to answer to 'Old Cock'. Evelyn, the baby, was 'Babs'. Denis was the black sheep and, being largely absent and/or in disgrace (it wasn't clear which), was simply referred to as 'Denis'. There had also been some sort of incident with Keith; the family evidently never spoke about him.

With that, we made plans to talk further once he had recovered from his surgery. In the meantime, he promised to send me some photographs.

When the photographs arrived, my favourite was one taken by a press agency in the 1930s, which offered me my first glimpse of Harry. Although dwarfed by Edith and her matronly bosom, he looked surprisingly debonair. They'd been captured standing in the dappled shade of a London street, dressed up for some smart event. A wedding, perhaps? It was the first time I'd seen Maud genuinely smile. They made a handsome couple.

Another was of Cecil and two boys sitting on a sand dune. Handwriting on the reverse identified one of the boys as a family friend and the other as 'No idea!', but the most eye-catching aspect of the photo was the large revolver Cecil was pointing at the camera.

It was an odd toy to take to the beach, but then the Elliott family weren't bound by convention. They seemed drawn to adventure. A case in point was something I'd discovered since speaking to Brian: in 1931, three years before he earned his aviator's certificate, Cecil had been involved in the first fatal gliding accident in Britain.

Gliding as a sport was in its infancy at the time. German engineers had perfected the aeronautics and worked out how to land, but what hadn't been determined was the best method of getting into the sky in the first place. And so it was that Cecil (masquerading as Charles) found himself with a group of friends on a farm in Hertfordshire one gusty Sunday afternoon, rigging up an experimental launching apparatus for a small Scud glider using a winding drum attached to the drive shaft of a car.

The pilot was thirty-six-year-old Thomas Eaton Lander, an ex-RAF officer and one of the founders of the British Gliding Association. The launch started well, with the glider being drawn towards the car, but then? As Cecil told a reporter, 'I think the apparatus was more effective than we anticipated, for he was shipped skywards at a terrific rate, and before we realised what had happened the machine crashed to the ground.'[26] Cecil and his friends pulled the unconscious Lander from the wreckage and carried him to a nearby house, but he died half an hour later.

The coroner's verdict was 'death by misadventure'.[27] The line between adventure and misadventure was thin, but, still, I couldn't help but wonder: if Cecil had been forgiven for identity theft and catapulting a friend into the air at eighty miles per hour, what on earth had Denis and Keith done to merit their status as the black sheep of the family?

I could find no dirt on Denis. He appeared to have led a scandal-free life. He'd joined the Merchant Navy in his teens – I found him returning from Rio on board a Royal Mail ship in 1925 – but also occasionally helped out with divorce investigations. In 1931, for example, he'd worked alongside Harry on a case in Gloucester,[28] and the following year secured the evidence Vera needed to divorce her first husband.[29]

Keith's story, however, was more of a shock.

It began in 1922, when Australia launched a charm offensive on Britain to support its plan to tempt 6,000 boys between the ages of fifteen and nineteen to start a new life Down Under, the aim being to replace those killed in the war.[30] This was an extension of the Dreadnought Scheme, so named because it had originally used money donated by the Australian people to build a British warship to patrol their seas, a plan which had been superseded by the formation of a dedicated Australian navy in 1911. The funds were used instead to supply and train British boys to work on Australian farms.

The official 1922 pamphlet promised a Boys' Own adventure, a country life of rounding up cattle on horseback, hunting kangaroos and bears, and playing cricket in the sunshine. Yes, life in the bush could be tough, it said, but 'it will make a man of you.'[31] All a boy needed was a willing heart, the signature of a parent or guardian and a contribution towards his passage to Australia.

The newspapers were also full of the wonders awaiting such recruits. 'What a world of adventure and desire is conjured up by the name Australia!' gushed the Elliotts' local paper. 'To the boy, it opens up scenes wherein Capt. Cook, Aborigines, and Ned Kelly, the bush ranger, hold sway.'[32] In July 1923, the *Hendon & Finchley Times* also printed a letter written by a local boy who had emigrated with the Dreadnought Scheme the previous year:

> I feel absolutely like a farmer now, and everything is going along as it should . . . it does not seem long before I shall be my own boss and go out with all my strength and will power to face the world on my own . . . For it is Fortune that I set out to make and I will not return until I have achieved the same.[33]

Less than a month later, and just two days shy of his fifteenth birthday, Keith Elliott packed his bags and, with Edith and Harry's blessing, set sail for Sydney on the SS *Euripides*.

His adventure started well, with a six-week journey via Tenerife and Cape Town in the company of forty-two like-minded boys. When the ship docked on 10 October, they were taken to a training farm just outside Sydney to learn how to ride horses, plough fields, dress sheep and milk cows. It was a tough three months – the conditions were deliberately spartan to prepare the boys for their first posting – but the novelty made up for it.

In March 1924, Keith was billeted with a twenty-nine-year-old farmer called Malcolm McLeod and his wife Dot, in Coolac, New South Wales (population 150). In the lottery of farm placements, he'd struck lucky. The work was relatively light, and he had his own bedroom. McLeod was, by all accounts, a kind and fair man, and an excellent farmer who would go on to become 'the top sheep man' in Australia.[34] Even Coolac itself, despite its small size, offered everything a Dreadnought Boy could hope for. When not working on the farm, Keith could swim in the nearby Murrumbidgee River or head into the bush to shoot parrots and other wildlife.[35] The town even managed to muster enough men to field a football team against neighbouring settlements on Sunday afternoons. Keith seemed 'bright and happy' and 'apparently contented with his lot.'[36]

But, underneath his sunny exterior, all was not well. He confided as much in Malcolm McLeod and asked for a pay rise. Was he thinking of returning home? If so, he was out of luck. His wages were automatically banked for safekeeping and the pocket money he received would barely get him to Sydney, let alone London.

On Easter Sunday, six months after Keith arrived in Australia, the morning started as usual. Keith lit the fire and milked the cows. Dot McLeod was away, so Malcolm swept out the house and prepared some lunch for Keith before leaving to visit his mother; Keith said he planned to join in the Sunday football game. When Malcolm returned at ten o'clock that evening, however, he found the back door jammed shut. Entering the house by the front, he went to the kitchen and discovered Keith's lifeless body slumped in front of the door, a Winchester rifle at his feet. He had shot himself through the heart.[37]

The End of His Tether

BY MAUD WEST

Some years ago I brought to justice a young girl who had cleverly forged a will. My chief assistant and myself had practically forgotten the case when late one evening, while motoring in an open two-seater through a narrow lane in Buckinghamshire, we were suddenly brought up by being 'roped'. As I tried to pull up, the car skidded and, running into a bank, overturned. Hastily picking myself up – I was luckily unhurt – I noticed eight men who had been holding a metal rope dashing towards us.

Crying to my assistant to 'run for it,' I set off as fast as I could go down the road. The pursuit, as it happens, was only half-hearted, and breathlessly we sought refuge in a small inn. The landlord, having listened sympathetically to our story, at once called to our aid a friend who had a fast car in the garage. Arming ourselves, we set out in search of our unknown attackers.

All the tyres of my car, we soon discovered, had been slashed. The assailants had flown. For more than two hours we searched the countryside and finally, some 10 miles from the inn, we passed three men whom I recognised in the moonlight. A little further along the road we pulled into a hedge, extinguished our lights, and got out.

Carefully and silently we picked our way along until we

heard a steady crunch, crunch on the gravel as the three men drew nearer. At a given signal we stopped and waited. Then the innkeeper's voice boomed through the night: 'Stop, you three. Put your hands up.' There was a sudden silence. Three pairs of hands slowly rose above three startled faces.

It was now my turn to speak, and keeping them covered I asked why they had roped my car. For a moment the three refused to talk. Then, realising they had no chance of escape, one of them broke the silence. He said he was the brother of the girl I had been responsible for sending to prison, and he had been awaiting his chance to have his revenge on me.

The other men who had helped him proved to be innocent of the real cause of the attack. They said they had been misled by the brother and treated the affair as a joke. It was not until they saw my car overturn after crashing into the bank that they became frightened, and five of them bolted.

By this time more assistance arrived, and after talking to the three men I decided to let the two go and took the brother along with us. On the way back to the village the man implored me not to take action against him. He was so obviously repentant that I decided to let him go after he had signed a full statement.

I have never had any further trouble from him. On the contrary, he took the trouble to ascertain the cost of my car repairs and sent me a packet containing the exact amount in treasury notes and a further apology![38]

Chapter Fourteen

Look to the Lady

It is by . . . putting my work before myself and
before everything that I gained any success I may
have made as a woman detective.

Maud West, 1928[1]

I'd been secretly hoping for a corpse, but not like this. Not so real,
not so damning. Brian had said no one ever spoke of Keith. It can't
have been the stigma of a suicide in the family, although enough
people felt that way. *What if everyone thinks we're mad?* No, the
Elliotts knew better. They must have come across enough distress
and mental illness in their work to understand. A more personal
shame, then. A deep wound. That nauseating mix of grief and regret.
Did they even have somewhere to grieve? What happened to the
body? I could find no grave.

They had a further blow to come. At the inquest into Keith's
death, it emerged that one of the last things he had done on that
Easter Sunday was write to his mother. The inquest documents
had long been destroyed, so I would never see a copy of the letter
that had been passed around for the court's inspection, but whatever it said – I love you? I hate you? *Help me?* – would have been
devastating to receive. I imagined the envelope dropping onto the
doormat one morning, months after the fact. Edith would live with
the pain of knowing her son had died alone and homesick for the
rest of her life.

Good, a small part of me whispered. He was just a boy, barely fifteen! Maybe he'd been a bit of a handful, even delinquent – who knew? – but a one-way ticket to the other side of the world? How *could* she?

I knew I was being unfair. I didn't have all the facts, and it was a different world. Besides, if I was going to blame Edith, I'd have to blame Harry, too, and Cecil and Vera and all the other supposedly responsible adults who could have stopped Keith boarding the SS *Euripides*. No, my anger was coming from somewhere else altogether. Frustration? Exhaustion? Maud was undeniably hard work, but she'd always managed to be funny, too. Not this time. This story had no punchline.

The floodgates opened. Was she even one of the good guys? It wasn't a question I'd allowed myself to ask before, although it was always there lurking in the back of my mind. She'd worked in one of the most despised and underhand professions going, but because she was *my* lady detective I'd imbued her with a moral superiority that allowed her to transcend all that. I'd wanted her to be good. But what kind of person would stitch up their own chimney sweep for an easy win in the divorce courts, or turn a blind eye, perhaps even provide encouragement, as her offspring indulged in a little career-enhancing identity theft? She wrote about how many lives she had restored, but how many had she ruined?

I knew I should be dispassionate; aim for an impartial appraisal of her life and career. But I didn't want to be dispassionate. I wanted to thump her. Not just for Keith and all the others who had fallen by the wayside as she ploughed through life, but because I'd begun to suspect that I had spent months enjoying the company of a woman who wasn't particularly nice.

For weeks, I couldn't look at her. I was tired of her games. I avoided my office, where her photographs were pinned to the walls, and changed the subject when friends asked after her. But something she'd said in 1926 was stuck to my fridge:

> . . . a detective who gives up hope, when things become too hard, had better stop working right away – as a detective, anyhow. Something nice and soft, with an armchair and a novel as soothing background, would be far more suitable![2]

Of course she was right, damn her. I had to carry on. I'd come so far, and there was still so much unexplained. Somehow, I needed to find a way back to the state of open-minded curiosity with which I had begun. Ironically, she'd given me an idea about how that could be achieved: armchairs and novels. The one person who could lift me out of my fug was inextricably linked to both in my mind: Dorothy L. Sayers.

What was the name of the club where she'd given that talk on murder?

The Efficiency Club had been formed in the summer of 1919 by Viscountess Rhondda, the equal-rights campaigner and formidable director of numerous manufacturing and shipping companies. At a public meeting that November, the vast Central Hall at Westminster was packed as she explained her vision for the club. It would have four key aims, she said: to promote greater efficiency and cooperation amongst established business and professional women; to encourage leadership and self-reliance amongst all women workers; to form a link between professional and business women for their mutual advantage; and, finally, to work towards the admission of women to British Chambers of Commerce.[3]

The membership included representatives from many large-scale employers of women, such as Selfridges and Lyons' Corner Houses, as well as doctors, dentists, aviators, lawyers, headmistresses, editors, saddlers, builders, artists, musicians, engineers and, of course, at least one private detective. It claimed to be the first organization of its kind in the world.

As for the name, 'efficiency' had been a buzzword in Britain for some time. It underpinned a broad spectrum of ideas that ranged from 'mental hygiene' systems such as Pelmanism to the horrific doctrine of eugenics, each with the aim of instilling order in a chaotic world. The first business efficiency clubs had been formed in 1916 to discuss how the new scientific approach to war being applied by the military might be used to rebuild the economy once the conflict was over.[4] But, whilst these male-dominated clubs focused on implementing efficiency measures with official names such as the Sheldon Method or the Bedaux System, the women in London took a broader approach.

Once a month, they held informal members' nights to share tips on day-to-day business practices – writing effective letters, training staff and so on – and debate issues such as how trade unionism could benefit women.[5] Networking was also encouraged at frequent dinners, musical evenings and social nights. Every fortnight, the club organized a public lecture on a loosely efficiency-based theme. This could be anything from the nationalization of coal mines to the perils of vanity.[6] Gladys Burlton, the director of education at Selfridges, for example, lectured on the psychology of efficiency; the 'Lady Icarus' Mary Heath, fresh from her triumph in becoming the first pilot to fly solo from Cape Town to London, spoke on developments in civil aviation.[7] One of the very first lectures was entitled 'Science as Applied to the Home',[8] which proved to be a recurring theme: an organized and efficient household, Viscountess Rhondda argued, was the first step towards a woman being able to combine both marriage and a career.[9] Maud's own contribution came in November 1931, when she delivered a lecture, sadly unreported, on 'Where A Woman Scores'.[10]

The club also attracted high-profile guest speakers, not all of whom took the subject seriously. In 1920, for example, Sir Robert Baden-Powell gave a talk on 'How to Track a Wife' in which he asserted that 43 per cent of women trod on the inside of one foot and the outside of the other. According to rules he had learned from trackers in the African desert, this meant that they were 'emotional and impulsive'. There was much laughter. Presumably, the women of the Efficiency Club counted themselves in the other 57 per cent.[11]

In November 1930, Dorothy L. Sayers also decided to have fun with her lecture, 'Efficiency in Murder'. Maud was in the chair that evening as Sayers put forward her argument that the most efficient murderer was George Smith of the Brides in the Bath case. It was an excellent choice. Smith's method was so effective that he had managed to dispatch three victims who were relaxing in the bath without leaving any trace of violence or struggle. At Smith's trial in 1915, various theories were put forward as to how this might be achieved, but the theory which carried the most weight was that of the Home Office pathologist Sir Bernard Spilsbury, who argued, based on meticulous forensic analysis, that the trick was to stand at the end of the bath, grab the victim firmly by the ankles and yank upwards, thereby causing a sudden rush of water into the nose and mouth. The victim would immediately lose consciousness through shock, and drown.[12]

Sayers concluded her talk with an idea to increase efficiency in murder by combining the training of future killers with the dispatching of those careless enough to be caught: a university course, in which students could practise their techniques on convicted felons.[13] As one journalist reported, 'Although Miss Sayers described the lecture as a leg pull, her audience listened to the tale of perfection in atrocity with a sang froid that made one very dubious about the ultra-efficient woman.' That composure wasn't to last.

At the end of the talk, a voice rang out: 'May I ask a question? Is this an open meeting?'

Maud hesitated a fraction too long.

The voice belonged to Mrs Harvey James, a member of the Howard League for Penal Reform and a vociferous opponent of capital punishment. She didn't wait for permission to continue. The lecture, she said, demonstrated a 'revolting cynicism and seventeenth-century savagery'. Had Miss Sayers not considered the psychological effect of her treatment of such an appalling subject? Did Miss Sayers perhaps regard 'state murder' with the same levity? The audience erupted into a chorus of 'ironical cheers and loud booing'. Maud made vain attempts to restore order, but Mrs James remained glued to her soapbox for several minutes.[14]

Sayers, however, took it all in her stride. Writing to her cousin a few days later, she said:

> I was lecturing to a club in London the other day on 'Efficiency in Murder' – a nice little ironical talk about how to dispose of corpses and so on – and at the end a hysterical female arose in wrath and said I was 'revolting,' and made said protests in the name of the Howard League for Penal Reform! I am sorry to say that everybody laughed unkindly at her, and I got quite a nice little advertisement. Such is life.[15]

She made no comment about the chairwoman.

Occasional failures in crowd control aside, the Efficiency Club gave women the opportunity to shine, and its formation had been timely, coinciding as it did with the surprise passing of the Sex Disqualification (Removal) Act and the opportunities that opened up for ambitious women. As regards the fourth aim of the club, by 1926 the London Chamber of Commerce had nearly fifty female members. The *Daily Sketch* reported that the traditional membership was viewing this tendency of women 'to force their way into the commercial circles of London' with a certain amount of dismay, but they were resigned to the inevitable. As one 'bachelor member' said of his fellow businessmen, '[they] philosophically attribute it to Kismet. Besides, what *could* they do?'[16]

He had a point. Many had been complaining about women in the workplace ever since the first soldiers returned from the front to reclaim their jobs after the First World War, but their petitions and threats of strike action had little effect due to the provisions of the Sex Disqualification (Removal) Act. Of course, that didn't stop some from continuing to rail loudly against the unfairness of it all and heap vitriol on prominent female figures.

One outfit guilty of direct and personal attacks on members of the Efficiency Club was the League of Womanhood, which believed motherhood was the 'best and highest walk of life'.[17] As the *Leeds Mercury* commented, however, 'like all leagues to put women in the place which according to man they should occupy, the League of Womanhood has a man for its organiser.'[18] In this case, it was Captain Alfred Henderson-Livesey, a former officer in the Household Cavalry, who had devoted himself to reclaiming public life as an exclusively male sphere.

He'd even written a book on the subject. *Sex and Public Life* was, naturally, dedicated to his mother, and had a bright yellow binding to match the bile within. The main thrust of his argument was that professional women were not real women but genetically abnormal 'sexual intermediates' whose second-rate achievements were of interest purely because of their sex. As such, they must be stopped from corrupting the nation's true womenfolk before the whole 'virile race' descended into debauched halfwittery. His views were extreme, with clear fascist undertones, but they gave some idea of the atmosphere in which Maud and her fellow businesswomen sometimes had to operate.

Fortunately, the business world itself was, for the most part, supportive of their achievements. The Publicity Club of London, for example, had been set up in 1913 for men in the advertising industry but had welcomed female members since 1919. In 1921, it also started holding ladies' nights with guest speakers chosen from the growing number of professional women who excelled in their fields.[19] This departure was, in the words of the *Vote*, the paper of the Women's Freedom League, 'probably the most novel ever made in business circles.'[20]

The first of these evenings took place at the Hotel Cecil in May 1921. The audience almost filled the hotel's Victoria Hall, which seated 350 diners, to hear the 'concourse of women experts' the club had gathered. This panel included Leila Lewis, press agent to various Hollywood stars including Charlie Chaplin and Mary Pickford, the barrister Helena Normanton, the illustrator Gladys Peto, a fashion editor, a prima donna, a socialite, two journalists, the wife of 'the Navvy Poet' Patrick MacGill – and Maud.[21]

This odd mix of women was invited to convey a female view of advertising practices, which they did with candour, making comments that wouldn't have been out of place in the twenty-first century. Helena Normanton, for example, read out a blacklist of products whose adverts were 'of the kind which disfigure beautiful landscapes and irritate railway travellers.' Another panellist complained that dress advertisements focused almost entirely on lithe models at the expense of women with 'gentle undulations in their figures.'[22]

Curiously, although Maud received a mention in practically all the newspaper reports about the event, not one recorded what she said. Eventually, in the Publicity Club archives, buried amongst detailed notes on the other speakers' opinions, I found one small, damning sentence:

> There was also a short speech by Miss Maud West, the lady detective, who had not been advertised to speak.[23]

Oh, dear. Had she clambered on to the podium, determined to have her say? Or was she a last-minute addition to the panel but proved to be a regrettable choice? Either way, it was a shame that there was no record of her speech, considering her own bold and somewhat cavalier approach to publicity.

I had found a record of one of her public speaking engagements, however. It occurred later in her career when she travelled to Birmingham to address a joint meeting of the city's Rotary Club and Soroptimists in 1937. By that point, she had been a member of the Soroptimists for some years.

The organization had originated in California in 1921 and was the female equivalent of the international Rotary movement. Its name came from the Latin *soror* (sister) and *optima* (best). The central London branch, to which Maud belonged, had formed three years later, merging with another club set up by Lady Rhondda and Lady Astor after their official request to join the Rotary movement was rejected.[24]

A list of the branch's early members gave more insight into the kind of people within Maud's network: it included the actresses Gwen Berryman and Sybil Thorndike, George Bernard Shaw's secretary and confidante Blanche Patch, the former suffragette 'General' Flora Drummond and Mary Allen of the Women's Police Service.[25] I'd also discovered that she must have known Lilian Wyles, a key figure in police history who had been one of Scotland Yard's first female recruits and progressed to the rank of chief inspector, as they both lived in Great Russell Mansions.

The Soroptimist meetings took place over lunch or dinner once a fortnight and included a guest speaker, who was often a member from another branch.[26] It was in this role that Maud found herself addressing the meeting in Birmingham whilst a reporter from the *Birmingham Gazette* jotted down a précis of her talk.

There was little in the report that I hadn't come across before.

This in itself was surprising. The occasion wasn't – or shouldn't have been – an opportunity for a comic turn. Yet, after emphasizing that the job was very often 'just hard work, with long hours of waiting and watching', she proceeded to tell versions of some of the more colourful adventures she'd written about over the years: her visit to the cocaine factory; her youthful sprint for the tram whilst disguised as an old lady in Paris; how she'd hired an actress to cause a scene in a restaurant to drive a wedge between a gigolo and his young prey.[27]

Had I got her wrong? She knew the limits of people's credulity – her everyday work demanded it – so why tell these tales in person, in public? Could they be based in truth, after all? Or was she so wedded to her public persona that she couldn't let the mask drop, even in front of a serious audience?

As I thought about it, I realized there was another possibility. In light of her involvement in women's networks, did she present these tales as encouragement to other women to be bold and unafraid of adventure? Was it not so much 'Look at *me*!' as 'Look at *you*! Look what *you* could do!'? The truth, as ever, was probably somewhere in the middle, but she was certainly beginning to redeem herself.

Something Brian had said came back to me: he thought his grandmother had been the first female mayor of Holborn. It had taken ten seconds on the internet to establish that she hadn't. That distinction went to another Edith – Edith Pooley – in 1955, so I'd dismissed it as another of Maud's inventions. But now, as I began to appreciate Maud as a businesswoman, I wondered if Brian been *almost* right.

I phoned Tudor Allen, the stalwart at the Camden archives centre where the civic records for Holborn were kept. Was an Edith Elliott ever associated with Holborn Borough Council in any way? Not as mayor, but in another capacity? A few days later, he got back to me. Yes, there had been a councillor by that name in the 1930s, but all he could find was that she was a married woman and lived at 8, Great Russell Mansions. That was enough for me. A few days later, I was back on the train to London.

I hadn't pegged Maud as a committee type – just reading the council minutes required a great deal of caffeine and willpower – but there she was between 1934 and 1937, sitting through endless reports, motions and divisions. She had stood in the local elections of November 1934 in the Central St Giles ward. There were only two types of candidate in Holborn that year: Labour and Municipal Reform, or, as the official council return put it, 'Socialist' and 'Anti-Socialist'. Maud was one of the latter.

The Municipal Reform Party, established in 1906, was essentially the Conservative Party in disguise, renamed and repackaged to appeal to a broader section of the electorate. A poster held at the Museum of London summed up its purpose:

The 35,000 residents of Holborn, it seemed, were especially protective of their hard-earned cash. Elsewhere in London that year, Labour and other progressive candidates sailed to victory and beat down the long reign of the right, but Holborn saw all but one of its forty-two seats go to Municipal Reformers. Maud wasn't there on sufferance, though. She'd had plenty of competition in her ward from other Municipal Reformers and had stormed to the top of the polls, a clear winner.[28]

The full council met twice a week in the domed chamber of the Town Hall on High Holborn, just five minutes' walk from both Albion House and Maud's flat opposite the British Museum. She threw herself into council business, sitting on six additional committees dealing with everything from public toilets and street musicians to tuberculosis care and strategic planning. She was also co-opted onto the committee of the Holborn Housing Trust, helping to oversee the development of social housing for the poorest residents of the borough.[29] When the nation celebrated King George V's silver jubilee in May 1935, she worked behind the scenes to ensure that Holborn could hold its head high when it came to flags, bunting and children's tea parties. That summer, she also attended the annual conference of the National Association for the Prevention of Infant Mortality along with one of the borough's health visitors.[30]

How did she fit it all in? After the first year, it seemed she didn't. Her attendance at full council meetings dropped off in 1936 – she'd be absent for weeks at a time – and she resigned from all council committees apart from two. The first, Maternity and Child Welfare, assessed applications for the subsidized home help, convalescent homes and dentures that new mothers could access in the days before the National Health Service, and oversaw the provision of minor-ailment clinics and other services for children.

The Public Health Committee offered slightly more excitement. Yes, there were the drainage works, rat infestations, vaccinations and public mortuary expenses to supervise, but these were interspersed with small flurries of intrigue: killer cans of tomato purée stalking the shelves of local grocery shops; a poisoning case in a laundry caused by the ink used for marking blankets.[31]

But Maud wasn't there for the drama. Her motives, I suspected, ran much deeper. It wasn't hard to see a correlation between the issues she prioritized – child welfare, public health, social housing – and the comforts lacking in her own childhood.

Maud's early years were still frustratingly elusive. I'd located her sister Nellie's birth certificate, which showed that she, too, was illegitimate, arriving in February 1898 when Mary Ann was thirty-nine and ostensibly working as a mangle-woman. But, beyond that, I'd drawn a complete blank.[32]

The most curious thing was that there was no sign of any of the girls in any census taken during their childhoods. Their mother was a constant presence in Staunton Street, along with her parents. Edith had been born there in September 1880, but she had vanished by the time of the 1881 census the following April. She was still missing in 1891, as was four year old Alice. Both girls were back in Deptford in 1901 when they were twenty and fourteen respectively, but by that time three-year-old Nellie had disappeared.

There were many places they could have been – with relatives or neighbours, in a workhouse or children's home – but they weren't. A search for the older girls, for two siblings of the right age called Edith and Alice with any nickname, any surname – even just initials – in any institution, school or private home anywhere in the United Kingdom in the 1880s or 1890s yielded no results. Had they been adopted and lived out their childhoods under other identities? But, if so, why return to Deptford and revert to their birth names later?

Perhaps they were abroad? Sending illegitimate offspring

overseas would be an unusual move for a working-class family from Deptford, but it was something that the wealthier classes – the aristocracy, along with lesser beings such as, say, barristers and solicitors – had been doing for some time. To them, the Continent was a great carpet under which all manner of indiscretions could be swept. There were 'don't ask, don't tell' expat communities dotted all over Europe, with France in particular being full of black sheep, indiscreet mistresses and misbegotten children. Adverts for 'A Continental Education' could be found in all the main papers, alongside those offering homes (for a fee) for unwanted wards and other inconvenient progeny.

Had Edith's father been a lawyer, after all? I played with the possibility, checking out all the lawyers with whom I knew she had connections, whether through her work or personal affairs. Where had they been around the time Edith was conceived? But they were all too old, too young or too elsewhere. Besides, if the girls had been spirited away one by one as they popped out of the womb, why leave Mary Ann behind with her parents, working a series of drudge jobs?

No, the most likely explanation was that Edith, Alice and Nellie had been in Deptford all along and, on the night of the various censuses, Mary Ann or her parents had hidden them away when the enumerator came to call to avoid the stigma of illegitimacy.

If, by this, they were hoping to give the girls a better start in life, it worked. According to her marriage certificate, Edith had landed a job as a sales assistant in a drapery store. It was a competitive field, requiring poise and good arithmetic skills, as well as the self-discipline to avoid any infractions of the rules and regulations employers imposed on women in shop work. Although preferable to many of the alternatives, it was by no means an easy job. Each slip could mean a fine docked from her meagre wages, and the hours could stretch from seven in the morning to eleven at night, six days a week.

But before that, when Edith first left school? Presumably this would have been at some point between the ages of ten (the minimum leaving age) and twelve (if she hadn't attained the government-prescribed educational standard earlier). She would have been too young for shop work, but she could have gone into domestic service, worked in a laundry or joined her schoolmates as a 'gut girl' – a Deptford speciality – slaughtering imported live-stock at the Foreign Cattle Market. Or, I wondered, had she left a clue in something she told the *Sunday Post* in 1927?

The paper had asked a variety of celebrities about their thwarted ambitions and childhood dreams. The matinee idol Carl Brisson explained that he'd wanted to be a polar explorer; the batsman Jack Hobbs that he'd only ever wanted to play county cricket; and the novelist Winifred Graham that she had dreams of being a trapeze artist. Maud replied:

> When I was a girl my ambition in life was to be a milliner. At the age of twelve I started making hats, and used to think how grand it would be to sell them to other people from a business address. But my ambition in this way was never realised.[33]

She'd gone on to trot out her usual story about her relatives push-ing her towards a career as a detective, but maybe the rest was true. She'd made it sound like a hobby, but hat factories and sweatshops used child labour, and all that experience with ribbons and trims could have helped her to secure the more refined job as a drapery assistant.

All of this was only speculation, of course. Between what seemed like a concerted effort to keep the Barber girls away from officialdom and a lack of surviving evidence, the finer details of Maud's biggest secret were safe.

The events after 1901 were easier to establish. Newly married and with her first child on the way, Edith was trying to make a new life for herself away from Deptford. But, as I discovered, an ongoing crisis at Staunton Street constantly called her back. The sickness that had caused Mary Ann to take to her bed on the night of the census hadn't been a passing ailment. When the diagnosis came in early 1902, it was a devastating blow: *carcinoma mammae*. Breast cancer.[34] Alice, at fifteen, was old enough to work and to help out at home, but four-year-old Nellie needed supervision and their grandparents were getting frail.

In the summer of 1903, Mary Ann took a turn for the worse. A secondary tumour at the base of her skull put pressure on her brain and the cancer spread to her liver. She died on 27 October 1903 at home in Staunton Street, with Edith, then four months pregnant with Vera, by her side.

What Edith did next showed that she had ambitions even then and, perhaps, had already gained some experience of how private detectives could dig up dirt from public records. When she went to register her mother's death, she repeated the lie she had told the vicar at her wedding and said Mary Ann was the widow of Robert Barber, a merchant seaman.[35]

Edith was left in charge of her sisters. Alice soon got married and started her own family with Geoffrey Palmer in Ilford,[36] but young Nellie joined Harry and Edith as they bounced around London, trying to keep a roof over the heads of their growing brood.[37]

Seven children.

A few short weeks ago, I had found Maud selfish and intolerable. Now, I decided, she was bloody amazing.

Such a Dull Job!
Or, Fifteen Minutes with
a London Woman Detective

INTERVIEW WITH MAUD WEST,
DAILY MAIL ATLANTIC EDITION,
17 JUNE 1931

When I called upon her at her New Oxford Street offices, Miss Maud West was not clad in a dressing-gown, sitting in a deep armchair and playing with a violin, with a hypodermic syringe of cocaine at her elbow. Nothing of the sort.

'Come along in,' she said briskly, from the other side of a frosted-glass panelled door. 'Sit down and tell me what you want, and excuse my looking for a number in the telephone directory.'

The office I entered was bright and ordinary. I sat and watched her forefinger sleuthing down the fugitive number.

'What do you deduce about me at first glance?' I asked.

'Smith, W., Smith, W., Smith, W.,' she muttered. 'I'm looking for someone called Smith, who has a Fulham number,' she explained distractedly, 'and I don't know his initials.' Then she looked up. 'Deduce? Oh, that's not the sort of thing I do. My job's very dull, you know, just inquiries and so on. Very dull indeed, though I couldn't live without it now, after 25 years of it.'

'Have you never had any excitement?' I asked.

'Smith, William, Smith, William,' said Miss West. 'No, I don't think so – or only once when two men who were drinking in a public house saw through the disguise one of the men on my staff was wearing. I was outside in a taxi, getting some information from a woman who was mixed up in the case – a criminal one – when out ran my man. He had a tumbler of whisky thrown in his face, and the suspects were after him. When they saw me with the woman, one of them pulled out an automatic pistol and levelled it at me. Luckily the taxi-driver grabbed his wrist and hung on to him, while my man wrestled with the second suspect. A policeman soon arrived, and I gave the criminals in charge. But that might have been a difficult situation.'

I admitted the possibility.

The telephone bell rang and Miss West left the directory to answer it, but even as she talked in short, vague sentences, I could see her eyes straying back towards the columns of Smiths, where lay the enigma of Mister (?) Smith of Fulham, the problem that would surely have defied all Holmes's powers of deduction.

The unheard speaker at the other end of the line was obviously one of Miss West's staff – she has a second office for her under-sleuths close by – who, I thought, must be making a sensational report.

Miss West's replies were maddeningly non-committal, and I found myself supplying the unheard voice.

'*That you, Chiefess?*' it began.

'Yes, speaking,' she said.

'*We've tracked the Slinker's death gang,*' said my imaginary voice. '*They're on the job all right.*'

'What time do you expect—?' asked Miss West.

'*The killing is scheduled for midnight,*' came the voice. '*Shall we call the Yard in?*'

'Oh, I don't think so.'

'*You think they'd muss it all up?*'

'Probably, yes.'

'*You want 'em bumped off?*'

'Yes, I think I should. You know where the place is?'

'*Sure. Down under Fan-chu's dope joint.*'

'That's right. You can walk straight in.'

'*Okay by me, Chiefess.*'

Miss West hung up.

'Was that a crime case?' I asked.

'Hardly that,' she smiled, returning to the directory. 'Only an eloped couple. Smith, W. E., Smith W. E.'

I came down to earth again.

'Was that taxi episode the only thrill of your professional life?' I asked.

'Yes,' said Miss West, 'except when a man came into this office one day and stood just about where you are sitting, and when I glanced up I found myself looking down the barrel of a revolver.

'There is always an automatic in this drawer,' she went on, 'but, of course I could not get at it. The only thing to do was to reason with the man and try to calm him down – he was talking excitedly about killing me. It seemed hopeless to try to calm him. The eyes staring at me about the revolver barrel had a strange gleam in them – they were mad. I saw the knuckles whiten as his finger pressed. Smith, W. E., Smith, W. E. D.'

'What happened?' I asked.

'Oh, a member of my staff, my right-hand man, in fact, is always here or hereabouts. He came in—'

'And hurled himself at the madman!' I exclaimed.

'No,' said Miss West. 'He said, "Did you ring?" And I said, "Yes. Will you please show this gentleman out?" And the man went out quite quietly.'

'What made you go in for such a dull occupation?' I asked.

'I was quite an anxiety to my people,' said Miss West, 'because I always wanted to do something out of the ordinary. Nearly all my family were either solicitors or barristers, and they didn't know what to make of me. Eventually I, well, almost pestered a solicitor uncle into giving me an inquiry to carry out in Paris. It was a case of petty thefts in a hotel, and I went there as a still-room maid. I had no idea what a still-room was, and still less how to be a maid in one; but I did my job quite efficiently and that led to more and more jobs, until I was in a position to start business on my own. But I do not think I should ever have been able to do so without my family's influence. Smith, Walter.'

As I rose and reached for my hat, 'Won't you try a deduction?' I asked.

She looked at me speculatively. Then, 'You owe your dentist money,' she said.

'Well, of course,' I concurred, 'but—'

'You have just had a new dental plate,' she explained.

'Dash it,' I cried, nettled, 'I've never even had an old one yet.'

'Well, I did my best,' she said. 'I'll try again.'

Her eye fell on my hat, a good hat, but it has lost some of its first time careless rapture.

'No, not that!' I said hastily, putting it behind me.

'We had better not go on,' said Miss West. 'I might say something uncomplimentary. Deductions aren't in my line – only inquiries.'

And as I slunk out, I heard behind me London's lady sleuth still persisting in the investigation of her insoluble mystery. 'Smith, Walter, Smith, W. A., Smith, V . . .'[38]

Chapter Fifteen

A Case of Identity

Well, well, a lady detective has, after all, to be
something of an actress occasionally.

Maud West, 1913[1]

Business Maud, Action Maud, Undercover Maud, Maternal Maud, Avenging Maud, Civic Maud. Maud came in many variations with accessories to match: magnifying glass, flat cap, garish earrings, revolver, gavel. *Collect them all!* I thought I had, but here was a new one: Grumpy Maud.

Armed only with a telephone directory and an air of mild irritation, Grumpy Maud could dispatch journalists to deadline hell in fifteen minutes flat. It didn't matter what paper they represented. The exclusive *Daily Mail Atlantic Edition*, printed onboard transatlantic liners full of wealthy people heading for London, some possibly with dark secrets and blackmailers in tow? *Whatever.* Grumpy Maud didn't give a damn.

The signs had been there for a while. Increasingly, she had been talking about the hardships of her job at the expense of the excitement. In 1926, for example, she'd said:

> I must admit that my life is full of thrills and interest. Yet it is extremely exhausting and tedious; it requires a large amount of physical strength, plus tenacity and a firm will that makes one say: 'I *won't* give in; I *will* succeed.' This takes some doing, when a case proves obstinate beyond all expectation.[2]

In her interview with the *Sunday Chronicle* that same year, in which she introduced the young Vera as head of the next generation of crime-fighting ingénues, Maud seemed to be distancing herself from the glamorous image she'd worked so hard to create. She didn't need to show off anymore – she'd made it – but there was also a sense that she was looking back over her lost youth:

> Maude West sat back in her office chair with a smile. 'You wouldn't think I could run very much now,' she said, 'but I wasn't bad at a sprint in those days. To be able to run was often as good a weapon in my armoury as my revolver.'[3]

Everything pointed towards a woman who was getting tired of the grind and of the pretence. She wasn't that old – only forty-five when she gave that interview – but it was understandable. Her counterparts in the police were pensioned off after twenty-five years' service, and she was edging towards that. She'd been walking her own bizarre beat for over twenty years and had also borne six children, raised seven, lost one, and intermittently supported a sickly husband, all whilst building a public persona to capture the eye of the press.

In one curious interview, however, she seemed to let the mask slip altogether. I'd come across it whilst pitting my poor language skills – and the limits of online translation software – against the myriad of tongues contained in European newspaper databases. The majority of pieces I found were variations of those published in the English-speaking press, but this one stood out. It was an exclusive interview Maud had given in March 1930 to a Dutch colonial newspaper published in Jakarta. Scanning through the text, one word caught my eye: *Selfridges.* I sent it off to be professionally translated.

When it came back a few days later, the translation said that Maud

had started her career 'as one of the many girls who were eking out
a living, working at Selfridges, the large department store.'[4] There
were two reasons this couldn't be true: firstly, Selfridges didn't
open until March 1909, which was just four months before Maud's
first adverts appeared in *The Times*, and, secondly, it didn't employ
married women. Still, it was closer to the truth than anything else
I'd seen about her early career. Maybe she, or the paper, was using
the world-famous name as shorthand for any London department
store. Who in Jakarta, after all, would have heard of Pyne Brothers,
Bland & Phillips or Chiesmans, where the women of Deptford did
most of their shoplifting?

Intrigued by this new, semi-truthful Maud, I read on: 'There
was a period in which she was drawn to the stage and during that
time she honed the art of make-up.' *What?* 'Very soon she became
famous for being a talented impersonator.' *WHAT?*

How had I been so blind?

*. . . One has to be a good many things in this profession . . . above
all an actress . . .*

*. . . I am able to imitate the tones of the majority of women, and
many men . . .*

*. . . I can alter my face quite easily by simply adopting another
expression for the time being . . .*[5]

The clues had been there all along. Even her choice of office at
Albion House was a giveaway, so close to theatreland and with
the Music Hall Ladies Guild and all those theatrical agents on her
doorstep. Her publicity photographs were just like the theatrical
cards circulated by performers, and she could weave a story like a
pro. Hadn't I even thought that 'Maud West' was akin to a stage
name?

Others had noticed, too. When the French *Police* magazine
showcased some of her disguise photographs in 1931, for example,
it said that should she ever decide to pack away her magnifying

glass she was assured of a career in theatre or film: 'For what inanimate photos cannot render is the ease with which she passes from one disguise to another . . . she modifies her size, her approach and her pace – stroll, fatigue or businesslike fever – at will!'[6]

The theatre was a gathering place for misfits and dreamers. Taboos in polite society could be enacted on the stage to laughter or tears, and often played out again in dressing rooms and boarding houses once the curtain had fallen. It was a refuge for those, like Willy Clarkson, who would have floundered in the wider world, and a route to independence and autonomy for working-class girls seeking to escape a life of drudgery. It gave them power and freedom.

Of course Maud had been on the stage. Proving it, however, was another matter.

In Victorian theatre, 'impersonator' invariably meant one thing: cross-dressing. The best-known impersonator was Vesta Tilley, who had been strutting her stuff on stage in male clothing since 1869, when she was five years old. As an adult, her music-hall

characters were always impeccably dressed gentlemen, the most famous being Burlington Bertie, the fading West End dandy with 'a Hyde Park drawl' and 'a Bond Street crawl'.[7]

Other big names were Hetty King, Ella Shields and Bessie Bonehill, but there were many more. Some played it straight, especially if they had boyish figures, whilst others made the most of their curves and hammed it up in a mishmash of corset, fishnets, top hat and tails. Either way, it was risqué stuff.

Whether consciously or not, these acts were loaded with meaning, music hall being one of the few outlets in which the broad range of human sexuality could be explored in public. Male impersonators would have been a sensational sight, but they also provided a service to society that went beyond entertainment, as the historian Anthony Slide has pointed out:

> An entire generation of sexually repressed men could live out their homosexual fantasies by watching one of the great male impersonators such as Vesta Tilley or Ella Shields perform. The natty clothes and the tight trousers, the bobbed hair and the masculine swagger were what the males in the audience desired and what they could watch and enjoy in a darkened theatre without fear of retribution.[8]

The same, I assumed, could be said for some female members of the audience. Of course, none of this went down well in more refined venues. Rumour had it that when Vesta Tilley brought her 'Algy, the Piccadilly Johnny' to the first Royal Variety Performance (then called the Royal Command Performance) in July 1912, Queen Mary hid behind her theatre programme until Algy had left the stage.

But where was Maud hiding? I started to look through the *Stage* and the *Era* in the British Newspaper Archive, searching for male impersonators active between 1893, when Maud would have been thirteen, and 1905, when she said she became a detective full-time. By the time I'd finished, I had a list of over 200 names, and those were just the ones looking for work or successful enough to be performing in the main London and regional theatres.

Maud West wasn't one of them, nor was Edith Barber or Edith Elliott, but that didn't surprise me. There were over 350 music halls in London alone, each hosting up to twenty acts per night, and hundreds more in towns and cities elsewhere. For every star performer, there were a thousand others who barely made an impression. Besides, if she had employed a stage name, I doubted it was Maud West. Music hall was entertainment for the masses; the audiences were overwhelmingly working class, with a smattering of bawdy young aristocrats out for a laugh. If Maud wanted to establish herself as a respectable lady detective, she would have been wise to choose a new pseudonym that had no association with that world.

Over the next few weeks, I managed to eliminate some of the names on my list through online photographs and biographies, but that still left a great mass of women hiding behind stage names. My only chance was to find a picture of her. I contacted the British Music Hall Society and scrolled through endless rolls of microfilm and pages of online images, but, eventually, I had to admit defeat.

It wasn't a complete dead end, however. Whilst searching for a booted and suited Maud, I'd come across another actress with a very familiar name: Kate Easton.

It couldn't be, could it?

Everything I knew about Kate Easton had come from the information contained in the 1911 census, in which she refused to participate, and the summary she gave of her progression from warehouse clerk to sleuth in an interview from 1910.[9] As I began to explore further, one of the first things I discovered was that the census enumerator had been generous with her age. He had guessed she was forty-five, whereas she was actually fifty-four. This was evidenced by her death certificate, which wasn't hard to track down as, refreshingly, she worked under her real name. From there, I was able to uncover more of her story.

Kate had been born in Lambeth in 1856, the youngest of four children. Her father was a tobacconist, but the performing arts clearly played a part in family life: her brother William would become a music teacher, and by the time Kate was twenty-one she had found success on the stage. A concert programme from 1877 listed her amongst the cast of a series of plays directed by the famous actor-manager Charles Wyndham at the Crystal Palace, and various reviews over the following years mentioned her skill as a vocalist.[10] She was still performing at the time of the 1901 census when, coincidentally, she was living with her widowed mother opposite the British Museum, just a few doors down from Great Russell Mansions.

Kate made her first appearance in the press as an assistant detective in 1904, when she was forty-eight, giving evidence at a divorce hearing in Dublin about how she had watched a Lady McConnell meet her lover at a private hotel in Brighton the previous year.[11] She would soon branch out on her own.[12] When a journalist from *Lloyd's Weekly News* visited her in her 'snug' Shaftesbury Avenue office a couple of years later, he reported:

> Miss Easton considers her profession a splendid one for women, but a candidate should be a first-rate actress, be able to efface self, possess indomitable pluck, an unshaken nerve, unlimited patience, powers of physical endurance, and excellent eyesight, hearing, and memory.[13]

It was practically a checklist for those wishing to tread the boards, although she never mentioned her previous career. Instead, she just quietly slogged away as a detective for the next twenty-four years until she retired at the age of seventy-three. She never married. At the time of her retirement in 1929, she was living in Notting Hill at what seemed to be a boarding house for women of slender means: 'Use of geyser bath,' promised one listing for two unfurnished rooms at the property. 'One or two ladies only.'[14] Within two years she would be dead, having seen out her last days at a hospital in Kensington after a fall.[15]

Out of curiosity, I decided to check out the other big-name female detective of the time. The official profile of Matilda Mitchell's work as head of Selfridges' secret service stated that she had worked as a railway detective and for the Royal College of Veterinary Surgeons before taking up the post, but it hadn't been clear as to how she got those positions. An interview she gave to a Sunday newspaper after her retirement in January 1914, however, filled in the gaps. Once again, the velvet curtain was drawn back: Matilda, too, had been on the stage.

Like Kate, she came from Lambeth. She had been born in 1873 and had first performed at the Royal Opera House at the age of fifteen before adopting the stage name Ethel Chester and moving into pantomime at the Drury Lane Theatre under the direction of the father of modern pantomime himself, Sir Augustus Harris. 'It was during this period,' Matilda said, 'that I frequently attended fancy dress balls at Covent Garden in all sorts and conditions of disguises, winning many first prizes. These successes, I may say, led to my first engagement as a lady detective.'[16]

Although she didn't say when this happened, she did mention the then-famous Hartopp divorce, a veritable mud bath of scandal involving a baronet, his wife, an earl and a society hostess, which had gone to trial in December 1902. By my reckoning, she'd had around fifteen years on the stage and at least seven as a private detective before joining Selfridges in 1909.

Had I stumbled across a secret cabal of actress-detectives looking to take down London's underworld with their crime-fighting prowess? Probably not. It was doubtful that they'd even met before entering the detective profession. Kate and Matilda may have both come from Lambeth, but there were fifteen years between them. Besides, each of the trio had her own theatrical discipline: Kate in traditional theatre, Matilda in opera and pantomime, and Maud, perhaps, in music hall. But after they became detectives? They must have known each other.

Still, something niggled. The timing of Maud's confession that she had been on the stage was suspicious, coming as it did just after Kate's retirement. Was she just weaving another tale, appropriating the background of her greatest rival when that rival could no longer fight back? But, if so, how did that explain the constant references to acting that she had made throughout her career?

I'd sensed from the beginning that there was something off in the relationship between Kate and Maud. At the time, I'd put it down to simple professional rivalry. London, after all, could only accommodate one leading lady detective. But now, I began to form a new theory and wondered if the one-upmanship they practised in their newspaper adverts was symptomatic of a deeper animosity.

How, exactly, had Maud got involved in detective work? It wasn't through her solicitor uncle or any other relative in the legal profession, because they didn't exist. So how had she learned what the job involved? It was possible that she'd just knuckled down and taught herself, as she claimed, but everything I'd learned about private detectives told me that wasn't how things worked. Inquiry agents didn't just dive in and make things up as they went along, however many criminology books they had read. They always served some form of apprenticeship, whether that was as a police officer or, like Kate and Matilda, as an assistant to a more experienced private detective. Even Maud admitted as much in an article she had written in 1928 about the secrets of her success:

> Of course, at the very beginning, one must know one's limitations if success is to be won! It is useless to imagine oneself a Napoleon or a Pinkerton; but it is equally fatal to lack courage to try. By beginning on small problems, whether of criminology or work, one must gain experience and graduate on to the big ones with some confidence.[17]

There wasn't any evidence, after all, to support her repeated claim that she had established her agency in 1905; there was nothing before 1909. Kate had, though. Her agency had been up and running by October 1905. Had Maud, twenty-five years Kate's junior, been her protégée?

It was a compelling theory. *Kate Easton, Maud West. Easton, West. East and West.* They even sounded like a double act. They could easily have worked together, whether Maud had been on the stage or not, with Kate passing on a few theatre tricks along the way. And if Maud then broke away to set up a rival agency right across the road? Such a betrayal, and her subsequent insistence on claiming all the credit of her success for herself, could easily have led to bad blood.

One thing was certain. Whether Maud got her first foot in the door of the detective profession through her own determination or by tap dancing down Shaftesbury Avenue arm in arm with Kate Easton, she was a self-made woman in every sense of the word. And now, in her fifties, she was reaping the rewards.

She was finally, and indisputably, London's leading lady detective. Longevity alone had ensured that. Furthermore, with her business at its peak, she could prioritize the work that interested her. According to the interview she gave to Margaret Gilruth of the *Hobart Mercury* in 1938, that no longer included divorce investigations. She left that kind of work to her staff so she could focus on worthier causes. 'She likes the humanitarian side of detecting,' Gilruth explained. 'She prefers the thought that, indirectly, she is doing good by stopping somebody doing harm. That spurs her on more than anything else.'[18]

For Maud, this meant blackmail and drugs investigations – 'although I have collaborated on murder cases,' she added. But it seemed to me that she had also found a new way of being.

During the 1930s, she became noticeably more political. There was her work on Holborn Council, of course, but she also started to comment more frequently on current affairs. In the early 1930s, for example, as the world was in the grip of the Great Depression, some had detected a rise in the number of women criminals. 'The honesty of women always wanes in times of economic stress,' Maud told one paper. 'Whenever money is scarce there is a perfect epidemic of thefts by women who, deprived of spending money, will have clothes at any price.'[19]

Elsewhere, however, she hinted at more political reasons, in line with her Conservative views. 'I cannot help thinking,' she told the *Daily Mail* in 1931, 'that our system of education is largely to blame. Girls and boys are taught little bits of this and that, and feel that they are too good for their own particular circle of life. Then they see girls and boys of their own age getting easy money by way of the "dole" and they jump at the suggestion that they, too, can get easy money if they will take a little risk and so they drift into criminal ways.'[20]

The following year, she turned her attention to the wider world after spending a month in America. The primary purpose of the trip was unclear – she had travelled with a friend from Finchley – but on her return she produced an article quite unlike anything she'd written before. It began with a lengthy scene in the back room of a Midwest precinct station, where a 'crumpled specimen of humanity' was receiving the attention of half a dozen detectives. She'd paid particular attention to the dialogue:

- Listen! I don' wanna get rough with you. Just come across an be quick. You know you gotta talk!
- I dunno, boss. I dunno a darn thing . . . honest I don't. I'd come clean if I did. I wasn't there . . . I . . .
- All right. If you want it you can have it. Give him the works, boys!

It wasn't for the squeamish – the use to which they put rubber tubing was enough to make anyone wince – but, having grabbed her readers' attention, Maud continued:

The 'Third Degree,' as practised in America, has for a long time constituted a disgrace to civilisation . . . I had heard tales of it, but believed these to be exaggerated. On my last visit to America, however, I made up my mind to investigate the truth of some of the reports I had heard. They were not exaggerated. They erred on the side of understatement.[21]

This, it turned out, was the introduction to a comparative essay on American and European investigative techniques. The American methods, she said, 'smack too much of the tortures of the Inquisition' and were unproductive to boot. Austria, on the other hand, was making great progress with their use of criminal psychologists; ditto France, to whom she awarded bonus points for their experiments with murder-scene reconstructions, which sometimes involved the actual corpse: 'A guilty person confronted with the corpse of the man he killed often gives himself away, but the same

process, even if unpleasant, has little effect on the mind of an innocent person.'

She also approved of the 'special department' in Berlin devoted
to checking the veracity of suspects and witnesses, resulting in an
unusually high clear-up rate for murders. As for the 'meek and
mild' Brits, they were efficient but hampered by suspects' right to
remain silent. 'This, in my opinion, places our police in an unfor-
tunate position,' she wrote. 'Close questioning, immediately on
arrest, before the suspect has time to prepare a story or alibi, may
result in important clues.'

Pragmatic or ruthless? I couldn't decide, but it was refreshing to
see her emerge from behind the fog of all the exploding safes and
screeching tyres to comment on the broader issues associated with
her work.

She hadn't completely abandoned her love of drama, however.
She was still capable of making a grand entrance, as she did in 1936
when she chugged up to an event in Mayfair, ostensibly straight
from a job. The *Daily Mirror* reported:

> A woman drove up to magnificent Sunderland House yester-
> day, having come from West Ham, in a dilapidated two-seater.
> From the back seat, where it lay hidden, she removed a fur coat.
> Putting this on, she swept into Sunderland House for the open-
> ing of the Exhibition of Women's Progress. She had a stall there.
> She was Maud West, detective, one of the most vivid characters
> in London.[22]

Nor had her scruples changed when it came to accepting clients.
The article from the Dutch East Indies had confirmed one of my
earliest assumptions, that none of Maud's stories could be true in
the strictest sense of the word: 'In all of London,' it said, 'there
is probably no other woman who knows more tragic secrets than

Maud West, but they are absolutely safe with her. She never even alludes to them, not even to her husband.'[23]

In 1938, she made an exception. Jimmy Brantley, a wealthy American manufacturer from Savannah, Georgia, was depicted in the international press as one of the world's greatest romantics, although to my eyes his actions were more akin to stalking. After being jilted in 1932 by his fiancée, an eighteen-year-old Southern belle called Constance Ryland, he refused to take no for an answer. 'I will wait until she says yes,' he said. 'I have the time.' In the meantime, he decided to send her a single Maréchal-Niel rose every day, wherever she was. Six years later, he was still at it.[24]

Constance didn't seem to mind. One photograph of her circulated by a press agency in 1937 showed her sniffing a rose delivered in London with an air of glamorous indifference worthy of the Hollywood career she was trying to cultivate. 'Postman and express messengers, porters on Pullman trains, hotel pageboys and ships' stewards have all played their part in delivering the daily reminder to Miss Ryland,' explained the caption.[25] Maud's somewhat dubious role in all this was to keep Mr Brantley informed of Constance's whereabouts, a task she delegated to her staff. The promised $10,000 bonus if the romance was ever rekindled was presumably never paid out, as Constance eventually, and sensibly, married someone else.

For the most part, however, Maud was slowing down. Harry was keen for her to retire, according to Margaret Gilruth, but she couldn't bring herself to do so: 'She tries, then somebody implores her to tackle some baffling case; she can't refuse, and back she comes to her offices.'[26] But, in September 1939, her hand was forced.

She'd known it was coming. The first Home Office instructions for air-raid precautions had arrived at Holborn Council in 1935; air-raid wardens had been recruited in 1937, gas masks issued in 1938, blackout curtains hung in the summer of 1939. She'd worked through one war. Now, with her sixtieth birthday on the horizon, could she face another?

It was time for Maud West to exit the stage. She made one last trip to Albion House to clear out her office, locked the door and, without so much as a final bow, disappeared. She was never seen again.

As for Edith Elliott, she was taking no chances. When asked for her occupation for the 1939 Register, a special census to gather information for identity cards, rationing and war work, she put 'Secretary'.[27] The message was clear. *Look elsewhere.* Maud West was no more, and Edith Elliott was unavailable – unless, that is, MI5 needed an elderly typist, and it wasn't difficult to imagine how she'd ham that one up. Then Edith, too, vanished. She packed her bags and went – *where*?

I had no idea. I'd lost her.

Chapter Sixteen

Farewell, My Lovely

If variety is the spice of life, then mine
has been more than ordinarily spicy.

Maud West, 1926[1]

I stood nervously outside the station, looking out for a red Saab convertible. Brian had recovered from his surgery and was on his way to pick me up. When I first came across Maud West, I'd never considered that one day I might be waiting to meet her grandson with some of the family's most intimate secrets smouldering away in my bag. It felt wrong. Almost creepy.

Hello, I'm your grandmother's stalker.

Doubt rippled through me. Had I got carried away? Were the dead fair game? And, if so, just how dead did they have to be to make it okay? Was Maud dead enough?

Every day it was becoming easier to scoot past the grand old men in their gilded carriages and observe the common folk as they trudged along. Archive catalogues, digitized newspapers, books, photographs, diaries and more were now only a Google search away; private lives made public with the click of a mouse. But these people hadn't invited scrutiny. Even Maud, for all her appreciation of publicity, had made it clear by her actions that her personal life was off-limits.

My main concern whilst I waited for Brian, however, was the effect such scrutiny could have on the living. The millions of genealogy enthusiasts building up their family trees knew the power of ancestry, of how the stories handed down or hidden over generations inform our sense of self. A noble lineage, centuries of hard graft, even a renegade skeleton or two, can shape how we see ourselves and the world around us.

Digging up the past could also lead to more disturbing discoveries: broken genetic links, unexpected siblings, a worrying pattern of premature mental decay. To root around in one's own family tree knowing these risks was one thing – I'd done it myself – but to do so in someone else's and then present them with the results? That seemed to hover somewhere between rude and dangerous.

But it was too late to back out now. The red Saab had arrived. I'd already alerted Brian to his grandmother's double life as Maud West, and now I had to tell him the rest.

We chatted about the weather and trains as he manoeuvred the car through the town towards the sea. I caught a glimpse of a harbour ahead as we pulled into a driveway next to a small Georgian

ONLY WOMAN DETECTIVE IN LONDON

Unique among London's strange occupations is that of Miss Maud West, who is London's lady detective. Miss West's experience in the crime world has been varied and thrilling. She often adopts masculine disguises, but in this picture is disguised as an old woman.

building where his wife Shirley was waiting in the flat upstairs.

Whilst Brian went into the kitchen to make some coffee, I took out a folder of photographs to show Shirley. The buck-toothed Salvation Army lass, the plump Charlie Chaplin and the aristocratic gent were each greeted with a gracious nod, but when we came to a picture of Maud disguised as a crotchety old woman, her eyes twinkled.

'That's just how I remember her,' she said.

When Brian returned with the drinks, we danced around the subject a little more. 'She was very good at getting people to fetch things for her,' he said. Edith, it seemed, had spent most of her retirement firmly plonked in an armchair, refusing to get up unless absolutely necessary.

'Perhaps she'd had enough of running?' I suggested. Shirley's polite smile suggested otherwise.

Any residual nerves I had were dispelled as the day went on. Brian was unfazed by the story I put before him about the life Edith – *Edie* – had created for herself as London's most famous lady detective. I left nothing out – her illegitimacy, Harry's gonorrhoea, Keith's suicide – and he took it all with the equanimity one would expect of a man who had spent a lifetime calmly sawing through people's bones day after day.

But what could he tell me about her life before retirement? Very little, it turned out. In the 1930s, when Maud West was still stalking the streets of London, Brian had been too young to take much notice of what the grown-ups were doing. To him, Edie was just his grandmother: she liked sitting down, disapproved of swearing and smoked Dr Blosser's herbal cigarettes because they were 'good for the lungs'.

Could she sing? Brian had never heard her do so. Was there anything else to suggest she might have once been on the stage? No. What about all the languages she claimed to speak? Was she a talented linguist? He didn't think so. Nor could he explain why she was the only one listed on the electoral roll at Great Russell Mansions in 1933 and 1934, or why she might have chosen to change her name by deed poll around that time. Perhaps it was related to her political career? To all my other questions, the answer was the same: she never talked about the past.

The conversation turned to Harry. History can be cruel to the common man – too often, the only surviving records are those connected with a person's lowest moments – and it soon became clear that Harry had been affected more than most. His health issues, juvenile crime record and debts had been mere blips in an otherwise healthy and happy life. Brian had been very fond of him, his abiding memory being of a crossword fiend who never went anywhere without a stubby pencil tucked into his waistcoat pocket.

I'd got Harry wrong. He wasn't just another encumbrance to Edith's peace of mind, dripping with germs and neuroses and blowing all her money on bad investments. He was a solid and supportive partner who cheered her on whilst quietly pursuing his own varied interests: motorbikes, advertising, the temporary storage of hats and coats. At one point between the wars, Brian said, he'd also worked as a tea taster. I'd been right about one thing, though: Harry was a shed man, although his shed was a bit larger than I had imagined. All those gentlemen's tricycles from the classified ads were bound for the successful bicycle-parts business he operated off the A3 near New Malden.

What about 1939 and beyond? Where had Edith and Harry gone? Brian knew the answer to that one because he'd been with them. His father had been drafted into the RAF as a flying instructor. Not wanting to stay in London, Edith and Harry, along with five-year-old Brian and his mother Mollie, had packed up their belongings and formed a little band of camp followers, trailing after Cecil as he moved from base to base.

I had another question. I'd recently discovered that when she left London Edith had put her business in the hands of her solicitors in Chancery Lane. She evidently had no intention of returning to it herself, but had she hoped that Evelyn or Vera would pick up where she left off? Did that happen? No. After being discharged from the SOE, Evelyn retrained as a chiropodist; Vera bought a pig farm in Scotland.

It struck me that both had chosen the reassuring honesty of flesh (whether porcine or human) over the ever-shifting moral sands of private detective work – as had Neville, who moved to New Zealand to try his luck as a sheep farmer. Cecil, of course, had his teeth. As for Denis, I had some more uncomfortable news for Brian: after the war, he had moved with his wife to a remote cottage near Ashford in Kent, where he died just eight years later at the age of forty-seven. His death certificate held uneasy echoes of another incident almost thirty years earlier:

> Laceration of brain owing to gunshot wound of the head. Killed himself whilst balance of mind was disturbed.[2]

Edith had lost two of her sons to suicide.

By that time, she had also lost her husband. In 1945, she and Harry had moved to Cheam in Surrey to enjoy a peaceful retirement, but the peace hadn't lasted long. Harry was soon diagnosed with stomach cancer and died in January 1950 at the age of seventy.

Edith, as ever, carried on. On 15 September 1960, she celebrated her eightieth birthday with her family, posing for a photograph at her new home in Bexhill-on-Sea:

She didn't need any disguise, now. She blended in with all the other elderly widows hiding their grief and lost youth beneath stiff tailoring and support stockings, any whiff of loneliness masked by the scent of powder and Parma Violets. Who would have guessed, to look at her, all that she had achieved? She certainly wasn't going to tell. She never spoke about the past.

As I was preparing to leave, I asked Brian, 'What do you think she would say if she knew I was writing this book?'

'She'd say, "Don't."'

A pause. We looked at the piles of papers and photographs I was packing into my bag.

'But I say do it, anyway,' he said.

The rental car had a sticky second gear. I cursed as I bunny-hopped my way out of London and headed south for the clear run down to the coast. I'd been feeling strangely bereft ever since Brian had dropped me back at the station. *Was that it?* After all those months in Maud's company, I couldn't just go home. There was one last place I had to visit.

Welcome to Bexhill-on-Sea.

The De La Warr pavilion gleamed in all its faded Art Deco glory as I juddered to a halt on the front. From there, it was just a short walk up a terraced street of smart boarding houses and tropical palms to Parkhurst Road. On the corner stood a dilapidated building covered in scaffolding, its paint peeling and rubbish strewn around the overgrown garden. So this was where Edith had whiled away her final years.

Apart from the eyesore that was No. 7, it was pleasant enough, but what kind of place was this for a lady detective to end her days? It wasn't as bad as the shared geyser bath and poky bedsit that Kate Easton had to endure, but I'd hoped for more. It had neither the bustle of Bloomsbury nor the deceptive calm of St Mary Mead. What was there to *do* here, except wait?

The end, at least, had been swift: a heart attack in March 1964, on Friday the thirteenth. One final dramatic flourish to a life filled with intrigue.

I walked back down to the front and onto the promenade. She'd led me a merry dance, but who *was* Maud West? A shameless attention seeker or private to the core? A champion of the downtrodden or the mortal enemy of chimney sweeps? A cosmopolitan adventurer or a suburban homebody? A witness to society's troubles or a brazen liar?

Looking out to sea, I thought of the great ocean liners that had once ploughed through the waves to New York, Cape Town, Valparaiso, Jakarta. Had she really been to all those places? Had she really hauled coke-addled debutantes out of Chinatown, punched men in Bond Street and faced down blackmailers with her trusty revolver?

Maybe. Did it even matter anymore? I'd gone looking for a lady detective and found so much more: a remarkably complex woman who'd taken the poor hand dealt her at birth and transformed it into a life that would be the envy of millions. She was bad-tempered and sharp and tender and kind. She loved her work, she loved her family; she was determined to have it all – and she'd almost succeeded.

Good for her, I thought.

THE END

Acknowledgements

Creating a book is a team effort. My heartfelt thanks, therefore, go to my editor George Morley and all at Picador, especially Marissa Constantinou, Laura Carr, Gaby Quattromini and Mel Four, and to my agent Tim Bates at Peters Fraser and Dunlop.

My enduring gratitude also goes to Brian and Shirley Elliott for sharing their memories with me and for their good humour in the face of unexpected revelations.

To all those slaving over hot scanners at the British Newspaper Archive, Trove, Gallica, Ancestry and other digitization projects throughout the world: thank you. Your work has opened up access to the past in ways unimaginable when I was a young researcher. The old ways are still indispensable, however, so equal thanks go to the staff at the British Library, National Archives and Camden Local Studies Centre, and to those who have undertaken lookups for me in far-flung places: Kevin Morse in California, Laura Schmidt in Illinois, Robyn Atherton in New South Wales and Alastair Moir in Norfolk.

For their friendly and excellent linguistic services, thank you to Alina Cincan, Yannis Tsitsovits, Elizabeth De Zoysa and Marion Pini-Overberg at Inbox Translation, and to Buffy Shaw for her help with transcribing Maud's articles.

Finally, a big cheer to everyone who cheered *me* on. You know who you are, but special mentions must go to James Hannah, Anna Dreda and the Lighthouse gang, to my husband Jim for enduring frequent and dramatic displays of creative angst, to my father for being a top-notch sounding board and image wrangler, and to my mother for so steadfastly 'keeping out of it'. I am indebted to you all.

Bibliography

Articles by Maud West

'The Adventures of a Lady Detective: My Early Cases', *Pearson's Weekly*, 29 Mar 1913, p. 1011

'The Adventures of a Lady Detective: Working in Big Hotels', *Pearson's Weekly*, 5 Apr 1913, p. 1045

'The Adventures of a Lady Detective: Work in Private Houses', *Pearson's Weekly*, 12 Apr 1913, p. 1058

'The Adventures of a Lady Detective: Lovers and Love Affairs', *Pearson's Weekly*, 19 Apr 1913, p. 1083

'The Adventures of a Lady Detective', *Pearson's Weekly*, 26 Apr 1913, p. 1107

'The Adventures of a Lady Detective: Hide and Seek Cases', *Pearson's Weekly*, 3 May 1913, p. 1137

'Blackmailing "Demobbed" Officers', *Pearson's Weekly*, 12 Apr 1919, p. 575

'New Frauds of Marriage Agencies', *Pearson's Weekly*, 17 May 1919, p. 671

'Why Sex Hate is Growing', *Pearson's Weekly*, 31 May 1919, p. 711

'Traps for Girls' War Savings', *Pearson's Weekly*, 7 Jun 1919, p. 731

'Dodges of Damage Hunters', *Answers*, 5 Jul 1919, p. 111

'How Rich Snobs Buy Society', *Pearson's Weekly*, 5 Jul 1919, p. 48

'Revelations of a Lady 'Tec', *Answers*, 2 Aug 1919, p. 183

'Crooks I Have Foiled', *Answers*, 9 Aug 1919, p. 209

'Jazz-Room Revelations', *Answers*, 23 Aug 1919, p. 248

'Real Life Love Stories', *Pearson's Weekly*, 13 Aug 1921, p. 171

'When Love Turns to Hate', *Pearson's Weekly*, 20 Aug 1921, p. 189

'Boy and Girl Lovers', *Pearson's Weekly*, 27 Aug 1921, p. 219

'Matter of Fact Lovers', *Pearson's Weekly*, 3 Sep 1921, p. 239

'Woman Detective's Theory of Inn Crime', *Lloyd's Sunday News*, 12 Mar 1922, p. 5

'How To Be a Detective', *Competitors' Journal & Everybody's Weekly*, 29 May 1926, p. 11

'Some Games of Bluff and Other Matters', *Pearson's Magazine*, 1 Nov 1926, pp. 430–4

'My Secrets of Success', *Pearson's Weekly*, 19 May 1928, p. 1323

'The Most Despicable Crime', *Derby Daily Telegraph*, 19 Nov 1929, p. 6

'How I Took Up the Work', *Weekly Irish Times*, 1 Feb 1930, p. 10

'The Clairvoyante Case', *Weekly Irish Times*, 8 Feb 1930, p. 3

'The Office Robbery', *Weekly Irish Times*, 15 Feb 1930, p. 3

'The German Spy Case', *Weekly Irish Times*, 22 Feb 1930, p. 3

'The Hotel Thief', *Weekly Irish Times*, 1 Mar 1930, p. 3

'The Country House Case', *Weekly Irish Times*, 8 Mar 1930, p. 3

'The Dope Fiend', *Weekly Irish Times*, 15 Mar 1930, p. 3

'Scoundrels in Love', *Weekly Irish Times*, 22 Mar 1930, p. 3

'The Fatal Letter', *Weekly Irish Times*, 29 Mar 1930, p. 3

'Who is to blame in divorce?', *Portsmouth Evening News*, 29 Apr 1930, p. 5

'Real-Life Adventures of Miss Sherlock Holmes', *Sunday Dispatch*, 15 Nov 1931, p. 4

'War Spies I Caught', *Sunday Dispatch*, 22 Nov 1931, p. 4

'Miss Sherlock Holmes's Adventures in Secret Dope Dens', *Sunday Dispatch*, 29 Nov 1931, p. 4

'Miss Sherlock Homes Reveals the Wiles of Hush-Money Parasites', *Sunday Dispatch*, 6 Dec 1931, p. 4

'Secret Gem Store of a Jekyll and Hyde', *Sunday Dispatch*, 13 Dec 1931, p. 8

'Forcing Confessions from Crooks', *Australian Worker* (Sydney), 9 Nov 1932, p. 19

'Beauty Wins, Woman Scorned: New Angle on Triangle', *Sunday Mail* (Brisbane), 29 Dec 1935, p. 17

'The Phantom Thief', *Huon and Derwent Times* (Australia), 4 Mar 1937, p. 3

'Prince of Lovers', *Times of India*, 11 Apr 1938, p. 22

Maud West: Select Profiles and Interviews

'Maud West: Woman Detective', *Sunday Press* (Pittsburgh), 27 Jul 1913, illustrated magazine section, p. 3

'Thrills of a Lady Detective', *Ideas*, 13 Mar 1914, p. 6

'A Woman Detects: Wiles and Disguises of a Charming Sleuth', *Daily Express*, 1 May 1914, p. 4

'The Lady 'Tec', *Camperdown Chronicle* (Australia), 17 Jul 1915, p. 6

'Women Detectives of London Threaten to Dim Holmes's Fame', *New York Tribune*, 10 Jul 1921, p. 2

'Work of a Woman Detective', *Manchester Guardian*, 21 Aug 1924, p. 6

'Meet Mrs Sherlock Holmes!', *Sunday Chronicle*, 14 Feb 1926, p. 3

'Exploits of London's Famous Woman Detective', *San Francisco Examiner*, 16 May 1926, 'American Weekly' section, p. 2

'Maud West, De Vrouwelijke Detective', *Het Nieuws van den Dag voor Nederlandsch-Indië* ('Woord en Beeld' supplement), 29 Mar 1930, pp. 288 and 290

'Maud West, Londen's Vrouwelijke Detective', *Het Nieuws van den Dag voor Nederlandsch-Indië*, 9 Jul 1930, p. 3

'A Woman Detective', *The Policewoman's Review*, Apr 1931, pp. 139–40

'Such a Dull Job! Or, Fifteen Minutes with a London Woman Detective', *Daily Mail Atlantic Edition*, 17 Jun 1931, p. 6

'Maud West: Détective à Transformations', *Police* (France), Vol. 54 (6 Dec 1931), p. 14

'Women Detectives: Maud West's Strange Work', *Hobart Mercury* (Australia), 21 Dec 1938, pp. 6 and 8

Other Lady Detectives: Select Articles and Interviews

Kate Easton

'Lady Detective: Knows not fear and can shoot straight', *Lloyd's Weekly News*, 19 May 1907, p. 6

'Blackmailers!', *New Zealand Truth*, 17 Oct 1908, p. 5

'My Work as a Lady Detective', *M. A. P. (Mainly About People)*, 5 Feb 1910, p. 171

Antonia Moser

'Adventures of a Woman Detective' (series):
  I.   'The Case of the Foreign Nobleman', *Weekly Dispatch*, 2 Jun 1907, p. 6
  II. 'The Gentleman Cracksman', *Weekly Dispatch*, 9 Jun 1907, p. 2

III. 'The Mystery of the Dead American', *Weekly Dispatch*, 16 Jun 1907, p. 2

IV. 'The First of the Gold Brick Swindles', *Weekly Dispatch*, 23 Jun 1907, pp. 6 and 13

V. 'A Case of Identity', *Weekly Dispatch*, 30 Jun 1907, pp. 6 and 13

VI. 'The Lady Who Disappeared', *Weekly Dispatch*, 7 Jul 1907, pp. 6 and 13

VII. 'A Criminal by Instinct', *Weekly Dispatch*, 14 Jul 1907, pp. 6 and 13

Anonymous

'A Lady Detective's Experiences', *The Sketch*, 24 Jan 1894, p. 704
'Adventures of a Woman Detective', *Weekly Dispatch*, 17 Oct 1909, p. 5
'Why I Shadow People', *Pearson's Weekly*, 4 May 1911, p. 759
'Life as a Lady Sleuth', *Answers*, 16 May 1925, p. 10
'Women Detectives and Their Work', *Midland Daily Telegraph*, 1 Mar 1938, p. 6

Books and Journal Articles

Allen, Mary S. *The Pioneer Policewoman*. Chatto & Windus, 1925
— *Lady in Blue*. Stanley Paul & Co., 1936
Anthony, Barry. *Murder, Mayhem and Music Hall: The Dark Side of Victorian London*. I. B. Tauris, 2015
Ashton, John. *The History of Gambling in England*. Duckworth & Co., 1898
Billington-Greig, Teresa. 'The Truth About White Slavery'. *The English Review*, Vol. XIV (April–July 1913), pp. 428–46
Brittain, Vera. *Lady into Woman: A History of Women from Victoria to Elizabeth II*. Andrew Dakers, 1953
Brunelle, Gayle K., and Finley-Croswhite, Annette. *Murder in the Métro: Laetitia Toureaux and the Cagoule in 1930s France*. Louisiana State University Press, 2010
Christie, Agatha. *Parker Pyne Investigates*. Penguin, 1953
Cobb, Irwin S. *Europe Revised*. George H. Doran Co., 1914
Cohen, Deborah. *Family Secrets: The Things We Tried to Hide*. Penguin, 2014

Connell, Nicholas. *Doctor Crippen: The Infamous London Cellar Murder of 1910.* Amberley Publishing, 2013

Craig, Patricia, and Cadogan, Mary. *The Lady Investigates: Women Detectives and Spies in Fiction.* Gollancz, 1981

Dark, Sidney. *The Life of Sir Arthur Pearson.* Hodder & Stoughton, 1922

Doughan, David, and Gordon, Peter. *Women, Clubs and Associations in Britain.* Routledge, 2006

Downer, Martyn. *The Sultan of Zanzibar: the bizarre world and spectacular hoaxes of Horace de Vere Cole.* Black Spring, 2010

Edwards, Martin. *The Golden Age of Murder: The Mystery of the Writers Who Invented the Modern Detective Story.* HarperCollins, 2015

Felstead, Sidney Theodore. *German Spies at Bay.* Hutchinson & Co., 1920

Foot, M. R. D. *SOE: An Outline History of the Special Operations Executive 1940–46.* British Broadcasting Corporation, 1984

Garth, Alan. *A History of the Publicity Club of London.* Publicity Club of London, 1978

Gibson, Colin. *Dissolving Wedlock.* Routledge, 1993

Gielgud, Sir John. *Backward Glances.* Hodder & Stoughton, 1989

Gillis, John R. *For Better, for Worse: British Marriages, 1600 to the Present.* Oxford University Press, 1986

Glazer, A. M., and Thomson, Patience (eds). *Crystal Clear: The Autobiographies of Sir Lawrence and Lady Bragg.* Oxford University Press, 2015

Goodwin, John C. *Crook Pie.* Alston Rivers, London, 1927

—*Sidelights on Criminal Matters.* Hutchinson, 1923

Graves, Robert. *The Long Weekend.* Second edition. Faber and Faber, 1950

Greenwall, Harry J. *The Strange Life of Willy Clarkson: an Experiment in Biography.* John Long, 1936

Greenwood, Colin. *Firearms Control: A Study of Armed Crime and Firearms Control in England and Wales.* Routledge and Kegan Paul, 1972

Haywood, Janet. *History of Soroptimist International.* Soroptimist International, 1995

Hazelgrove, Jenny. *Spiritualism and British Society between the Wars.* Manchester University Press, 2000

Herbert, A. P. *Holy Deadlock.* Methuen & Co., 1934

Hillman, June. *The Glass Ladder*. Heinemann, 1960

Hutchinson, Arthur Stuart Menteth. *This Freedom*. Fourth edition. Hodder
     & Stoughton, 1922

Hyde, H. Montgomery. *The Other Love: An Historical and Contemporary
     Survey of Homosexuality in Britain*. Mayflower, 1972

—*A Tangled Web: Sex Scandals in British Politics and Society*. Constable,
     1986

Hynes, Samuel. *The Edwardian Turn of Mind*. Princeton University Press,
     1968

Jackson, Louise A. 'The Unusual Case of "Mrs Sherlock": Memoir, Identity
     and the "Real" Woman Private Detective in Twentieth-Century Brit-
     ain', *Gender & History*, Vol. 15, No.1 (April 2003), pp. 108–34

Jones, Charles Sheridan. *London in War-Time*. Grafton & Co., 1917

Kerner, Annette. *Woman Detective*. T. Werner Laurie, 1954

—*Further Adventures of a Woman Detective*. T. Werner Laurie, 1955

Kestner, Joseph A. *The Edwardian Detective, 1901–1915*. Ashgate Publish-
     ing, 2000

Klein, Kathleen Gregory. *The Woman Detective: Gender & Genre*. Univer-
     sity of Illinois, 1988

Kohn, Marek. *Dope Girls: The Birth of the British Drug Underground*.
     Lawrence & Wishart, 1992

Lang, Elsie M. *British Women in the Twentieth Century*. T. Werner Laurie,
     1929

Le Queux, William. *German Spies in England: An Exposure*. Sixth edition.
     Stanley Paul & Co., 1915

Liddington, Jill, and Crawford, Elizabeth. *Vanishing for the Vote: Suffrage,
     Citizenship and the Battle for the Census*. Manchester University
     Press, 2014

Livesey, A. H. Henderson. *League of Womanhood Pamphlet No.1: The
     Women Police Question*. League of Womanhood, 1924

—*Sex and Public Life*. Social Services Ltd, 1926

Lock, Joan. *The British Policewoman: Her Story*. Robert Hale, 1979

Lodge, Sir Oliver. *Raymond, or Life and Death*. Thirteenth edition.
     Methuen, 1916

Luke, Thomas Davy. *Spas and Health Resorts of the British Isles*. A & C
     Black, 1919

Malcolm, Joyce Lee. *Guns and Violence: The English Experience*. Harvard University Press, 2002

McDonald, Brian. *Gangs of London: 100 Years of Mob Warfare*. Milo Books, 2010

McLaren, Angus. 'Smoke and Mirrors: Willy Clarkson and the Role of Disguises in Inter-war England', *Journal of Social History*, Vol. 40, No. 3 (Spring 2007), pp. 597–618

— *Sexual Blackmail: A Modern History*. Harvard University Press, 2002

Morn, Frank. *The eye that never sleeps: a history of the Pinkerton National Detective Agency*. Indiana University Press, 1982

Nicholson, Virginia. *Singled Out: How Two Million Women Survived Without Men after the First World War*. Viking, 2007

O'Sullivan, Frank Dalton. *Crime Detection*. O'Sullivan Publishing, 1928

Phillips, Roderick. *Untying the Knot: A Short History of Divorce*. Cambridge University Press, 1991

Rivers, Aileen. *A Brief History of the Private Detective*. Association of British Investigators, 2009

Robins, Jane. *The Magnificent Spilsbury and the Case of the Brides in the Bath*. John Murray, 2010

Savage, Gail. 'Erotic Stories and Public Decency: Newspaper Reporting of Divorce Proceedings in England', *Historical Journal*, Vol. 41, No. 2 (June 1998), pp. 511–28

Slide, Anthony. *Great Pretenders: A History of Male and Female Impersonation in the Performing Arts*. Wallace-Homestead, 1986

Stephen, Adrian Leslie. *The "Dreadnought" Hoax*. Hogarth Press, 1936

Tozer, Basil. *Confidence Crooks and Blackmailers: Their Ways and Methods*. T. Werner Laurie, 1929

Walton, John. *The Legendary Detective: The Private Eye in Fact and Fiction*. University of Chicago Press, 2015

Ward, Frederick W. *The 23rd (Service) Battalion Royal Fusiliers (First Sportsman's): A Record of Its Services in the Great War, 1914–1919*. Sidgwick and Jackson, 1920

West, Nigel. *Historical Dictionary of World War I Intelligence*. Scarecrow Press, 2014

White, Jerry. *Zeppelin Nights: London in the First World War*. Vintage (reprint ed.), 2015

Winter, J. M. *The Great War and the British People*. Second edition.
    Palgrave, 2003
Wood, Walter. *Survivors' Tales of Famous Crimes*. Cassell, 1916
Woollacott, Angela. '"Khaki Fever" and Its Control: Gender, Class, Age
    and Sexual Morality on the British Homefront in the First World
    War'. *Journal of Contemporary History*, Vol. 29, No. 2 (1994),
    pp. 325–47
Wyles, Lilian. *A Woman at Scotland Yard*. Faber, 1952
Young, Alexander Bell Filson. *The Trial of Hawley Harvey Crippen*.
    William Hodge & Co., 1920

Archives and Other Sources

Newspapers and Magazines

Unless otherwise stated, all newspapers and magazines cited were published
in Britain and are in the newspaper collections of the British Library. Some
have been digitized and are also available at www.britishnewspaperarchive.
co.uk

Sources for overseas titles include:

Australia – Trove (National Library of Australia) www.trove.nla.gov.au
France – Gallica (Bibliothèque nationale de France) www.gallica.bnf.fr
Netherlands and Dutch East Indies – Delpher (Koninklijk Bibliotheek)
    www.delpher.nl
New Zealand – Papers Past (National Library of New Zealand)
    www.paperspast.natlib.govt.nz
Singapore – NewspapersSG (Singapore National Library Board)
    www.eresources.nlb.gov.sg
Ukraine – The European Library (Conference of European National
    Librarians) www.theeuropeanlibrary.org
United States of America: www.newspapers.com and Chronicling America
    (Library of Congress) www.chroniclingamerica.loc.gov

Archives

Camden Local Studies and Archives Centre (Metropolitan Borough of
    Holborn records)
Cumbria Archives Service (Charles Richards detective reports)

History of Advertising Trust (Publicity Club of London archive)
The Marion E. Wade Center, Wheaton College, Wheaton, Illinois
(Dorothy L. Sayers papers)
The National Archives (Metropolitan Police, Home Office and security
service files; military records; divorce records)
The Women's Library, London School of Economics (WSPU and
Efficiency Club records)

Websites

Ancestry – www.ancestry.co.uk
Charles Booth Poverty Maps and notebooks – booth.lse.ac.uk
Find My Past – www.findmypast.co.uk
General Register Office – www.gro.gov.uk
London Gazette – www.thegazette.co.uk
Espacenet (European Patent Office) – worldwide.espacenet.com
United States Congressional Record – www.congress.gov/
congressional-record
World War Two London Bomb Census – bombsight.org

Notes

Chapter One: The Documents in the Case

1 *Ideas*, 13 Mar 1914, p. 6
2 *Time*, 19 Nov 1934, p. 22
3 *Perth Daily News*, 25 Jun 1926, p. 5 (Original in *Sphere*, 24 Apr 1926, p. 112)
4 *Czernowitzer Allgemeine Zeitung* (Ukraine), 6 Jul 1913, p. 7; *New Zealand Herald*, 28 Dec 1927, p. 1
5 *Camperdown Chronicle* (Australia), 17 Jul 1915, p. 6
6 *Adelaide Saturday Journal* (Australia), 10 Jul 1926, p. 4
7 Ibid.
8 Ibid.
9 *Adelaide Express and Telegraph* (Australia), 18 Apr 1914, p. 7
10 Ibid.; the *Singapore Free Press and Mercantile Advertiser,* 5 Sep 1925, p. 6
11 *Sunday Press* (Pittsburgh), 27 Jul 1913, illustrated magazine section, p. 3
12 *Pearson's Weekly*, 26 Apr 1913, p. 1107
13 *Adelaide Express and Telegraph* (Australia), 18 Apr 1914, p. 7
14 *Sunday Dispatch*, 6 Dec 1931, p. 4

Chapter Two: The Body in the Library

1 *Weekly Irish Times*, 1 Feb 1930, p. 10
2 Annette Kerner, *Woman Detective*, T. Werner Laurie, 1954; Annette Kerner, *Further Adventures of a Woman Detective*, T. Werner Laurie, 1955. For an appraisal of Kerner's career, see Louise A. Jackson, 'The Unusual Case of "Mrs Sherlock": Memoir, Identity and the "Real" Woman Private Detective in Twentieth Century Britain', *Gender & History*, Vol. 15, No. 1 (April 2003), pp. 108–34, which also mentions Maud West.
3 *Daily Express*, 12 Mar 1913, p. 4

4   *The Times*, 5 Nov 1904, p. 6; Proceedings of the Central Criminal
     Court, 14 Nov 1904, pp. 33–7

5   *Daily Express*, 12 Mar 1913, p. 4

6   *Britannia and Eve*, Dec 1931, p. 126

7   *Daily Mail*, 14 Jul 1919, p. 5; 15 Jul 1919, p. 3

8   *Daily Mail*, 22 Jul 1919, p. 4

9   *Daily Mail*, 15 Jul 1919, p. 3

10   *Daily Mail*, 21 Jan 1914, p. 3

11   *The Times*, 9 Nov 1905, p. 4

12   *Hearth and Home*, 11 Jan 1900, p. 414; *Spectator*, 18 Feb 1893,
     p. 13

13   Gail Savage, 'Erotic Stories and Public Decency: Newspaper Reporting
     of Divorce Proceedings in England', *Historical Journal*, Vol. 41, No. 2
     (June 1998), pp. 513–14

14   *Sporting Times*, 1 Dec 1894, p. 4

15   *Nelson Evening Mail* (New Zealand), 18 May 1904, p. 3

16   *The Times*, 4 Apr 1855, p. 9

17   *Hearth and Home*, 13 Oct 1892, p. 730

18   Quoted in *North Wales Times*, 4 Apr 1896, p. 6

19   *The Times*, 22 Jul 1890, p. 3; Divorce Court File, National Archives,
     ref: J77/447/3639

20   *Manchester Guardian*, 28 Aug 1908, p. 8; *London Gazette*, issue 29828,
     17 Nov 1916

21   According to the *Clerk* in 1908, office workers were often paid as little
     as 25 to 30 shillings a week. *Clerk*, Feb 1908, p. 6

22   *The Times*, 27 Jan 1912, p. 3; 30 Jan 1912, p. 7

23   *Lloyd's Weekly News*, 19 May 1907, p. 6

24   *Irish Times*, 9 Jan 1913, p. 9; *Western Times*, 10 Jan 1913, p. 12

25   For details of the census boycott, see Jill Liddington and Elizabeth
     Crawford, *Vanishing for the Vote: Suffrage, Citizenship and the Battle
     for the Census*, Manchester University Press, 2014. Kate Easton's par-
     ticipation in the boycott was unusual, given that she appeared to have
     no official link to any of the suffrage organizations involved.

26   *M. A .P. (Mainly About People)*, 5 Feb 1910, p. 171

27   *Lloyd's Weekly News*, 19 May 1907, p. 6

28   *Sunday Post*, 14 Mar 1926, p. 11

29   *Adelaide Saturday Journal* (Australia), 10 Jul 1926, p. 4

30 *Perth Daily News* (Australia), 25 Jun 1926, p. 5
31 *Sunday Dispatch*, 15 Nov 1931, p. 4
32 *Hobart Mercury* (Australia), 21 Dec 1938, p. 6
33 *Pearson's Weekly*, 29 Mar 1913, p. 1011
34 *Weekly Irish Times*, 1 Feb 1930, p. 10
35 *Pearson's Weekly*, 29 Mar 1913, p. 1011

Chapter Three: Crooked House

1 *Answers*, 9 Aug 1919, p. 209
2 *Sunday Times*, 4 Jul 1909, p. 1
3 *Sunday Press* (Pittsburgh), 27 Jul 1913, illustrated magazine section, p. 3; *Daily Mail Atlantic Edition*, 17 Jun 1931, p. 6
4 See map at bombsight.org
5 *Building News*, 17 Mar 1899, p. 371
6 *Manchester Courier*, 18 Nov 1909, p. 3
7 *Review of Reviews for Australasia*, Jul 1909, p. 428; *The Times*, 6 Oct 1908, p. 1; 22 Dec 1909, p. 2; *Sheffield Daily Independent*, 18 Oct 1909, p. 8; *Western Times*, 22 May 1908, p. 3
8 *Financial Times*, 18 Sep 1909, p. 4
9 *British Medical Journal*, 6 Jun 1908, pp. 1375–6.
10 *Teesdale Mercury*, 24 Jul 1907, p. 3; *Financial Times*, 12 Jun 1909, p. 8; *Lancet*, 29 Jan 1910, p. 308
11 *Dundee Evening Telegraph*, 2 Jun 1909, p. 5; 15 Jun 1909, p. 4
12 Walter Wood, *Survivors' Tales of Famous Crimes*, Cassell, 1916, pp. 270–1
13 *Sydney World's News* (Australia), 20 Aug 1910, p. 13
14 *Pearson's Weekly*, 3 May 1913, p. 1137
15 *Pearson's Weekly*, 29 Mar 1913, p. 1011
16 *Illustrated Police News*, 13 Mar 1909, p. 2
17 *Pearson's Weekly*, 26 Apr 1913, p. 1107
18 *Daily Telegraph*, 22 Nov 1911, p. 6
19 *Daily Mail*, 22 Nov 1911, p. 8
20 *Croydon Guardian and Surrey County Gazette*, 18 Jun 1910, p. 2; *Yorkshire Post*, 18 May 1908, p. 7; *Pall Mall Gazette*, 27 Aug 1913, p. 8
21 *Nottingham Evening Post*, 26 Mar 1903, p. 3
22 *Lloyd's Weekly Newspaper*, 7 Jan 1872, p. 7

23   *London Evening Standard*, 19 Aug 1871, p. 7; 15 Apr 1896, p. 4; *Morning Post*, 26 Feb 1873, p. 7; *Daily Telegraph*, 5 Jul 1907, p. 4

24   *London Evening Standard*, 20 Aug 1898, p. 2

25   *Pall Mall Gazette*, 22 Jul 1913, p. 10

26   *Irish Times*, 3 Dec 1952, p. 10

27   *Huddersfield Chronicle*, 15 May 1894, p. 4

28   *London Gazette*, issue 33991, 31 Oct 1933

29   *Pearson's Magazine*, Nov 1926, p. 434; *Sunday Chronicle*, 14 Feb 1926, p. 3

Chapter Four: They Do It With Mirrors

1   *Pearson's Magazine*, Nov 1926, p. 431

2   *Détective* (France), 22 Nov 1928, p. 7

3   *Pittsburgh Press*, 27 Jul 1913, p. 43; *San Francisco Call*, 3 Aug 1913, p. 17

4   *Pearson's Weekly*, 29 Mar 1913, p. 1011

5   *Pearson's Weekly*, 12 Apr 1913, p. 1058

6   *Sunday Dispatch*, 15 Nov 1931, p. 4

7   *Daily Mirror*, 3 Sep 1913, p. 5

8   *Gloucestershire Echo*, 27 Sep 1913, p. 5

9   *Luton Times and Advertiser*, 29 Aug 1913, p. 6

10   *Taunton Courier*, 23 Jul 1913, p. 1; 4 Aug 1913, p. 1; *Dundee Evening Telegraph*, 30 Sep 1913, p. 1

11   *Globe*, 6 Sep 1913, p. 4; *Sheffield Evening Telegraph*, 25 Aug 1913, p. 7; *Aberdeen Press and Journal*, 23 Aug 1913, p. 2; *Sheffield Daily Telegraph*, 21 Aug 1913, p. 7; *Lincolnshire Standard and Boston Guardian*, 6 Sep 1913, p. 2; *Sheffield Evening Telegraph*, 23 Aug 1913, p. 4

12   *Sporting Times*, 30 Aug 1913, p. 1

13   *The Times*, 8 Oct 1913, p. 3; *Dundee Evening Telegraph*, 18 Jul 1913, p. 2; *Yorkshire Evening Post*, 14 Jul 1913, p. 6; *Dundee Courier*, 15 Jul 1913, p. 5; *Yorkshire Post*, 17 Jul 1913, p. 6

14   *San Francisco Examiner*, 16 May 1926, 'American Weekly' section, p. 2

15   *Sunday Dispatch*, 15 Nov 1931, p. 4

16   *Pictorial Review*, Apr 1926, p. 20

17   Sir John Gielgud, *Backward Glances*, Hodder & Stoughton, 1989, p. 50. For an earlier description of Clarkson's, see 'Wiggery, London: A look around Mr Clarkson's New Home in Wardour Street', *Music Hall and Theatre Review*, 26 May 1905, p. 330

18 *Daily Mirror*, 3 Sep 1913, p. 5

19 *Pearson's Magazine*, 1 Nov 1926, p. 431

20 *Weekly Dispatch*, 17 Oct 1909, p. 5

21 Martyn Downer, *The Sultan of Zanzibar: the bizarre world and spectacular hoaxes of Horace de Vere Cole*, Black Spring, 2010, p. 111

22 Adrian Stephen, *The 'Dreadnought' Hoax*, Hogarth Press, 1936

23 *San Francisco Examiner*, 16 May 1926, 'American Weekly' section, p. 2

24 *Manchester Guardian*, 21 Aug 1924, p. 6

25 *Hobart Mercury* (Australia), 21 Dec 1938, pp. 6 and 8

26 *Sunday Press* (Pittsburgh), 27 Jul 1913, illustrated magazine section, p. 3

27 *Britannia and Eve*, Dec 1931, p. 126

28 *Birmingham Gazette*, 16 Jun 1937, p. 9

29 *Manchester Guardian*, 21 Aug 1924, p. 6

30 *Ideas*, 13 Mar 1914, p. 6

31 Ibid.

32 *Hobart Mercury* (Australia), 21 Dec 1938, pp. 6 and 8

33 John Goodwin, *Crook Pie*, Alston Rivers, 1927, p. 195

34 Ibid., pp. 196–7

35 Ibid. See also John Goodwin, *Sidelights on Criminal Matters*, Hutchinson, 1923, pp. 193–4

36 *Ideas*, 13 Mar 1914, p. 6

37 *Sunday Dispatch*, 15 Nov 1931, p. 4

38 Ibid.

39 *Hobart Mercury* (Australia), 21 Dec 1938, pp. 6 and 8

40 *Weekly Irish Times*, 1 Feb 1930, p. 10

41 *Pearson's Magazine*, Nov 1926, pp. 430–4

42 *Sunday Press* (Pittsburgh), 27 Jul 1913, illustrated magazine section, p. 3

43 *Dundee Courier*, 7 Oct 1909, p. 5

44 *The Times*, 28 Oct 1916, p. 11; *Daily Mirror*, 28 Oct 1916, p. 10

45 *Pearson's Weekly*, 12 Apr 1913, p. 1058

Chapter Five: The Shadow in the House

1 *Sportsman's Gazette*, 11 Jun 1915, p. 360

2 *Portsmouth Evening News*, 23 May 1913, p. 5

3 *Women's Social & Political Union Seventh Annual Report* (1913), p. 14

4 *Women's Social & Political Union Eighth Annual Report* (1914), p. 22

5 *Portsmouth Evening News*, 23 May 1913, p. 5

6   *Czernowitzer Allgemeine Zeitung* (Ukraine), 6 Jul 1913, p. 7

7   *The Times*, 9 Jul 1913, p. 8

8   *Sunday Dispatch*, 13 Dec 1931, p. 8; *Sunday Dispatch*, 6 Dec 1931, p. 4

9   *San Francisco Examiner*, 16 May 1926, 'American Weekly' section, p. 2

10 *Pearson's Weekly*, 14 Mar 1912, p. 915

11 *Czernowitzer Allgemeine Zeitung* (Ukraine), 6 Jul 1913, p. 7

12 *Maitland Daily* (Australia), 15 Jan 1907, p. 2

13 *Czernowitzer Allgemeine Zeitung* (Ukraine), 6 Jul 1913, p. 7

14 Ibid.

15 Ibid.

16 *Portsmouth Evening News*, 28 Mar 1911, p. 6. See also 'The Immorality of Women at Bridge', *Grand Magazine*, Feb 1905, p. 44

17 *Belfast Evening Telegraph*, 17 Jun 1908, p. 4

18 *Pearson's Weekly*, 12 Apr 1913, p. 1058

19 *Pearson's Weekly*, 12 Apr 1913, p. 1058

20 *The Times*, 10 Jun 1891, p. 9

21 *Pearson's Weekly*, 12 Apr 1913, p. 1058

22 *Daily Telegraph*, 19 Sep 1906, p. 5

23 *Daily Express*, 22 Jun 1912, p. 1

24 *The Times*, 21 Jan 1911, p. 10

25 *The Times*, 25 Jan 1911, p. 8

26 *The Times*, 30 Jan 1911, p. 10

27 *The Times*, 11 Feb 1911, p. 8

28 *The Times*, 31 Jan 1911, p. 12

29 *Belfast Evening Telegraph*, 23 Sep 1907, p. 5

30 *Washington Post*, 16 Jun 1914, p. 3; *New York Tribune*, 16 Jun 1914, p. 3

31 *Washington Post*, 16 Jun 1914, p. 3

32 *Nottingham Evening Post*, 9 Jun 1914, p. 3

33 *The Times*, 5 Jun 1914, p. 8

34 *Yorkshire Evening Post*, 17 Jun 1914, p. 4

35 *Belfast Evening Telegraph*, 23 Sep 1907, p. 5

36 *The Times*, 7 Jan 1913, p. 2; 12 Mar 1913, p. 4; 14 Mar 1913, p. 2

37 *Daily Mirror*, 14 Mar 1913, p. 4

38 *Daily Telegraph*, 15 Nov 1905, p. 6

39 *Bystander*, 7 Mar 1906, p. 464

40 *Daily Telegraph*, 21 Oct 1909, p. 20

41 *Vanity Fair*, 7 Jul 1909, p. 13
42 *Times of India*, 11 Apr 1938, p. 22

Chapter Six: To Love and Be Wise

1   *Sunday Press* (Pittsburgh), 27 Jul 1913, illustrated magazine section, p. 3
2   *Birmingham Gazette*, 16 Jun 1937, p. 9
3   *San Francisco Examiner*, 16 May 1926, 'American Weekly' section, p. 2
4   *Pearson's Weekly*, 4 May 1911, p. 759
5   *Sunday Press* (Pittsburgh), 27 Jul 1913, illustrated magazine section, p. 3
6   *Pearson's Weekly*, 19 Apr 1913, p. 1083
7   *Pearson's Weekly*, 13 Aug 1921, p. 171
8   Ibid.
9   *Times of India*, 11 Apr 1938, p. 22
10 *Weekly Irish Times*, 22 Mar 1930, p. 3
11 *Weekly Irish Times*, 1 Feb 1930, p. 10
12 *Hobart Mercury* (Australia), 21 Dec 1938, pp. 6 and 8
13 *Sunday Press* (Pittsburgh), 27 Jul 1913, illustrated magazine section, p. 3
14 *Britannia and Eve*, Dec 1931, p. 126
15 *Ideas*, 13 Mar 1914, p. 6
16 *Weekly Irish Times*, 22 Mar 1930, p. 3
17 *Pearson's Weekly*, 12 Apr 1919, p. 575
18 *Pearson's Weekly*, 5 Apr 1913, p. 1045
19 *Belfast Evening Telegraph*, 23 Sep 1907, p. 5
20 *Pearson's Weekly*, 4 May 1911, p. 759
21 John Goodwin, *Crook Pie*, Alston Rivers, 1927, p. 189
22 John Goodwin, *Sidelights on Criminal Matters*, Hutchinson, 1923, pp. 190–1
23 *Pearson's Weekly*, 5 Apr 1913, p. 1045
24 *Daily Express*, 28 Jan 1914, p. 4
25 *Daily Herald*, 29 Nov 1919, p. 2
26 *The Times*, 29 Nov 1919, p. 4
27 *Nottingham Daily Express*, 30 Oct 1912, p. 6; *The Times*, 30 Oct 1912, p. 4
28 *Sunday Dispatch*, 22 Nov 1931, p. 4

Chapter Seven: A Kiss Before Dying

1   *Pearson's Weekly*, 29 Mar 1913, p. 1011

2   *Mataura Ensign* (New Zealand), 10 Jul 1914, p. 3

3   *Daily Express*, 1 May 1914, p. 4

4   Jerry White, *Zeppelin Nights: London in the First World War*, Vintage (reprint ed.), 2015, p. 181

5   Joan Lock, *The British Policewoman: Her Story*, Robert Hale, 1979, p. 61

6   *Daily Express*, 4 Mar 1916, p. 1

7   *London Evening News*, 30 Apr 1918, p. 4

8   *The Times*, 20 May 1915, p. 5

9   *Sunday Dispatch*, 22 Nov 1931, p. 4

10 *Sunday Dispatch*, 22 Nov 1931, p. 4

11 Aileen Rivers, *A Brief History of the Private Detective*, Association of British Investigators, 2009, p. 44

12 Thomas Davy Luke, *Spas and Health Resorts of the British Isles*, A & C Black, 1919, pp. 185–6

13 *Weekly Irish Times*, 22 Feb 1930, p. 3

14 National Archives KV1, KV2, HO45/10727/254753 and WO141

15 William Le Queux, *German Spies in England: An Exposure* (sixth edition), Stanley Paul & Co., 1915, p. 8

16 Sidney Theodore Felstead, *German Spies at Bay*, Hutchinson & Co., 1920, pp. 42–3

17 *Post Sunday Special*, 5 Aug 1917, p. 7; 12 Aug 1917, p. 7

18 65 Cong. Rec. 1515 (1918), Statement of Senator Owen

19 *Divorces in England and Wales: Number of couples divorcing, by party petitioning/decree granted, 1858–2014*, Office of National Statistics

20 *Summary of Recorded Crime Statistics for England and Wales 1898–2001/02*, Home Office

21 *Army and Navy Gazette*, 11 Aug 1917, p. 13

22 *Sporting Times*, 19 Sep 1914, p. 9

23 *Globe*, 14 Jan 1915, p. 8

24 A. M. Glazer and Patience Thomson (eds), *Crystal Clear: The Autobiographies of Sir Lawrence and Lady Bragg*, Oxford University Press, 2015, p. 7

25 Frederick W. Ward, *The 23rd (Service) Battalion Royal Fusiliers (First Sportsman's): A Record of Its Services in the Great War, 1914–1919*, Sidgwick and Jackson, 1920, p. 17

26 *Sportsman's Gazette*, 11 Jun 1915, p. 360
27 National Archives MH 47/115/77, Case Number RM1/819
28 Charles Booth survey notebooks B353, p. 131, booth.lse.ac.uk
29 *Lloyds Weekly Newspaper*, 13 Aug 1893, p. 11
30 *Pearson's Weekly*, 12 Apr 1919, p. 575

Chapter Eight: The Secret Adversary

1   *Derby Daily Telegraph*, 19 Nov 1929, p. 6
2   *Camperdown Chronicle* (Australia), 17 Jul 1915, p. 6
3   *Sunday Dispatch*, 6 Dec 1931, p. 4
4   *Answers*, 2 Aug 1919, p. 183; *Pearson's Weekly*, 12 Apr 1919, p. 575
5   *Pearson's Weekly*, 12 Apr 1919, p. 575
6   Robert Graves, *The Long Weekend* (second edition), Faber and Faber,
     1950, pp. 14–15
7   *The Times*, 25 May 1916, p. 3
8   *Sunday Post*, 2 Mar 1924, p. 9; *Sheffield Daily Telegraph*, 29 Feb 1924, p. 5
9   Basil Tozer, *Confidence Crooks and Blackmailers: Their Ways and
     Methods*, T. Werner Laurie, 1929, p. 234
10 Ibid., p. 227
11 *Sunday Dispatch*, 6 Dec 1931, p. 4
12 *Derby Daily Telegraph*, 19 Nov 1929, p. 6
13 *Daily Herald*, 28 Sep 1921, p. 1
14 *Answers*, 2 Aug 1919, p. 183
15 *Sunday Post*, 15 Apr 1923, pp. 1–2
16 *Dundee Evening Telegraph*, 29 Jun 1928, p. 1
17 *Yorkshire Post*, 26 Aug 1925, p. 8
18 *Era*, 5 Mar 1919, p. 18
19 *New Zealand Truth*, 17 Oct 1908, p. 5
20 *The Times*, 7 Mar 1919, p. 5; *Globe*, 19 Jan 1920, p. 7; *Northern Whig*,
     21 Jun 1928, p. 7; *West London Observer*, 22 Nov 1929, p. 9
21 *Globe*, 19 Jan 1920, p. 7
22 *Yorkshire Post*, 24 Sep 1934, p. 2
23 *Daily Herald*, 18 Nov 1920, p. 2
24 *West London Observer*, 23 Oct 1931, p. 7
25 *The Times*, 26 May 1925, p. 13; *Bucks Herald*, 13 Jun 1925, p. 8
26 *M. A. P. (Mainly About People)*, 19 Nov 1910, p. 611; *Ideas*, 22 Jan
     1913, p. 12; *Derby Daily Telegraph*, 17 Nov 1928, p. 4

27 *Nottingham Journal*, 12 Feb 1924, p. 5; *Nottingham Evening Post*, 1
    Apr 1924, p. 6
28 *Derby Daily Telegraph*, 19 Nov 1929, p. 6
29 *New Zealand Truth*, 17 Oct 1908, p. 5
30 *Good Housekeeping*, Sep 1927, pp. 74, 157–8
31 Tozer, p. 228; see also Sir Basil Thompson, 'Beware of Hyde Park',
    Sunday News, 30 May 1926, p. 1
32 H. Montgomery Hyde, *The Other Love: An Historical and
    Contemporary Survey of Homosexuality in Britain*, Mayflower,
    1972, pp. 206–7
33 Angus McLaren, 'Smoke and Mirrors: Willy Clarkson and the Role of
    Disguises in Inter-War England', *Journal of Social History*, Vol. 40, No.
    3 (Spring 2007), pp. 597–618
34 *Lloyd's Weekly News*, 19 May 1907, p. 6
35 *Pearson's Weekly*, 5 Apr 1913, p. 1045
36 *Answers*, 2 Aug 1919, p. 183
37 *The Times*, 24 May 1927, p. 13
38 *Sunday Dispatch*, 6 Dec 1931, p. 4
39 Ibid.
40 *New Zealand Truth*, 17 Oct 1908, p. 5
41 *Manchester Guardian*, 21 Aug 1924, p. 6
42 *Northern Whig*, 5 May 1922, p. 7; *Chemist and Druggist*, 29 Apr 1922,
    p. 52
43 *Belfast Newsletter*, 8 Feb 1928, p. 11
44 *Manchester Guardian*, 21 Aug 1924, p. 6
45 *Hendon and Finchley Times*, 12 and 26 Apr 1918, p. 4; 16, 23 and 30
    Apr 1920, p. 4; 23 Jan 1920, p. 4; 7, 14 and 21 Oct 1921, p. 4
46 *Hendon and Finchley Times*, 18 Nov 1927, p. 5
47 National Archives WO364/1124
48 *Hendon and Finchley Times*, 8 Oct 1920, p. 7
49 *Hendon and Finchley Times*, 15 Oct 1926, p. 7
50 *Royal Aero Club Aviators' Certificates, 1910-1950*, ancestry.co.uk
51 *Weekly Irish Times*, 8 Feb 1930, p. 3

Chapter Nine: Wanted – Someone Innocent

1   *Pearson's Weekly*, 19 May 1928, p. 1323
2   *Portsmouth Evening News*, 5 Oct 1920, p. 1

3   *Era*, 2 May 1923, p. 14

4   UK Patent number GB283359: Suction hat and coat hook, published
    12 Jan 1928

5   *Hendon and Finchley Times*, 15 May 1925, p. 10

6   See, for example, pantomime audition call for Brown's Agency, *Era*,
    20 Oct 1920, p. 3. Other agencies and production companies at Albion
    House included Nat Day, Joe Collins, Fred Peel, Macmaric produc-
    tions and Collins & Gladwin Theatres.

7   *Leeds Mercury*, 3 Apr 1920, p. 2

8   *Queenslander* (Australia), 3 Dec 1921, p. 47

9   *Pearson's Weekly*, 7 Jun 1919, p. 731

10 Ibid.

11 *Globe*, 3 Mar 1920, p. 6

12 *Ballymena Weekly Telegraph*, 29 Sep 1928, p. 11

13 *Aberdeen Press and Journal*, 24 Oct 1928, p. 7

14 *Sunday Dispatch*, 22 Nov 1931, p. 4

15 Sir Oliver Lodge, *Raymond, or Life and Death* (thirteenth edition),
    Methuen, 1916, p. xv

16 *Illustrated Police News*, 20 Sep 1934, p. 4

17 *Daily Mail*, 7 Jul 1904, p. 3. See also 10 Aug 1904, p. 3; 1 Sep 1904, p. 3;
    7 Oct 1904, p. 3

18 *Morning Post*, 5 Oct 1904, p. 3

19 *Sheffield Daily Telegraph*, 1 Sep 1904, p. 5

20 *Morning Post*, 18 Aug 1904, p. 7

21 *Globe*, 29 Dec 1916, p. 5; *Daily Mail*, 13 Dec 1916, p. 3

22 *Sunday Post*, 14 Mar 1926, p. 11

23 *Daily Sketch*, 22 Mar 1926, p. 2

24 *Light*, 13 Mar 1926, p. 125

25 For a description of Munnings' seances and trickery see *Journal of the
    Society for Psychical Research*, May 1926, pp. 73–5; *Daily Sketch*, 16
    Mar 1926, p. 2

26 *Sunday Post*, 14 Mar 1926, p. 11

27 *Sunday Dispatch*, 22 Nov 1931, p. 4

28 *New York Tribune*, 10 Jul 1921, p. 2

29 *Pearson's Weekly*, 17 May 1919, p. 671

30 *Answers*, 9 Aug 1919, p. 209

31 *People*, 11 Jun 1939, p. 9; *Globe*, 7 Aug 1911, p. 7

32 *Illustrated Police News*, 10 Dec 1925, p. 6; *Aberdeen Press and Journal*, 3 Dec 1925, p. 7

33 *Answers*, 6 Sep 1919, p. 285

34 *Good Housekeeping*, Feb 1928, p. 120

35 *Answers*, 5 Jul 1919, p. 111

36 *Mackay Daily Mercury* (Australia), 3 Jun 1938, p. 3; *New Zealand Herald*, 6 Jan 1938, p. 3

37 *Daily Mail*, 29 Oct 1937, p. 8

38 *Mackay Daily Mercury* (Australia), 3 Jun 1938, p. 3

39 General Register Office. Birth Certificate. Willesden. 1913 Jun Q. Vol. 3a, p. 641. Elliott, Evelyn

40 *Sunday Dispatch*, 29 Nov 1931, p. 4

Chapter Ten: Tracks in the Snow

1   *News Chronicle*, 24 Nov 1938, p. 8

2   Frank Dalton O'Sullivan, *Crime Detection*, O'Sullivan Publishing, 1928, p. 193

3   John Goodwin, *Crook Pie*, Alston Rivers, 1927, pp. 191–2

4   *The Times*, 22 Jul 1890, p. 3

5   *Pearson's Magazine*, Nov 1926, p. 431

6   *Illustrated Police News*, 1 Sep 1921, p. 2

7   *The Times*, 20 May 1913. p. 9

8   *Answers*, 23 Aug 1919, p. 248

9   *Gloucester Citizen*, 10 Nov 1929, p. 4

10 See, for example, 'Women Blackmailers', *Cornishman*, 14 Apr 1920, p. 2

11 *Het Nieuws van den Dag voor Nederlandsch-Indië* (Dutch East Indies), 29 Mar 1930, pp. 288 and 290

12 *Sunday Chronicle*, 14 Feb 1926, p. 3

13 *Sunday Dispatch*, 29 Nov 1931, p. 4

14 *The Times*, 16 Feb 1916, p. 9

15 *The Times*, 12 Feb 1916, p. 3

16 See, for example, the case of the Kosmo Dance Club in Edinburgh, as reported in the *Daily Herald*, 30 Nov 1933, p. 7

17 *Sunday Chronicle*, 14 Feb 1926, p. 3

18 *Het Nieuws van den Dag voor Nederlandsch-Indië* (Dutch East Indies), 29 Mar 1930, p. 290; *Sunday Chronicle*, 14 Feb 1926, p. 3

19 *Weekly Irish Times*, 15 Mar 1930, p. 3

20 *Het Nieuws van den Dag voor Nederlandsch-Indië* (Dutch East Indies), 9 Jul 1930, p. 3

21 *Sunday Dispatch*, 29 Nov 1931, p. 4

22 *Scotsman*, 13 Jan 1927, p. 7

23 *Daily Herald*, 10 May 1924, p. 3

24 Mary S. Allen, *Lady in Blue*, Stanley Paul & Co, 1936, p. 229; *Aberdeen Press and Journal*, 2 Nov 1925, p. 3

25 *Sunday Post*, 22 Aug 1926, p. 11; *The Times*, 23 June 1926, p. 5

26 *Mooi Limburg* (Dutch East Indies), 10 Sep 1938, pp. 6-7

27 Teresa Billington-Greig, 'The Truth About White Slavery', *The English Review*, Vol XIV (April–July 1913), p. 428

28 Ibid., p. 445

29 Joan Lock, *The British Policewoman: Her Story*, Robert Hale, 1979, p. 19

30 Billington-Greig, p. 434

31 General Register Office. Marriage Certificate. Lewisham. 1901 Jun Q. Vol 1d, p. 1843. Barber, Edith Maria

32 General Register Office. Birth Certificate. Greenwich. 1885 Mar Q. Vol 1d, p. 1017. Barber, Edith Maria

33 General Register Office. Death Certificate. Greenwich. 1887 Jun Q. Vol 1d, p. 585. Barber, Edith Maria; Register of Burials, Royal Borough of Greenwich, May 1887, no. 104, www.deceasedonline.com

34 *San Francisco Examiner*, 16 May 1926, 'American Weekly' section, p. 2

Chapter Eleven: Partners in Crime

1 *Policewoman's Review*, Apr 1931, pp. 139–40

2 *Scotsman*, 7 Mar 1922, p. 8; *Nottingham Evening Post*, 6 Mar 1922, p. 1; *Pall Mall Gazette*, 6 Mar 1922, p. 1

3 *Lloyd's Sunday News*, 12 Mar 1922, p. 5

4 *Nottingham Evening Post*, 8 Apr 1922, p. 1

5 *Account to Hart Jackson from private detective Charles Richards, 11 Nov 1906*. Cumbria Archives Service BDHJ/88/10/8

6 *Perth Daily News* (Australia), 4 Jul 1907, p. 9

7 *Ideas*, 13 Mar 1914, p. 6

8 *Het Nieuws van den Dag voor Nederlandsch-Indië* (Dutch East Indies), 29 Mar 1930, pp. 288 and 290

9 *Policewoman's Review*, Apr 1931, p. 140

10 *The Times*, 26 May 1925, p. 16

11 Quoted in *Western Chronicle*, 20 Oct 1899, p. 3

12 *Leicester Daily Post*, 17 Feb 1914, p. 5

13 *Daily Mirror*, 27 Jun 1914, p. 3

14 Joan Lock, *The British Policewoman: Her Story*, Robert Hale, 1979, p. 99

15 Ibid., p. 107

16 A. H. Henderson Livesey, *League of Womanhood Pamphlet No.1: The Women Police Question*, League of Womanhood, 1924

17 *The Times*, 15 Aug 1924, p. 7

18 Lock, p. 15

19 *Vote*, 25 Jul 1913, p. 9

20 Lock, p. 16

21 *The Times*, 12 Aug 1920, pp. 7 and 11

22 Lock, p. 126

23 *The Times*, 25 Feb 1921, p. 15

24 Lock, pp. 100–1, 154

25 *Manchester Guardian*, 21 Aug 1924, p. 6

26 *New York Tribune*, 10 Jul 1921, p. 2

27 *Bruce Herald* (New Zealand), 18 Oct 1901, p. 2

28 *Manchester Guardian*, 21 Aug 1924, p. 6

29 *Competitors' Journal and Everybody's Weekly*, 29 May 1926, p. 11

30 Ibid.

31 *Sunday Press* (Pittsburgh), 27 Jul 1913, illustrated magazine section, p. 3; *New Zealand Herald*, 26 Sep 1931, p. 3

32 Ibid.

33 *Mooi Limburg* (Dutch East Indies), 10 Sep 1938, pp. 6–7

34 *Sunday Dispatch*, 15 Nov 1931, p. 4

35 *Hobart Mercury* (Australia), 21 Dec 1938, p. 6

36 *Policewoman's Review*, April 1931, pp. 139–40

37 *Competitors' Journal and Everybody's Weekly*, 29 May 1926, p. 11

38 John Goodwin, *Sidelights on Criminal Matters*, Hutchinson, 1923, p. 195

39 *Hobart Mercury* (Australia), 21 Dec 1938, p. 6

40 *Manchester Guardian*, 5 Aug 1925, p. 16

41 *Competitors' Journal and Everybody's Weekly*, 29 May 1926, p. 11

42 Charles Booth Poverty Map 1889, Square M10, www.booth.lse.ac.uk

43 General Register Office. Birth Certificate. Greenwich. 1880 Dec Q. Vol 1d, p. 940. Barber, Edith Maria
44 General Register Office. Birth Certificate. Greenwich. 1886 Sep Q. Vol 1d, p. 1020. Barber, Alice
45 John R. Gillis, *For Better, for Worse: British Marriages, 1600 to the Present*, Oxford University Press, 1986, p. 234
46 *Weekly Irish Times*, 29 Mar 1930, p. 3

Chapter Twelve: The Wrong Man

1 *Pearson's Magazine*, Nov 1926, pp. 430–4
2 Irwin S. Cobb, *Europe Revised*, George H. Doran Co., 1914, p. 337; Langham Hotel brochure c.1920
3 *Portsmouth Evening News*, 29 Apr 1930, p. 5
4 *Pearson's Weekly*, 31 May 1919, p. 711
5 *Portsmouth Evening News*, 29 Apr 1930, p. 5
6 *Divorces in England and Wales: Number of couples divorcing, by party petitioning/decree granted, 1858–2014*, Office of National Statistics
7 A. P. Herbert, *Holy Deadlock*, Methuen & Co., 1934, p. 27
8 *Sphere*, 23 Jan 1932, p. 115
9 Ibid.
10 John Goodwin, *Crook Pie*, Alston Rivers, 1927, pp. 201–2
11 *Sunday Dispatch*, 13 Dec 1931, p. 8
12 *The Times*, 15 Dec 1937, p. 4
13 *Daily Express*, 12 Apr 1905, p. 5
14 *Globe*, 28 Nov 1919, p. 9
15 *Globe*, 2 Nov 1920, p. 8
16 *The Times*, 29 Nov 1919, p. 4
17 June Hillman, *The Glass Ladder*, Heinemann, 1960, p. 17
18 Ibid., p. 230
19 Ibid., p. 231
20 Petition for nullity, 1930. National Archives, J77/2806/6904
21 Hillman, p. 247–8
22 Ibid., p. 272
23 Ibid., p. 273
24 Ibid., p. 276
25 Ibid., p. 281
26 *Edinburgh Evening News*, 16 Nov 1933, p. 9

27 *Dundee Evening Telegraph*, 22 Dec 1933, p. 1
28 Hillman, p. 281
29 *Dundee Evening Telegraph*, 22 Dec 1933, p. 1
30 Ibid., p. 4
31 Ibid.
32 *Yorkshire Post*, 23 Dec 1933, p. 10
33 Ibid.
34 *Dundee Courier*, 23 Dec 1933, p. 7
35 *Western Daily Press*, 2 Dec 1927, p. 3
36 General Register Office. Birth Certificate. Lewisham. 1902 Jun Q. Vol. 1d, p. 1200. Elliott, Cecil Henry; Greenwich. 1904 Jun Q. Vol. 1d, p. 1035. Elliott, Vera Edith; Wandsworth. 1907 Jun Q. Vol. 1d, p. 801. Elliott, Denis Frank; Brentford. 1908 Dec Q. Vol. 3a, p. 93. Elliott, Keith Eugene; Fulham. 1910 Sep Q. Vol. 1a, p. 334. Elliott, Neville John; Willesden. 1913 Jun Q. Vol. 3a, p. 641. Elliott, Evelyn
37 *Sunday Dispatch*, 15 Nov 1931, p. 4

Chapter Thirteen: Sweet Danger

1 *Sunday Dispatch*, 15 Nov 1931, p. 4
2 *Pearson's Magazine*, Nov 1926, pp. 430–4
3 *Sunday Post*, 14 Mar 1926, p. 11
4 *Lloyd's Weekly News*, 19 May 1907, p. 6
5 *Sheffield Daily Telegraph*, 4 Nov 1921, p. 7; *Gloucester Citizen*, 9 Apr 1926, p. 6
6 *Ideas*, 13 Mar 1914, p. 6
7 *Pearson's Magazine*, 1 Nov 1926, pp. 433–4
8 *Manchester Guardian*, 21 Aug 1924, p. 6
9 *Pearson's Magazine*, Nov 1926, pp. 430–4
10 *Globe*, 2 Sep 1911, p. 1
11 *West London Observer*, 28 Jun 1935, p. 11. See also *The Times*, 23 Feb 1935, p. 4; 25 Feb 1935, p. 9
12 *Globe*, 8 Jul 1920, p. 7; *The Times*, 2 Jul 1920, p. 4
13 Gayle K. Brunelle and Annette Finley-Croswhite, *Murder in the Métro: Laetitia Toureaux and the Cagoule in 1930s France*, Louisiana State University Press, 2010
14 A. S. M. Hutchinson, *This Freedom*, Hodder & Stoughton, 1922, p. 9

15 Ibid., p. 186
16 Ibid., p. 239
17 *Pall Mall Gazette*, 1 Aug 1922, pp. 1–2. See also 3 Aug 1922, pp. 8–9 and 4 Aug 1922, p. 7
18 *New York Tribune*, 10 Jul 1921, p. 2; *New Zealand Herald*, 13 Aug 1921, p. 2; *Perth Daily News*, 20 Aug 1921, p. 6
19 *Perth Daily News*, 20 Aug 1921, p. 6
20 *New Zealand Herald*, 13 Aug 1921, p. 2
21 *Perth Daily News*, 20 Aug 1921, p. 6
22 *Sunday Chronicle*, 14 Feb 1926, p. 3
23 National Archives HS9/22/10
24 M. R. D. Foot, *SOE: An Outline History of the Special Operations Executive 1940–46*, British Broadcasting Corporation, 1984, p. 48
25 Divorce Court File, National Archives J77/2949/1180
26 *Ballymena Weekly Telegraph*, 14 Mar 1931, p. 11
27 *Lancashire Evening Post*, 9 Mar 1931, p. 2; 12 Mar 1931, p. 5; *Scotsman*, 13 Mar 1931, p. 11
28 *Western Daily Press*, 29 Jan 1931, p. 3
29 *Hendon and Finchley Times*, 11 Mar 1932, p. 7
30 *Exeter and Plymouth Gazette*, 25 Mar 1922, p. 1
31 *Australia's Offer to the British Boy*, Melbourne: Albert J. Mullett, Government Printer, 1922, p. 12
32 *Hendon and Finchley Times*, 12 Sep 1924, p. 10
33 *Hendon and Finchley Times*, 27 Jul 1923, p. 8
34 Sir John McEwen quoted in G. P. Walsh, 'McLeod, Malcolm Athol Wallace (1894–1989)', *Australian Dictionary of Biography*, Vol. 18, Melbourne University Publishing, 2012, p. 95
35 Letter from Percy Lord (aged 9), 'The Letterbox', *Freeman's Journal* (Australia), 17 Jun 1920, p. 46
36 *Farmer and Settler* (New South Wales), 24 Apr 1924, p. 4
37 *Gundagai Independent and Pastoral, Agricultural and Mining Advocate* (Australia), 2 Jun 1924, p. 2
38 *Sunday Dispatch*, 15 Nov 1931, p. 4

Chapter Fourteen: Look to the Lady

1 *Pearson's Weekly*, 19 May 1928, p. 1323
2 *Competitors' Journal and Everybody's Weekly*, 29 May 1926, p. 11

3 *Sunday Times*, 30 Nov 1919, p. 16; Efficiency Club membership form, Women's Library, London School of Economics SE 7/PHS/1/A/3

4 *Derbyshire Advertiser and Journal*, 21 Jul 1916, p. 3

5 *Dundee Evening Telegraph*, 13 Dec 1922, p. 9; *Pall Mall Gazette*, 25 May 1920, p. 9

6 *Pall Mall Gazette*, 15 Jan 1920, p. 9; *Gloucestershire Echo*, 8 Feb 1933, p. 6

7 *Pall Mall Gazette*, 26 Nov 1919, p. 11; *Sunday Times*, 1 May 1927, p. 15

8 *The Times*, 20 May 1919, p. 7

9 *Sunday Times*, 30 Nov 1919, p. 16

10 *Daily Mail*, 6 Nov 1931, p. 10

11 *Portsmouth Evening News*, 18 Nov 1920, p. 2

12 Jane Robins, *The Magnificent Spilsbury and the Case of the Brides in the Bath*, John Murray, 2010, pp. 207–18

13 *Daily Telegraph*, 14 Nov 1930, p. 16

14 *Lancashire Evening Post*, 14 Nov 1930, p. 6

15 Dorothy L. Sayers to Ivy Shrimpton, 19 Nov 1930, Dorothy L. Sayers Papers, folder 60, p. 46. The Marion E. Wade Center, Wheaton College, Wheaton, Illinois

16 *Daily Sketch*, 14 Jan 1926, p. 16

17 Livesey (League of Womanhood pamphlet), back cover

18 *Leeds Mercury*, 19 Feb 1926, p. 4

19 Alan Garth, *A History of the Publicity Club of London*, Publicity Club of London, 1978, pp. 34–6

20 *Vote*, 27 May 1921, p. 2

21 *Dundee Evening Telegraph*, 30 May 1921, p. 6

22 Ibid.; *Advertising World*, Jun 1921, p. 584

23 *History of the Publicity Club* (Vol. 1), History of Advertising Trust archives

24 David Doughan and Peter Gordon, *Women, Clubs and Associations in Britain*, Routledge, 2006, p. 128

25 Janet Haywood, *History of Soroptimist International*, Soroptimist International, 1995, p. 3

26 *Adelaide Advertiser* (Australia), 25 Jan 1932, p. 88

27 *Birmingham Gazette*, 16 Jun 1937, p. 9

28 *Holborn Guardian*, 9 Nov 1934, p. 5

29 *Annual Report of the Medical Officer of Health for 1935*, Metropolitan Borough of Holborn, p. 29

30 *Council Minutes 1935*, Metropolitan Borough of Holborn, p. 211

31 Ibid., p. 360; p. 359

32 General Register Office. Birth Certificate. Greenwich. 1898 Mar Q. Vol. 1d, p. 1053, Barber, Ellen

33 *Sunday Post*, 24 Apr 1927, p. 12

34 General Register Office. Death Certificate. Greenwich. 1903 Dec Q. Vol. 1d, p. 556, Barber, Mary Ann Elizabeth

35 Ibid.

36 Geoffrey Charles Palmer and Alice Barber, 17 Dec 1903. All Saints Church, Rotherhithe, Marriages. London Metropolitan Archives

37 Ellen Barber, 29 May 1906, Colls Road School Admission Register, London Metropolitan Archives

38 *Daily Mail Atlantic Edition*, 17 Jun 1931, p. 6

Chapter Fifteen: A Case of Identity

1 *Pearson's Weekly*, 5 Apr 1913, p. 1045

2 *Competitors' Journal and Everybody's Weekly*, 29 May 1926, p. 11

3 *Sunday Chronicle*, 14 Feb 1926, p. 3

4 *Het Nieuws van den Dag voor Nederlandsch-Indië* (Dutch East Indies), 29 Mar 1930, p. 288

5 *Daily Express*, 1 May 1914, p. 4; *Pearson's Magazine*, Nov 1926, p. 431; *Weekly Irish Times*, 1 Feb 1930, p. 10

6 *Police* (France), Vol. 54, 6 Dec 1931, p. 14

7 From 'Burlington Bertie', composed by Harry B. Norris and performed by Vesta Tilley

8 Anthony Slide, *Great Pretenders: A History of Male and Female Impersonation in the Performing Arts*, Wallace-Homestead, 1986, p. 61

9 *M.A.P. (Mainly About People)*, 5 Feb 1910, p. 171

10 *Crystal Palace. Season 1877-78. October 6th, 1877–May 18th, 1878*. MS Crystal Palace Saturday Concerts. British Library.

11 *Northern Whig*, 21 Jun 1904, p. 10

12 *Daily Telegraph*, 16 Oct 1905, p. 15

13 *Lloyd's Weekly News*, 19 May 1907, p. 6

14 Advertisement for rooms at 20 Arundel Gardens W11, *West London Observer*, 14 Oct 1927, p. 13

15   General Register Office. Death Certificate. Kensington. 1931 Dec
     Q. Vol. 1a, p. 147, Easton, Kate
16   *People*, 25 Jan 1914, p. 1
17   *Pearson's Weekly*, 19 May 1928, p. 1323
18   *Hobart Mercury* (Australia), 21 Dec 1938, pp. 6 and 8
19   *Winnipeg Free Press* (Canada), 16 Jul 1932, p. 14
20   *Daily Mail*, 9 Jun 1931, p. 9
21   *Australian Worker*, 9 Nov 1932, p. 19
22   *Daily Mirror*, 5 Mar 1936, p. 11
23   *Het Nieuws van den Dag voor Nederlandsch-Indië* (Dutch East
     Indies), 29 Mar 1930, p. 288
24   *Mooi Limburg* (Dutch East Indies), 10 Sep 1938, p. 7
25   Press photograph of Constance Ryland, 25 Jun 1937. topfoto.co.uk, ref:
     EU054457
26   *Hobart Mercury* (Australia), 21 Dec 1938, p. 8
27   1939 Register, RG101/0383D/011/28 Letter Code: AOCA. www.
     findmypast.com

Chapter Sixteen: Farewell, My Lady

1   *Sunday Post*, 14 Mar 1926, p. 11
2   General Register Office. Death Certificate. Ashford. 1953 Jun Q. Vol.
     5b, p. 14. Elliott, Denis Frank

Picture Acknowledgements

1. *Solicitors' Journal and Weekly Reporter*, 13 Dec 1924, p. 184 / British Library; 5. Contains public-sector information licensed under the Open Government Licence v3.0; 8 (top). *Sunday Times*, 4 July 1909, p. 1 / British Library; 8 (bottom). *The Times*, 13 Mar 1936, p. 1 / British Library; 9. *Sunday Times*, 9 Nov 1930, p. 15 / British Library; 11 (first). Ville de Paris / BiLiPo; 11 (second). State Library of New South Wales: BN249; 11 (third). National Library of Australia, *Adelaide Saturday Journal* (Australia), 10 July 1926, p. 4 6449460; 11 (fourth). ANNO / Austrian National Library, *Czernowitzer Allgemeine Zeitung*, 6 July 1913, p. 7; 14 (first). The Phantom Thief (1937, March 4). *Huon and Derwent Times* (Tas: 1933–1942), p. 3. Retrieved 12 Dec 2018 from http://nla.gov.au/nla.news-article136031669; 14 (second and third). State Library of New South Wales: TN201; 15. CROOKS I HAVE FOILED. (1920, Sept 3). *Huon Times* (Franklin, Tas: 1910–1933), p. 6. Retrieved 12 Dec 2018 from http://nla.gov.au/nla.news-article135831129; 19, 50, 67, 75 (right) and endpapers. By courtesy of the author; 28. Library of Congress, Prints & Photographs Division, Civil War Photographs, [LC-DIG-CWPB-03861]; 29 (first). Two Clever Sisters, *Daily Mail*, 15 July 1919, p. 3 / British Library; 29 (second). N-P-Manawatu-Standard-29-12-1923-p11, Alexander Turnbull Library, Wellington, New Zealand; 29 (third). *Daily Mail*, 14 July 1919, p. 5 / British Library; 31. Fox Photos / Stringer; 35. *Sporting Times*, 1 Dec 1894, p. 4 / British Library; 40 (top and bottom). *Sunday Post*, 14 Mar 1926, p. 11 / British

Library; **47.** *Sunday Times*, 4 July 1909, p. 1 / British Library; **63, 105.** *London Gazette*, issue 33991, 31 Oct 1933 / British Library; **68 (left and right), 75 (left).** *The San Francisco Call* (San Francisco [Calif.]), 3 Aug 1913. Chronicling America: Historic American Newspapers. Lib. of Congress. http:// chroniclingamerica.loc.gov/lccn/sn85066387/1913-08-03/ ed-1/seq-17/; **98.** *New York Tribune*, 16 Jun 1914, p. 3 / British Library; **103.** *Daily Telegraph*, 11 Apr 1911, p. 20 / British Library; **104.** Archives and Local History, Manchester Central Library; **114, 128.** Courtesy of Camden Local Studies and Archives Centre; **127.** *Nottingham Journal*, 30 Oct 1912, p. 6 / British Library; **134.** *Daily Express*, 1 May 1914, p. 4 / British Library; **149.** *Sportsman's Gazette*, 11 Jun 1915, p. 360 / British Library; **163.** *Era*, 5 Mar 1919, p. 18 / British Library; **172.** *Hendon and Finchley Times*, 18 Nov 1927, p. 5 / British Library; **173.** Royal Aero Club Trust; **180. 283, 359.** Elliott, H. G. Feb 18 1927, worldwide.espacenet.com; **194.** *Daily Mail*, 29 Oct 1937, p. 8 / British Library; **196, 217.** By courtesy of the author, Crown Copyright; **227.** Cumbria Archive Service, Barrow; **231.** Topical Press Agency / Stringer; **256.** Anonymous / AP / REX / Shutterstock; **284, 285, 333.** By courtesy of Brian Elliott; **287.** National Archives Australia: A461, G349/1/7; **301.** © Museum of London; **316 (left).** Public Domain, https://commons.wikimedia.org/w/index.php?curid=607490; **316 (right).** © Victoria and Albert Museum, London; **330.** State Library of New South Wales: BN217